PRAISE FOR
THE EMERGENCE OF MODERN SHI'ISM

"This is an absorbing account of the rise of modern Shi'ism and of the rise of the Shi'i clergy as authoritative interpreters (*mujtahids*) of theology, religious practice, and the law. Zackery Heern aptly situates the 'triumph of Usuli Shi'ism' in Iraq and Iran, brought to fruition by Vahid Bihbihani and his disciples during the late eighteenth and early nineteenth centuries, within broader contemporary currents of Islamic religious revival and reform."

Peter Sluglett, Director,
Middle East Institute, National University of Singapore

"A major achievement. This original new work explains not only the roots of modern Shiite thought but also places these roots into the context of Middle Eastern religious reformism since the second half of the 1700s. An excellent and timely introduction for students as well as general readers seeking to understand the beginnings of modern Islam."

Peter Von Sivers,
Associate Professor, History, University of Utah

"Zackery Heern has produced a very important and deeply researched contribution to the history of Shi'ism. At last there is a book that sets developments in Shi'ism in the context of the larger Islamic world. Scholars of Islamic studies will greatly benefit from reading this book."

Roy P. Mottahedeh,
Gurney Professor of History, Harvard University

"Heern not only provides the most thorough intellectual, social and organizational analysis of the rise of the rationalist Usuli school in Shi'ism, but contextualizes it within the framework of local, regional and global changes of the eighteenth and nineteenth centuries. Significantly, he posits these developments as an important manifestation of the global phenomenon of multiple modernities."

Meir Litvak, Associate Professor,
Department of Middle Eastern History, Tel Aviv University

The Emergence of Modern Shi'ism

Islamic Reform in Iraq and Iran

ZACKERY M. HEERN

ONEWORLD

A Oneworld Book

First published by Oneworld Publications, 2015

Copyright © Zackery M. Heern 2015

The moral right of Zackery M. Heern to be identified as the
Author of this work has been asserted by him in accordance
with the Copyright, Designs, and Patents Act 1988

ISBN 978-1-78074-496-4
ISBN 978-1-78074-497-1 (eBook)

Typeset by Tetragon, London
Printed and bound in Great Britain by
TJ International Ltd, Padstow, Cornwall

Oneworld Publications
10 Bloomsbury Street
London WC1B 3SR
England

Contents

For Mona, Liya, and Jamal

If you would understand anything,
observe its beginning and its development.

ARISTOTLE

PREFACE

I initially began research for this book for my PhD dissertation. I had already written an MA thesis on the development of Shi'ism in the nineteenth century, focusing on the figure of Murtada Ansari who, in many ways, brought the Usuli movement to a logical conclusion. For the PhD I decided to investigate the earlier developments of Usuli Shi'ism. All roads initially led to Wahid Bihbihani, who remains the lead actor of this book. After completing the chapters on the emergence of the Usuli movement and the figure of Bihbihani, my advisor, Peter von Sivers, encouraged me to contextualize Usulism within the history of the Middle East. He continually asked me why and how the Usuli movement emerged at this particular time and place in history. We came to the conclusion that it was largely a response to the fall of the Safavid Empire and the decentralization of Ottoman rule. I then became interested in additional Islamic responses to the socio-historical conditions of the late eighteenth century, which prompted a comparison of the Usuli movement with the movements of Wahhabism and neo-Sufism, or the *tariqa Muhammadiyya*.

After completing the dissertation, I began teaching at Murray State University, where much of my teaching work focused on world history. As my understanding of global trends increased, I could not help but notice parallels between Usulism and seemingly unrelated movements throughout the world – including the Enlightenment and Neo-Confucianism. Prior to teaching world history, I was questioned in a job interview by a Europeanist whether Usulis borrowed the rationalist element of their movement from the Enlightenment. My response was definitively, "No, the rationalist tradition in Islam predates the Enlightenment by a thousand years." I still do not think that Usuli rationalism is a direct result of the Enlightenment, but the syncronicity and convergence of the two movements is certainly striking. Therefore, I focused much of the revision work for this book on situating Usulism in a global context. Additionally, I rewrote the entire book, partially in an attempt to make it accessible to a wider audience. In the process, I added and deleted entire chapters.

The book was made possible by the generosity and assistance of scholars, institutions, and my family. I owe a special debt of gratitude to Professors Peter von Sivers, Peter Sluglett, and Bernard Weiss. I will never be able to repay the countless hours they spent imparting knowledge, sharing wisdom, writing letters of recommendation, and of course guiding my dissertation project. I will be ever grateful to Novin Doostar and everyone at Oneworld Publications for publishing this book. I also thank Robert Gleave who included me in the Clerical Authority in Shi'i Islam Project, lent me countless books, and was also on my PhD committee. I am also thankful to Moojan Momen, Meir Litvak, Sholeh Quinn, Marjorie Hilton, and William Schell for their comments on earlier drafts of my manuscript.

This book would not have been possible without the support of several universities and their libraries. I thank UCLA and the University of Utah, especially the History Department and the Middle East Center at the University of Utah, for providing institutional support for my studies. I am also grateful to Murray State University, particularly my colleagues in the History Department. An additional debt of gratitude is owed to the Aziz S. Atiya Middle East Library at the University of Utah and the University of Cologne for granting me unlimited access to its lithograph collection in the Schia-Bibliothek. Finally, Firestone Library at Princeton University, The Library of Congress in Washington, DC, the Young Research Library at UCLA, and Waterfield Library at Murray State were of great help.

My entire course of study would have remained a dream without generous fellowships and grants from multiple donors and institutions. At the University of Utah, I thank the History Department for the three-year Burton Teaching Assistant Fellowship, the Middle East Center for five Arabic and Persian FLAS Fellowships, and the Graduate School for the Marriner S. Eccles Graduate Fellowship in Political Economy and two University Teaching Assistantships. I also thank the University of Utah Middle East Center and the Graduate School for multiple conference travel grants. I am likewise thankful for the Reza Ali Khazeni Memorial Scholarship for Graduate Study Abroad. Further, I am grateful to the Institute of Ismaili Studies in London for its generous Dissertation Scholarship as well as the British Academy, the British Institute for Persian Studies, and the British Society for Middle East Studies for funding the Clerical Authority in Shi'i Islam Project. Finally, thanks to Murray State University for two CISR grants and the History Department for research and travel grants.

My family and friends have been an immovable support system throughout the arduous process of writing this book. Thank you first and foremost to my wife, Mona Kashani Heern, for being a constant source of hope and encouragement, and to the lights of my life, Liya and Jamal Heern, for consistently bringing me joy. I hope to follow in the footsteps of my first teachers, Bobette and Jim Heern, who instilled within me a love for learning and taught me the value of hard work.

INTRODUCTION

THE TRIUMPH OF NEO-USULISM

In the late eighteenth century, a debate between Usuli and Akhbari Shiʻis gripped the scholarly community in the holy city of Karbalaʾ in southern Iraq. Akhbaris argued that the foundational Islamic texts (the Qurʾan and Hadith) are the only living sources of knowledge, authority, and law in Islam. Because of their emphasis on scripture, especially the traditions (*akhbar* or Hadith) of the Prophet Muhammad and the Shiʻi Imams, Akhbaris are commonly referred to as scripturalists or traditionists.[1] While Akhbaris rejected the use of reason (*ʻaql*) as a source of Islamic law, Usulis accepted it. Therefore, Usulis are often referred to as rationalists.

A century before the Usuli-Akhbari dispute came to blows, Akhbaris had consolidated their control over the complex of Shiʻi seminary colleges (*hawza*s) in Iraq. Shiʻi sources tell us that Usulis ran the risk of being beaten if Akhbaris caught them with Usuli books.[2] Therefore, Usulis met in secret and hid their books in handkerchiefs. By the turn of the nineteenth century, Usulis overcame the Akhbari leadership and claimed their role as the guardians of Shiʻi Islam, or "custodians of the saved sect" as Wahid Bihbihani, the founder of the modern Usuli movement, put it.[3] Usulis violently expelled Akhbaris, Sufis, and other would-be challengers from Karbalaʾ and consolidated their control over the Shiʻi communities of southern Iraq, Iran, and the majority of the Shiʻi world.

This book is primarily concerned with the modern Usuli movement, which I argue is the single most dominant Shiʻi trend of the past several hundred years. The intellectual foundations of Usulism and Akhbarism are not new to the modern period. In fact, rationalism and traditionism represent two of the most prevalent currents that stretch back to the foundational period of Shiʻi intellectual history. However, in the late eighteenth century, Usulism emerged as something more than an intellectual trend. It became a powerful social movement, which has largely defined the course of modern Shiʻism and has played a critical role in the social, economic, and political development of the modern Shiʻi world.

Therefore, I refer to the Usuli movement that began in the eighteenth century as neo-Usulism or modern Usulism. In what follows, I will also use Usulism for shorthand, just as Shi'ism will be shorthand for Twelver or Imami Shi'ism. This is not to exclude the importance of Zaydism, Isma'ilism, or other branches of Shi'ism. However, Usuli Shi'ism is a movement within the dominant branch of Shi'ism often referred to as the Twelvers (or Imamis) because they accepted twelve Imams, whereas Zaydis accepted five Imams and the Isma'ilis believe in seven.

More than one thousand years before the Usuli-Akhbari dispute took place, Karbala' was the site where Husayn (the third Shi'i Imam) and a small band of his followers were massacred by forces of the 'Umayyad clan, who established the first dynasty in Islamic history from 661–750. The martyrdom of Husayn was a decisive moment in the transformation of the followers of the Imams from a political party to the full-blown sectarian movement that we now know as Shi'ism. Similar to Christian commemorations of the crucifixion of Jesus, Shi'i observances dedicated to Husayn still rouse passion among participants.[4] Karbala' eventually developed as a Shi'i center of pilgrimage, learning, and leadership where Shi'is pray at the shrine of Imam Husayn and learn at the feet of Shi'i scholars. In addition to Karbala', the Iraqi city of Najaf, as well as Qum in Iran, are the most influential Shi'i cities. Najaf became the center of gravity for the global Shi'i community in the nineteenth century and remains the most important Shi'i center outside Iran. Prior to the rise of Qum in the twentieth century, aspiring clerics had to study in the shrine cities of southern Iraq (Najaf and Karbala') if they wanted to be taken seriously in the rest of the Shi'i world.[5] Since the mid-twentieth century, Qum and Najaf have become relatively independent of each other, which is illustrative of the nationalization of Shi'ism over the course of the past century.[6]

Relative to Sunnis, Shi'i scholars played a limited role in the political development of Islam going all the way back to the foundational period of Islamic history.[7] The term Shi'i or Shi'a originally referred to the "party" of 'Ali ibn Abi Talib (d. 661) – the son-in-law of the Prophet Muhammad. Shi'is claim that 'Ali was the rightful successor of Muhammad and the first Imam.[8] According to Shi'is, 'Ali and subsequent Imams inherited a measure of Muhammad's divine knowledge as his male heirs. Therefore, Shi'is often refer to themselves as the "People of the House" (*ahl al-bayt*) of Muhammad. Even though 'Ali did have some political success and is considered by Sunnis as one of the four "rightly guided" (*rashidun*) Caliphs, Shi'is did not initially win the day politically. The first Islamic dynasties associated with Shi'ism, the Fatimids (909–1171) and the Buyids (934–1055), did not appear until the tenth century – two and a half centuries after Imam 'Ali. Shi'is played a relatively limited role in mainstream politics after the fall of the Fatimids and Buyids. That is, until the Safavids came to power in 1501. This, of course, is not to say that Shi'is were completely kept out of politics between the twelfth and sixteenth centuries. For example, Nasir al-Din al-Tusi (d. 1274) served as advisor to Hulugu Khan after the Mongol invasion of the Middle East. Additionally, local Shi'i dynasties of this period include the Sarbardarids of Sabzivar.

For much of Islamic history, Shi'i scholars associated the rejection of worldly affairs, including politics, with piety. Many Shi'i scholars have claimed that all governments are illegitimate until the promised Mahdi (the Twelfth Imam, Muhammad al-Mahdi) returns to establish everlasting peace and justice on earth. This ideological position stemmed from the development of Shi'ism as a minority movement, which was often divorced from the political establishment. As Said Amir Arjomand points out, the sixth Imam Ja'far al-Sadiq (d. 765) "transformed the early political Shi'ism into an introverted and quietist religious movement. The Imams ceased to be anticaliphs ... and became the spiritual guides of the Shi'ite (Imami) sectarians."[9] Additionally, Hamid Algar argues that "after the occultation of the Twelfth Imam, Shi'ism became even more quietist in its attitude to worldly power."[10] Therefore, the rise in socio-political involvement of Shi'i clerics in the modern period may seem surprising.

What accounts for the increase in the socio-political position of Shi'i clerics in the modern period? The answer to this question begins with the adoption of Shi'ism as the state religion of the Safavid dynasty (1501–1722) in Iran. As Henry Corbin argues, Safavid Shi'ism gave rise to "something like an official clergy, exclusively concerned with legality and jurisprudence, to such a point that original Shi'ism, in its essence gnostic and theosophic, has, so to speak, to hide itself."[11] The Shi'i clerical establishment consisting of religious professionals came into existence during the Safavid period "with firm roots among the people and therefore with a power base independent of the state."[12] By the time the Safavid dynasty fell, the majority of people within the empire had converted to Shi'ism and clerics retained their strong base of popular support.

The Qajar (lit. "marching quickly") dynasty (1785–1925), which was superimposed on the ruins of the Safavid Empire, adopted Shiʿism as the state religion in an attempt to legitimize their rule. The early Qajar shahs especially supported Usuli scholars (*mujtahids*), who began publicizing their claim to be the deputies of the Hidden Imam. Usulis proclaimed that the Qajar shah ruled on their behalf and made it clear that the Qajars were only authorized to enter the Russo-Persian war after they issued declarations of *jihad*. One Usuli *mujtahid* (Kashif al-Ghita'), in fact, equated the authority of Shiʿi scholars (*ʿulama'*) to the authority of God. In his declaration of *jihad* against Russia, Kashif al-Ghita' states: "He who disobeys the most distinguished *ʿulama'*, by God, disobeys the *imam*, and who disobeys the *imam* disobeys the prophet of God, the best of creation, and who disobeys the best of creation disobeys Almighty God."[13]

The Qajar central government was not particularly strong, partially because of the intrusion of Russian and British imperialists, who propped up the weak regime. Instead of colonizing Iran, Russia and Britain established spheres of influence in northern and southern Iran, respectively. Escaping formal colonization in the nineteenth century, modern Iran emerged with the potent mix of a strong transnational clerical establishment and a weak central government. In addition to the relationship between high-ranking clerics and the national government, the religio-political balance of power also played out on the local stage in which politicians and clerics competed for the upper hand.

In addition to political and popular support, the transformation of clerical status required an equally grand reinterpretation of clerical authority, a process that began with Usulis in the pre-modern period. The French traveller Jean Chardin famously reported that Usulis had already protested the Safavid political establishment in the following manner:

> How can it be possible, say the clergy, that these impious kings – consumers of wine carried away by their passions – to be the vicars of God, communicate with heaven, and receive the necessary enlightenment to guide the faithful believers? How could they resolve a case of conscience and the doubts of faith, in the required manner of the lieutenant of God, they who can barely read? The supreme throne of the universe belongs only to a *mujtahid*, or to a man who possesses sanctity and the sciences, transcending the community of men. However, as the *mujtahid* is peaceable,

he should have a king at his service to exercise his sword to the cause of justice as his minister.[14]

In other words, the political system should be in service of the Usuli establishment, not the opposite. In this way, Usuli clerics continued to justify their appropriation of the role played by the Imams. That is, they claimed the right to declare war (*jihad*), collect *zakat* and *khums* money, and issue binding legal judgments. Some Usulis also claimed to possess the spiritual authority of the Imams.

Such authority was revived and reformed by the founder of the modern Usuli movement, Muhammad Baqir "Wahid" b. Muhammad Akmal Bihbihani, who is scarcely known in Western scholarship – even in Islamic studies. His life spanned most of the eighteenth century (1704–91) and his students were the most dominant Shi'i figures during the foundational period of the Qajar regime. Although Wahid Bihbihani has received little scholarly attention, his importance is not lost in Shi'i sources. Shi'i biographers and historians unanimously cite him as the primary catalyst for the establishment of neo-Usulism. Authors writing in both Persian and Arabic call him the "teacher of all" and the "reviver" of the twelfth Islamic century (roughly eighteenth century CE). Bihbihani's successors also describe him as the one who was inspired by God to overcome the Akhbari establishment. The leadership of Bihbihani was indeed largely responsible for the success of the initial phase of the neo-Usuli movement. But, we are getting ahead of ourselves. Before returning to the topic at hand, let us consider the broader context in which modern Usulism emerged.

THE EIGHTEENTH-CENTURY MOMENT

This book specifically focuses on the origins and early development of the modern Usuli movement, a period that roughly spans the late eighteenth and early nineteenth centuries. A central argument of the book is that the recent ascendancy of Shi'ism is a culmination of the neo-Usuli movement. Therefore, I agree with Arjomand who states that "the establishment of an Islamic theocracy ruled by the Shi'ite 'ulama [was] the last stage of the evolution of clerical authority in Shi'ite Islam."[15] This book, therefore, examines the historical roots of the contemporary stage of the Shi'i establishment.

Similar to the revival and reform of Islam in the past several decades, the foundational period of the modern Usuli movement was also an age of reform in the broader Islamic world. Put differently, neo-Usulism emerged as part of a wider trend of Islamic reform and revival that began in the eighteenth century. The most prominent examples of such movements are Sunni Wahhabism and neo-Sufism. The conservative Wahhabi movement started by Muhammad Ibn 'Abd al-Wahhab (1703–92) remains to this day the ideological basis for Saudi Arabia, and the alliance between the Saudi clan and Wahhabi ideology has continued to the present day. In the past several decades, Wahhabism has spread throughout much of the world, partially as a result of Saudi oil revenue.[16] Otherwise, it might have remained a fringe movement. The term neo-Sufism has been vigorously debated by scholars, but is generally associated with Ahmad Ibn Idris al-Fasi (1760–1837), who emphasized a close orientation toward the Prophet Muhammad. Mark Sedgwick and other scholars have rejected the concept of neo-Sufism in favor of "the *tariqa Muhammadiyya* movement, the movement of the Muhammadan way."[17] Although Ibn Idris was less known for his political influence than Ibn 'Abd al-Wahhab, Ibn Idris's successors did involve themselves in politics.

I argue that these three networks (Usuli Shi'ism, Wahhabi Sunnism, and Idrisi Sufism) are the most powerful Islamic movements that emerged in the modern period prior to European imperialism. Although the movements were not Islamist organizations per se, the roots of contemporary Islamist movements can be found in them.

The three movements began at a critical moment in modern world history – simultaneous with monumental changes in the "West" and elsewhere, including the industrial revolution, the Enlightenment, the American, French, and Haitian revolutions, Christianity's Great Awakening, as well as the ideologies of nationalism, secularism, communism, and capitalism. Primarily focusing on Euro-American changes, the well-known historian Eric Hobsbawm calls the period from 1789–1848 the "Age of Revolution."[18] Enlightenment thinkers and historians alike have also referred to this period as the "Age of Reason."[19] Because of the critical developments of this period, historians often divide the modern period into two parts: early modern (c. 1450–1750) and late modern (c. 1750–1950).

What occurred in the late eighteenth century that warrants this split in time, which separates one age from the previous age? Historians have vigorously debated this question, but it seems that three changes stand out above others, which include new forms of industrialization, a new global economic system, and the emergence of the nation-state system from a collection of empires and kingdoms. Each of these changes had global roots and implications, which were not simply confined to Europe or the "West." Indeed, the age of "revolution" and "reason" were not limited to the Western experience as illustrated by the Islamic reform movements.

The eighteenth-century Islamic revival was specifically linked to the decentralization of the Ottoman and Mughal Empires and the collapse of the Safavid Empire, a process that preceded the emergence of nation-states in the Islamic world. The Ottomans, Safavids, and Mughals are often referred to as "Islamic gunpowder empires" or "military-patronage" states. Several scholars, including Marshall Hodgson, who popularized the term "Islamic gunpowder empires," have pushed back against exaggerating the importance of gunpowder in the formation of these empires.[20] Likewise, we should be weary of overstating the role that Islam played in these empires. Nevertheless, I will continue to refer to the three empires with references to Islam and gunpowder for shorthand. By the sixteenth century, the Ottomans, Safavids, and Mughals dominated the swath of earth that includes Eastern Europe, West and South Asia, North Africa, and the Middle East. Similar to the empires that developed in Russia, China, and Western Europe, the Islamic empires reached their height in the seventeenth century. By the eighteenth century, gunpowder empires throughout the world began to decentralize, often resulting in the emergence of nation-states.

This process of political decentralization is the subject of considerable debate among historians, some of whom argue that the decentralization of Safavid, Mughal, and Ottoman territory in the eighteenth century began a period of "decline" from which the Islamic world has not yet recovered.[21] Indeed, the Ottomans lost direct control of several imperial provinces, including Iraq. European imperialists eventually began referring to the Ottoman Empire as the "sick man of Europe" and debated how its territory might be divided up once the dynasty fell. To them the "Eastern Question," as it was known, was not a question of whether the Ottoman Empire would fall, but when. Unable to reach a consensus about how to divide it without disrupting the European balance of power, imperialists maintained the Ottomans in power until World War One, which resulted in the final collapse of the Ottoman Empire and the end of the Islamic Caliphate for the first time in history.

In the past few decades, however, scholars of the Middle East and Islam have generally rejected the "decline" thesis, partially on the basis of cultural studies related to issues of revival and reform.[22] Decline has, in fact, become the politically incorrect "d-word" in Middle East Studies.[23] Instead of an age of decline, some scholars proposed that the eighteenth-century Islamic world experienced its own enlightenment.[24] I suggest that the terms "decline" and "enlightenment" are too simplistic and do not add to a nuanced view of the eighteenth-century Islamic world. The issues at the heart of the two debates, however, are interconnected. The political decentralization in the eighteenth century produced conditions that led to Islamic revival and reform. It is no coincidence that new, semi-independent Islamic movements emerged as the early modern empires decentralized and collapsed. Neo-Usulism, Wahhabism, and neo-Sufism were direct responses to the changing sociopolitical conditions of the Islamic world by reformers who attempted to breathe new life into their societies.

These movements, therefore, are part and parcel of the modern experience. In addition to reviving Islamic traditions, they also initiated reforms in an attempt to adapt to the emerging modern world. As Ira Lapidus puts it, reform (*tajdid*) movements "are a response to and expression of Muslim modernity, but they are also rooted in a deep historical and cultural paradigm."[25] Lapidus defines *tajdid* movements as "universalistic" projects that "emphasize correct ritual legal practice," provide a "mechanism for political organization," and look to the Prophet as the model of Islam.[26] Lapidus, like many scholars, however, ignores Shi'i reform movements altogether and only focuses on what he calls "the Sunni-Shari'a-Sufi synthesis."[27] One of the goals of this book, therefore, is to add Shi'ism to the history of eighteenth-century Islamic reform.

CONTEMPORARY SHI'ISM AND ITS ROOTS

Since the late eighteenth century, Usuli Shi'ism has been dominant in Iran and Iraq and throughout the Shi'i world. Although Iran has been the locus of global Shi'i trends since the mid-twentieth century and especially since 1979, it does not completely define the transnational Shi'i community. While Shi'is are as little as ten percent of the global Muslim population, Shi'is in the Middle East may be as much as thirty percent. Over ninety percent of Iranians are Shi'is and roughly sixty percent of Iraqis are Shi'is, the majority of whom live in southern Iraq. Mass conversion to Shi'ism in Iran and Iraq is a modern phenomenon and Usulism played a critical role in the Shi'ification of both countries. The majority of Iranians converted to Shi'ism during the Safavid period (1501–1722) and most of the tribal confederations in southern Iraq began converting in the eighteenth century.[28] Yitzhak Nakash argues that this point also "marked the beginning of a process of Shi'i state formation in southern Iraq," which was specifically associated with the emergence of Najaf and Karbala' as desert market towns.[29] In addition to Iran and Iraq, Bahrain has a majority Shi'i population. Although roughly two-thirds of Bahrainis, approximately a million people, are Shi'i, the Sunni al-Khalifa family has ruled Bahrain since the eighteenth century. Lebanon also has a significant Shi'i community, which is one of the three confessional groups in the political system. Shi'i communities also exist in Syria, Northern India, Pakistan, Afghanistan, Saudi Arabia, and other Gulf states. The majority of Shi'is in Saudi Arabia live in the oil-rich al-Ahsa province. The epicenter of Shi'ism in India is Lucknow, once the capital of the Shi'i state of Awadh. In Pakistan, Shi'is comprise roughly fifteen percent of the total population and primarily reside in Lahore. In Afghanistan, Hazaras and many Tajiks are Shi'is. In Africa, Shi'i communities are primarily composed of Indian Khojas, who are organized under the Federation of Khoja Shia Ithna-Ashari (Twelver) Jamaats of Africa. The largest communities in Africa reside in Tanzania, Kenya, and Uganda, although none of these communities number above the tens of thousands.[30]

After the post-world war period of secularization in the Islamic world, masses of Iranians, led by Ayatollah Khomeini and other Usuli clerics, succeeded in overthrowing the Iranian government in one of the most spectacular revolutions in modern history.[31] What made the revolution particularly stunning was that it brought a religious establishment (Usulis) to power. The secularization of much of the Middle East (except for Saudi Arabia) in the decades leading up to the 1979 revolution made the emergence of a theocratic government unthinkable to many analysts. After all, the struggle between secularism and traditional religious establishments is a hallmark of modern history. Although many scholars assume that secularism is a pillar of modernity, Khomeini and many of his Usuli colleagues disagreed. Usulis successfully established themselves in power as champions of Shi'i Islam and moved to eliminate those who did not fit their ideological vision, including Marxists, secularists, royalists, and Baha'is.

The theocratic political system that Usulis have built in Iran is a unique innovation in Islamic history. It is a culmination of the modern revival and reform of Shi'ism that started with the Usuli movement. It is no secret that the most powerful figures in the government are Usulis. This is not to say that all Usuli clerics support(ed) the Iranian revolution or the Islamic Republic. Additionally, not all of the architects of the revolutionary government were Usuli clerics. Like any complex social or religious organization, Usulism is not monolithic. In fact, the revolution made the networks of Usuli clerics more diverse. Ardent supporters of the Islamic Republic are at one end of the spectrum, while those who denounce it as un-Islamic are at the other end. The influence of the Iranian revolution was also not confined to Usulism, Shi'ism, or Iran; it reverberated throughout the Middle East and the Islamic world. Many scholars argue that the Iranian revolution signaled or at least contributed to a more general revival of Islam since the 1970s.[32] Therefore, the Usuli movement has been a major part of this shift in the history of the Islamic world.

The context for the revival of Islam in the twentieth century included the fall of the Ottoman Empire, the creation of new nation-states after World War One, and decolonization after World War Two. By the end of this chain of events, the number of sovereign countries in the world more than tripled. In 1945 there were roughly fifty sovereign states in the world and by the 1970s, there were approximately 150 countries. The new states in the Middle East, with the exceptions of Iran, Turkey, and others, were based on the territorial divisions of the Sykes-Picot Agreement recognized in the League of Nations Mandate System after World War One. Britain and France had won most of the territory in the Middle East and created new states on the basis of their own interests and the perceived realities on the ground. Justifications for national unity often came in the form of ethnic or sectarian identity, which had also been the basis for the creation of national identities in Europe. While calls for unity in Islam often transcended ethnic identity, ethnic nationalism transcended religion.

Despite appeals to Islamic solidarity and the pan-Islamism associated with figures like Jamal al-Din al-Afghani (d. 1897), secular governments generally prevailed in the Middle East in the first two-thirds of the twentieth century. This was especially the case in Turkey, Iran, and Egypt. Secularism in these countries was specifically associated with Mustafa Kamal Ataturk, Reza Shah Pahlavi, and Gamal 'Abd al-Nasser respectively – each of whom had been military officers before seizing power. These figures perceived Islam as an obstacle to modernization, which they attempted to achieve through Westernizing reforms. Such reforms included the prohibition of religious dress, banning of Islamic organizations, and the establishment of secular educational and legal institutions. Culture associated with Islam was officially replaced by European fashion and attempts to import European-style institutions.

Islamism (or political Islam), therefore, emerged in the context of nation-state building and the Westernizing secularism of the twentieth century. To borrow Peter Mandaville's definition, Islamism "refers to forms of political theory and practice that have as their goal the establishment of an Islamic political order in the sense of a state whose governmental principles, institutions, and legal system derive directly from the shari'ah."[33] Muslim theorists had been discussing methods and ideals associated with socio-political organization long before the modern period. However, a new impetus for the development of political Islam came when Mustafa Kemal abolished the caliphate in 1924. For the first time in Islamic history, the Muslim world was without the authority of a caliph (*khalifa*). Four years after the end of the Ottoman caliphate, Hasan al-Banna (1906–49) formed the Muslim Brotherhood, which is often referred to as the quintessential Islamist organization.[34] The founders of the Muslim Brotherhood advocated a greater socio-political role for Islam and pushed back against the importation of Western culture and secularism. Emphasizing a holistic conception of Islamic society, Hasan al-Banna defined the Brotherhood as "a Salafi movement, an orthodox way, a Sufi reality, a political body, an athletic group, a scientific and cultural society, an economic company and a social idea."[35] Although originating in Egypt, branches of the Muslim Brotherhood, including Palestine's HAMAS, spread throughout much of the Islamic world.

Islamist trends proliferated as new states developed. Sayyid Abu al-'Ala Mawdudi, for example, established Jam'at-e Islami, an organization similar to the Muslim Brotherhood, in the early 1940s in the midst of the independence movements that created the new nations of India and Pakistan. In 1932 Abdulaziz Ibn Saud founded the Kingdom of Saudi Arabia as an "Islamic" state. Indeed, the Saudi government protested the Universal Declaration of Human Rights because it guaranteed individuals the right to change their religion. King Faysal (r. 1964–75) continued to resist secularism by incorporating religious figures into the state. He also established the global Organization of Islamic Cooperation, which has fifty-seven member states and a regular delegation to the United Nations.

The Cold War, the Arab-Israeli conflict, and particularly the Iranian revolution accompanied the rise of additional Islamist organizations after World War Two. The Iranian revolution pioneered a new model of political organization and ushered in a new phase of Islamism. For many Muslims around the world, Iranians had bucked the global order of superpower patronage. Inspired by the revolution and partially supported by the new Iranian government, Shiʻis in Lebanon founded Hezbollah for the expressed purpose of providing assistance to the Lebanese Shiʻi community and fighting Israeli forces that had been stationed in southern Lebanon.[36] Resistance to the Soviet invasion of Afghanistan, which began simultaneously with the Iranian revolution, led to the development of the Taliban and transnational *jihad* organizations, like al-Qaeda. Additionally, HAMAS, which emerged in Palestine in the late 1980s, conducted terrorist attacks against Israelis and provided social services to disenfranchised Palestinians.

Although no other country has copied the model of the Islamic Republic of Iran, the influence of the new system has been far reaching. When Israel invaded Lebanon, Iran armed and trained Hezbollah fighters who rose in opposition. Seeing Iran's regional reach, Saddam Hussein feared that Iran's revolution might spread to Iraq's Shiʻi population. Also hoping to score the oil-rich region of Khuzistan, Saddam Hussein invaded Iran. The Iran-Iraq war raged on for nearly ten years until it finally ended in a stalemate, with Khomeini and his revolutionary forces more deeply entrenched in power.[37] The war also allowed Saddam to tighten his grip on power and prevent any would-be Iraqi Shiʻi revolutionaries from initiating change in Iraq. However, the 2003 American invasion and overthrow of Saddam Hussein afforded Shiʻis in Iraq an opportunity to gain political power for the first time since the creation of the Iraqi state in the early twentieth century. Realizing the opportunity this presented, Ayatollah al-Sistani – the head of the Usuli establishment in Iraq – supported Iraqi elections. His role, therefore, has been decisive in post-Saddam Iraq.

Shiʻi influence in the Islamic world over the past three decades elicit mixed reviews. No matter how historians eventually treat this period, it seems clear that Shiʻi influence has been on the rise since the 1979 revolution in Iran. Although contemporary Islamism is not the central theme of this book, any understanding of contemporary Islam is impossible without knowledge of Islamic history. Marshall Hodgson referred to the tenth/eleventh century as the "Shi'i century."[38] Only future historians will be able to assess whether the twentieth/twenty-first century, a millennium later, will also be considered a Shi'i century. In addition to discussing issues related to sectarianism and nationalism, historians will be tasked with answering the question of how and why Shi'i clerics reversed a longstanding policy of staying out of politics. One of the aims of this book, therefore, is to contribute to this question, which is closely linked to matters of Islamic knowledge and authority.

SHI'I KNOWLEDGE AND AUTHORITY

Knowledge and authority stand at the heart of questions related to the emergence of modern Usulism. In practical terms, Usulis and Akhbaris debated the problem of how to rule on new issues not explicitly addressed in the Qur'an and Hadith. For example, is it permissible to drink coffee or make use of new technologies? In the twenty-first century, we debate whether cloning is morally acceptable and how to handle climate change. Settling the big questions of the day is an eternal human problem. Historically speaking, the duty of answering such big (and small) questions was often the domain of religious officials, who were supposed to possess the knowledge and authority to guide entire societies on the right path. Similarly, the Usuli-Akhbari debate was about the relationship of Shi'i scholars to Islamic knowledge and authority. More specifically, Usulis and Akhbaris argued over proper methodologies for interpreting the Qur'an and Hadith, the permissibility of handing down legal judgments with the aid of reason, and the authority of Shi'i scholars in relation to Muhammad and the Imams.

In fact, the rationalist-scripturalist dispute is one of the most persistent debates in the history of Islam.[39] It is a fundamental question faced by every society because it has to do with change. How does a society adapt to change without losing its core traditions, identity, and culture? Who in the society has the power to effect change or define the tradition in the first place? The question for many Muslims is, what constitutes "Islamic" knowledge and authority? The relation between knowledge and authority, therefore, is intimately interconnected. As far as Shi'ism is concerned, it was the divine knowledge inherited from the Prophet

Muhammad that authorized the Imams to lead the community. When the twelfth Imam disappeared into mystical occultation (*ghayba*) in 874, the problem of knowledge and authority became a pressing issue in Shi'ism – just as it had been after the death of Muhammad for Muslims in general.[40] On what basis would the new leader(s) of Muhammad's community claim authority?

After the death of Muhammad, his divine revelations were canonized into the Qur'an and his sayings and deeds were compiled as Hadith collections. These two sources became the ultimate foundations of knowledge and authority, which unified the majority of the Muslim community. In addition to these sources, the authority of the Imams became a unifying factor for Shi'is. After the disappearance of the Twelfth Imam, Shi'is also relied on Hadith reports attributed to the Imams. In practice, Muslim scholars (*'ulama'*, literally "those who know") claimed that their knowledge of the Qur'an and Hadith gave them authority to lead the community. The following tenth-century report, attributed to the concealed Twelfth Imam, is illustrative of the delegation of authority from the Imam to the Shi'i scholars during the occultation: "Concerning the new cases that occur, refer to the transmitters of our Traditions, for they are my *hujja* (proof) unto you and I am God's proof unto them."[41] This reference specifically refers to the authority of Hadith transmitters, which indicates the textualist bent of clerical authority in Islam.[42]

However, the authoritative textual sources (i.e. Qur'an and Hadith) of Islamic law, and that of other text-based traditions, are finite in the sense that they do not contain explicit rulings on all legal matters, which are potentially infinite. The question, then, is how do Muslim scholars rule on cases that are not found in the texts, if at all? Similarly, American legal experts must create new laws within the textual framework of the Constitution, which contains little content from which legal norms can be derived. Like the Constitution and any other text-based tradition, the Qur'an contains a limited amount of textual sources that explicitly relate to law. It is often suggested that the Qur'an contains roughly five hundred verses of "legal" content. Hadith compilations contain far more legal statements that instruct Muslims on how to act in order to adhere to the divine law (*shari'a*). However, the traditions found in the Hadith are not exhaustive.

Questions related to the extraction of rulings from the texts and the creation of new rules are the domain of Islamic law (*fiqh*). The importance of law to Islam cannot be overstated as indicated by its designation by Muslims as the "queen of the sciences." If philosophy was the defining feature of ancient Greece and the modern world is a civilization characterized by science and technology, then Islam is a civilization of law. As many scholars have pointed out, the Islamic legal system is "something grander than law: it aspired to classify and categorize all human acts."[43] Therefore, Muslim legal experts assume that God has a ruling or law (*hukm*) for every human behavior and that their duty is to uncover whether each act is forbidden, discouraged, permissible, recommended, or mandatory according to the Lawgiver (*al-Shari'*). *Shari'a* is divine law as it exists in the mind of God, the Lawgiver, whereas *fiqh* is the human understanding of *shari'a*. Islamic law, therefore, is much more than a list of do's and don'ts for which one will be punished or rewarded by governmental or religious authorities. It is a complex divine moral code of conduct that encompasses all areas of social, economic, political, cultural, religious, and other human spheres of activity.[44]

The process or exercise in which Muslim jurisconsults (*mujtahids*) endeavor to derive new rulings is called *ijtihad*. The famous Iraqi *mujtahid*, Muhammad Baqir al-Sadr (1935–80), succinctly defined *ijtihad* as "the effort which the jurist expends in extracting a divine-law ruling from its arguments and sources."[45] A central question for those who engage in *ijtihad* concerns the non-textual sources that a legal expert has at his disposal. In other words, in conjunction with the Qur'an and Hadith, on what sources should new rulings be based? This question is the foundation for the subfield of jurisprudence (*usul al-fiqh*) in Islamic law, which is the "theoretical and philosophical foundation of Islamic law."[46] *Usul al-fiqh* literally means the "sources" or "principles of the law" and is the origin of the term Usuli. It is also one of the primary distinguishing features of both Sunni and Shi'i legal schools of thought. Many Sunni Muslim scholars agreed that consensus (*ijma'*) and analogy (*qiyas*) are legitimate sources to be used by *mujtahids* in addition to the Qur'an and Hadith.

Usuli scholars accepted consensus (*ijma'*) and reason (*'aql*) as the third and fourth sources. The first scholar to define Shi'i *usul al-fiqh* in this way was Shaykh al-Mufid (d. 1022), who was influenced by rationalist Mu'tazili and Sunni legal scholars.[47] Mufid's work was the first to clearly move beyond the transmission of textual sources. He maintained the superiority of the foundational texts by arguing that reason needed the help of the texts, not the opposite. Prior to Mufid, the task of scholars was to collect traditions, not give their opinions on them. Mufid harshly attacked scripturalists and accused them of being too liberal in their collection of traditions, without investigating or thinking critically about what they were reporting.[48] Whereas Sharif al-Murtada's (d. 1044) system favored a more prominent role for reason, Shaykh al-Ta'ifa al-Tusi (d. 1067) struck a balance between reason and revelation, which was followed for at least a century after him. These eleventh-century Usulis argued that Shi'i scholars were permitted to fulfill functions that had previously been associated with the Imams, including the collection of and distribution of *zakat* and *khums*, the implementation of criminal punishments (*hudud*), and leading congregational prayers. Usulis of this period also developed theories of the Imamate which suggested that the Hidden Imam's return was not imminent and would not be hastened by human action. Although they upheld the notion that all political institutions are illegitimate in the absence of the Imam, they encouraged political quietism and a willingness to work more closely with those in power during the Imam's occultation.[49] In fact, the newly established Shi'i Buyid dynasty (945–1055) in Baghdad welcomed such theories and promoted Usuli scholars, partially because their school of thought allowed for greater pliability of the law.

The Usuli school was later developed by scholars working during the Mongol period who continued to expand the authority of Shi'i scholars. Al-Muhaqqiq al-Hilli (d. 1277), whose emphasis on *ijtihad* increased the authority of *mujtahids*, claimed that Shi'i scholars are the deputies of the Hidden Imam during the occultation and insisted that a ruling from a *mujtahid* is like "talking with the tongue of [God's] law."[50] Muhaqqiq's nephew (al-Allama al-Hilli, d. 1327), who became an official in the Ilkhanid court of Sultan Oljaitu (d. 1316), argued in favor of the division of the Shi'i community into *mujtahids* and emulators (*muqallids*) of *mujtahids*. He contended that an emulator who failed to comply with the rulings (sing. *hukm*) of a *mujtahid* was a sinner.

Akhbari scholars, however, rejected Usuli rationalism, charged them with adopting Sunni methods of jurisprudence, and maintained a reliance on the texts. In other words, Akhbaris insisted that the Qur'an and Hadith are the only authoritative sources of knowledge and authority and, therefore, viewed *ijtihad* and the authority of *mujtahids* as illegitimate. Although Akhbari sentiments existed prior to the modern period, Akhbarism was articulated by Muhammad Amin al-Astarabadi (d. 1627), who attacked rationalist methodology and contributed to the development of what has become known as the Akhbari school.[51] Astarabadi rejected *ijtihad* as a tool of Sunnis and argued that it only produced conjectural knowledge (*zann*) at best. Instead, his methodology was limited to sources that would produce certainty (*qat'*), especially Hadith reports (*akhbar*), which perfectly reflect God's will.[52] Astarabadi suggests that the authority of deducing new rulings rest with *muftis* and judges (*qadis*), instead of *mujtahids*.[53]

In addition to the textualism of Akhbaris and the rationalism of Usulis, a third response to the question of knowledge and authority emerged under the rubric of Illuminationism (*ishraqiyya*), which emphasizes intellectual intuition in the formation of knowledge. The emergence of the Illuminationist school is often traced back to the figure of Shihab al-Din al-Suhrawardi (d. 1191), who promoted the idea that true knowledge was the result of both rational and intuitive emanations from the mind.[54] During the Safavid period, Illuminationism was associated with the School of Isfahan, especially Mulla Sadra Shirazi (d. 1640), whose cosmology included rationalism and visionary experience, and required purification of the soul through asceticism, mysticism, and gnosis. Mulla Sadra also developed a new synthesis for Shi'i authority in the absence of an earthly Imam. He writes:

> The earth cannot be devoid of a person upon whom the proof [*hujja*] of God rests ... Thus, in each time, there must be a saint (*wali*) who worships God by his personal experience and possesses the knowledge of the divine book as well as what the 'ulama' and mujtahids have learned. He has absolute supervision and leadership in both religious and temporal affairs.[55]

In the early nineteenth century, Illuminationism was associated with the Shaykhi movement, founded by Shaykh Ahmad al-Ahsa'i (d. 1826), who was a student of the founders of the modern Usuli movement.[56] Dissatisfied with his Usuli education, Ahsa'i claimed that his knowledge was the result of intuitive experiences with the Imams.[57] Therefore, he rejected the idea that *mujtahids* were the vicegerents of the Hidden Imam and instead suggested that living authority was with the "Perfect Shi'i" (*Shi'i kamil*) or the "Fourth Pillar" (*rukn al-rabi'*), who would be in direct contact with the Hidden Imam.[58] Responding to the Shaykhi challenge of their authority, Usulis eventually declared infidelity (*takfir*) on Shaykhis as they had done with Akhbaris.

As we have seen, therefore, three broad sources of Shi'i knowledge and authority are discernable: the foundational texts (*naql*, i.e. the Qur'an and Hadith), reason (*'aql*), and intuition (*kashf*). Although the majority of Muslims accept the authority of texts, the second two sources have caused divisions. Some scholars accept reason and intuition as methods of textual exegesis while others believe that these two sources can be used independently of the texts to arrive at new knowledge. Still other scholars have accepted a synthesis of the three sources. While appeals to the texts, reason, and intuition are fairly consistent throughout Shi'i history, periodic shifts in Shi'i thought often result from emphasis on one of the three sources.

SUMMARY OF CHAPTERS

As indicated already, this book examines the rise of the modern movement of Usuli Shi'ism. In addition to contextualizing Usulism within the Shi'i intellectual tradition, I analyze the rise of the Usuli movement within the framework of global, regional, and local changes of the eighteenth and nineteenth centuries. Much of this book focuses on the individuals and groups associated with Usuli Shi'ism, which is loosely organized. Therefore, I look at Usulism from the perspective of informal networks of students–teachers and patrons–clients, which are not always related to formal institutions. At the highest level, Shi'i clerics are engaged in scholarly activity, teaching, issuing legal judgments, and maintaining networks of supporters. Therefore, much of what follows will be associated with these activities. I argue that the Usuli movement prevailed as a result of a variety of factors, including the ability of Usulis to survive independently of state sponsorship during a period of political decentralization with support from Iraqi tribes and the international Shi'i business community. Additionally, Bihbihani and his disciples consolidated leadership of the Shi'i intellectual community.

The first chapter develops a theoretical basis for the remainder of the book. I argue that the eighteenth-century Islamic reform movements were responses to the changing socio-political landscape of the Middle East and were, therefore, intimately linked to modernity. The Islamic movements do not fit into the traditional Eurocentric framework of modernity, largely because modernity is a global phenomenon and "multiple modernities" have prevailed in the modern world. Chapters 2 and 3 discuss the local and regional forces that contributed to the making of the transnational Usuli movement. Chapter 2 illustrates that Usulism was one of the competing trends in Iran during the Safavid period, which contended with Akhbarism, Illuminationism, and exaggerated (*ghuluww*) Shiʻism. The neo-Usuli movement emerged victorious out of the wreckage of the Safavid Empire and was adopted as the state ideology during the early Qajar period. Chapter 3 moves to southern Iraq, where a small diaspora of ex-Safavid Shiʻis and Iraqis established the modern Usuli movement in a Mamluk-controlled province of the Sunni Ottoman Empire. Much to the dismay of the Ottomans, Usulis came to exert immense popular influence in southern Iraq, especially after the majority of Arab tribesmen converted to Shiʻism from Sunnism as they settled near Karbala' and Najaf.

Chapters 4, 5, and 6 explore the emergence of Usulism at ground level by examining the thought and activism of the first generation of Usuli scholars. Chapter 4 focuses on the life of the "founder" of modern Usulism, Wahid Bihbihani, who is remembered in the Shiʻi tradition as the "reviver" (*mujaddid*) of the eighteenth century because he put an end to Akhbari dominance. Chapter 5 illustrates that one of the primary reasons for the longevity of the Usuli school is that Bihbihani trained a network of disciples, who became immensely powerful as the supreme religious figures in Iran and southern Iraq in the early nineteenth century. Bihbihani's successors upheld the appearance of granting legitimacy to the Qajar dynasty, while arrogating supreme authority to themselves. As *mujtahids*, they claimed to be the "general deputies" (*niyaba ʻamma*) or "guardians" (*wilayat al-faqih*) of the Imams and the "sources of emulation" (*marjaʻ al-taqlid*) for all Shiʻis. The subject of Chapter 6 is Bihbihani's methodology of producing knowledge, which is rooted in the legalistic tradition of Islam. Bihbihani argued that jurists who misinterpret Islamic law are the enemies of religion because their rulings can last an eternity, unlike the mistakes of physicians, which can only cause short-term bodily harm. Building on his Usuli predecessors, Bihbihani advocates a theory of Islamic law in which *mujtahids* derive knowledge from the Qur'an, Hadith, consensus (*ijmaʻ*), and reason (*ʻaql*).

In the final chapter, I discuss the broader Islamic revival and reform by comparing Bihbihani's Usulism with the contemporaneous movements of Wahhabism and neo-Sufism. I argue that the Shiʻi, Sunni, and Sufi movements associated with Bihbihani, Ibn ʻAbd al-Wahhab, and Ibn Idris are among the most influential and enduring Islamic trends in the modern world.

Chapter 1

The Times and Places of Reform in the Modern World

INTRODUCTION

The late eighteenth century witnessed an increase in ideological reform movements in various parts of the world – none of which has become a universal political, religious, or economic system. Although ideological diversity has prevailed in the modern world, we can conclude that the late eighteenth century ushered in a new age of ideological reform movements. Neo-Usulism was one such movement. Although the Enlightenment spread beyond Europe, it did not become as pervasive as many modernization theorists might have hoped. Additionally, the Great Awakening had little influence outside the Christian world. Similarly, Islamic reform movements hardly extended beyond Islamic societies. Although not as well known, Chinese Confucianism also witnessed a period of reform simultaneous to reforms in the Middle East and Europe. As Jonathan Spence argues, eighteenth-century Confucianism "began to develop in new directions, paralleling changes in the society and the economy."[1] Spence points out that Confucian scholars began searching for certainty with the use of a new methodology (*kaozheng*) more than in the texts (like Usulis) and those who were inclined to studying the texts, focused on older works that were closer to the time of Confucius (similar to Akhbaris).

No matter how innovative they might have been, Islamic and Confucian reform movements are hardly considered as "modern" by scholars who suggest that Europe or "the West" is the birthplace of all things modern. By this Eurocentric perspective, neo-Usulism is simply a continuation of age-old Islamic ideals and practices, and Shi'is still languish in a pre-modern state of static tradition. Similar to a growing number of scholars, I propose that our conception of modernity must be unhinged from Eurocentrism, which will show that Usulism is one of many modern movements responding to problems that have arisen since the eighteenth century.

Usulism became one of the most powerful expressions of modernity in the Shi'i world similar to the Enlightenment, the Great Awakening, Communism, and other ideological movements that articulated "modern" ideals. That reform movements in various parts of the world developed simultaneously in the eighteenth century is not coincidental. Scholars within each movement were responding to the social, economic, and political changes of their societies, which were often tied to changes in emerging global systems. Indeed, this was a period of convergence as eighteenth-century reformers even came to some of the same conclusions. The acceptance of rationalism, for example, seems to have been on the rise in the eighteenth century, as evidenced by the Enlightenment, Usulism, and *kaozheng* Confucianism.

The period was also one of divergence as scholars attempted to come to grips with changing times in a variety of ways, producing a proliferation of social movements, which has made the emergence of a universal global ideology more difficult. The search for a global ideology, therefore, is still on and only the future will tell whether a global ideology will materialize at all. The ideologies, movements, and cultures of modernity represent a kaleidoscope of diverse positions – including religious, secular, rational, textual, socialist, and individualist prescriptions for life in the modern world. In the study of social movements, then, we are left with "multiple modernities," which overlap, acculturate, interact, coexist, interconnect, compete, and fight with one another.[2] Since ideological movements are not created equally and are able to marshal a varying amount of resources, some have become more pervasive than others. State-sponsored ideologies that have access to the coercive power of finances, warfare, and politics (such as capitalism, Communism, and Usulism) often become more prominent than their competitors. Therefore, Communism and Liberalism have indeed been immensely prominent forces in the modern world and have expanded beyond the regions in which they were created, but neither has become universal. Additionally, some ideologies were more innovative than others. Some reform movements attempted to reinvent or revise established traditions, while others proposed radical change and a revolutionary break with tradition.

THE PLACE OF MODERNITY

The holy grail of modernity studies has to do with questions related to the transformation of the world in the past several hundred years. There is little disagreement that a monumental change took place in nearly every realm of human activity as attested by population growth, technological development, urbanization, etc. However, there is little consensus among historians or social scientists in terms of how, when, where, or why the "great transformation" occurred.

Historians and social scientists have often concluded that modernity resulted from the "rise of the West" and the "decline of the Rest." As Andre Gunder Frank rightly argues, such "Eurocentric historiography and social theory looks for these roots only under the European street light" to explain that the modern world emerged from the genius of European culture, which then diffused throughout the world.[3] Therefore, neglecting the histories of the "non-West" has resulted in assumptions that modernity is a European phenomenon, often explained as the "European Miracle." Even worse, it leads to the unfortunate conclusion that those who have resisted "European cultural genius" continue to wallow in the stagnant, putrefying state of their unchanging pre-modern traditions. The economic, military, scientific, artistic, and moral gap between European culture and pre-modern, non-Western traditions, therefore, presumably allowed the superior Europeans to dominate the "rest" of the world. Such assumptions have led to doomsday conclusions that the modern West is locked in a "clash of civilizations" with traditional societies as proposed by Samuel Huntington, or that "the end of history" was achieved with the fall of the Soviet Union as suggested by Francis Fukuyama.[4]

European exceptionalism, however, fraudulently disregards geography, assumes that Europe is homogeneous, and downplays the dark side of modern European history. Never mind that Japan, which is indisputably central to the modern world economic system, is not located in "Europe" or the "West." Never mind the heterogeneity produced by violent sectarianism, ethnic nationalism, and the competing ideologies of capitalism, socialism, Nazism, and fascism in modern Europe. Never mind that European colonialism constitutes one of the most immoral endeavors in human history, which was justified by irrational pseudo-scientific theories of the inherent inferiority of the non-white, non-European, non-male, non-Christian Other. Never mind that economic power which fueled military and political might was won by orchestrating the largest slave trade in human history, peddling opium, engaging in wanton acts of piracy, and committing genocide. Such criticisms of modern European history are not often included in the selective evidence at the heart of Eurocentric explanations of modernity.

Because the term modern and its derivatives (modernity, modernization, postmodern, pre-modern) are so often used and in so many different contexts, they run the risk of becoming meaningless for historians, vaguely associated with ill-defined notions of advancement or progress – whether in technology, religion, politics, economics, literature, philosophy, or art. Progress, after all, is often in the eye of the beholder, and as modern world systems developed, progress for one social group spelled regress for another. Therefore, modern here does not refer to something positive, good, or progressive as it did for many Enlightenment thinkers.[5] Instead, it has to do with change. This is not necessarily the change that classic Western social theorists (Marx, Weber, Durkheim, etc.) described as the "modern moment," which was assumed to be a rupture between tradition and modernity.[6] As Marshall Hodgson rightly argues, "every society is traditional in that it operates through cultural traditions."[7] Traditions are not inert, unchanging objects; they have the ability to adapt, reform, fragment, and metamorphose. And when they do so in response to conditions in the new world, they indeed modernize.

Some scholars insist that explanations of modernity must be universal.[8] Certainly, there are common experiences, trends, patterns that contribute to an understanding of global phenomena. However, the reality is that even if the world has become more integrated and interrelated in recent times, it is not homogenous. Therefore, we must be content with understanding the world in terms of its unity and its diversity. I agree, then, with scholars such as Frank who call for a "holistic analysis to explain any part of the system" which is "humanocentric" instead of Eurocentric.[9] However, since perfect holism cannot be reached unless each part is factored into the system and no trend is fully universal, the concept of "multiple modernities" pioneered by Shmuel Eisenstadt and others is a good counterweight to those who insist on holism.[10] In other words, the world and its parts must be understood simultaneously. Since the whole and its parts can never be fully understood, conclusions should be formed tentatively. Even if the parts do not neatly explain global forces, they interact with broader trends and necessarily provide us with a picture of a whole that is complex. Additionally, I argue that paradigms must be "historocentric" rather than primarily theory-based. Theories, then, must be grounded in a wide reading of history instead of formed around selective cases that fit carefully into narrow models. In fact, the very problem with Eurocentrism is that it disregards the history of the majority of the world and narcissistically assumes that since Europe is at the center of the world, the rest of the world must be understood from its vantage point.

When asked to define modernity, scholars might fire off a list of social, political, and economic concepts such as equality, freedom, rational thought, constitutionalism, popular sovereignty, capitalism, and secularism. Many of these ideas are specifically associated with the Enlightenment and the spread of "Western" culture. As Arjun Appadurai suggests, these ideas are not universal, but part of a "teleological theory, with a recipe for how modernization will universally yield rationality, punctuality, democracy, the free market, and a higher gross national product."[11] Historically speaking, global participation in Enlightenment thought varied tremendously, and Enlightenment philosophers themselves did not reach a high level of unanimity. They especially differed on religion. Some Enlightenment thinkers continued to accept Christianity, albeit in an "enlightened" form. In the wake of intense sectarian Christian warfare, many Enlightenment scholars argued that secularism was a viable solution to religious violence. Others completely rejected religion, arguing that it was incompatible with scientific rationalism, which led to atheistic and anti-religious theories and movements.

Notions of a single modernity are so pervasive that even critics of Eurocentrism often end up supporting its most basic premises – especially the theory that traditional societies will eventually become modernized as they become more rational and that a single modernity originated in Europe. Samir Amin begins his book titled *Eurocentrism* by arguing that "modernity arose in Europe, beginning with the Renaissance, as a break with the 'traditional' culture" and that "modernity is constructed on the principle that human beings ... make their own history" as opposed to God.[12] Amin goes on to argue that Christianity has adapted to modernity by accepting the "new emancipatory conception of reason," whereas Arab societies have not entered modernity because they have not successfully secularized.[13] As Appadurai and others have pointed out, modernization theorists have generally assumed that the space of religion is shrinking in the modern world.[14] I agree with his assessment that it is premature to suggest that religion is on its deathbed, especially when the argument that religion has experienced a revival in the modern world is just as plausible.

As Timothy Mitchell and many others have noted, Edward Said's *Orientalism* "stands as the most powerful account of how Europe's sense of cultural identity was constructed in the business of colonizing and getting rich overseas."[15] However, even postmodernists assume that modernity is a European product, even if it was manufactured in South American, African, Asian, or Middle Eastern colonies. Indeed, many postmodern theorists grew up in, lived in, or reflected a colonial environment. Edward Said, Jacques Derrida, Frantz Fanon, Jean-Francois Lyotard, and Michel Foucault focused on global interactions and dichotomies related to the colonized and colonizer, often equating imperialism with modernity.

Mitchell explains how the "staging" of Eurocentrism has become imbedded in the notion of modernity. In his words, the West is the "product of modernity," which "depends upon the representation of an homogenous space."[16] If the West is the place that occupies the time of modernity, the non-West, therefore, has been demoted to the periphery of modernity and is imagined as "the non-place, terra incognita, the wasteland," and the space without time in which history has not yet begun.[17] From this perspective, then, the monumental achievements in science and technology in the Islamic world during the pre-modern period are of little consequence, even if they are, in fact, the building blocks on which modern Europe was built.

Mitchell concludes, therefore, that modernity is not necessarily a stage of history but the staging of it.[18] In other words, Eurocentric modernity involves the depiction or representation of differences between modern and pre-modern, West and non-West. Becoming modern, then, is often viewed as a rejection of tradition and the adoption of Western ideals, institutions, culture, language, etc. Therefore, one might assume that the centrality of rationalism to the Usuli movement is the result of importing Enlightenment philosophy into the Islamic world, even though Islamic rationalism is nearly as old as Islam itself. According to Eurocentric modernity, the Usuli movement cannot be fully modern because it has not completely replaced its tradition with the whole pantheon of modern/Western ideals. Even if Muslims did accept the entire toolkit of modern Western ideas – whatever those might be – the copy would never be as good as the original.

One of the most powerful representations of Eurocentrism is, in fact, the classic history of "Western" civilization, which moves westward as an "Orient Express" – from the ancient Middle East (the biblical Orient) to Greece, Rome, France, England, and finally America. As J. M. Blaut, Marshall Hodgson, and others have pointed out, this "tunnel history" suggests "that every important thing that ever happened to humanity happened in one part of the world," namely "Greater Europe," which has come to dominate modernity.[19] (The Bible lands only factor into the ancient world.) Historians, therefore, often ignore the contributions of peoples from the non-West. Asian societies are generally caricatured and essentialized as Oriental despotisms and Africans are depicted as savages. As Said's *Orientalism* articulates, Muslims were particularly despised as the reverse negative of Europe – the Orient instead of the Occident, the deviants of Western civilization.[20] In his *Black Athena*, Martin Bernal pushes back against the "Oriental Express" model of history by demonstrating the African and Asian roots of "Western" culture.[21]

THE TIME OF MODERNITY

Whether we like it or not, historians must choose or manipulate time periods, which they do on the basis of their field of study, data, region of interest, and, unfortunately, their desired outcome. Some historians choose the arbitrary time period associated with a century or decade, while others use important events as the start and finish lines. The reality is that we can go as far back in time as we want to understand the roots of more current trends. Certainly, to get a better grasp of the modern Middle East it is crucial to understand the early period of Islam, which occurred a millennium and a half ago. But, we have to start somewhere and by choosing a starting point, a historian argues (wittingly or not) that the point of departure illustrates the root or origin of the subject under question.

Even though historical periodization often devolves into hair split-ting and we should be wary of rigid categorizations of historical time, assigning time to modernity is incredibly important. It indicates how we conceive of change and from where we assume that change has come. Therefore, narratives of the Middle East and Islamic world suggesting that the modern period began in the nineteenth century run the risk

of overstating the importance of Europe in the process of modernization in the Middle East. Indeed, many histories of the modern Middle
East begin in 1798 with Napoleon's invasion of Egypt, or even later.[22]
Although this was a momentous development in the Islamic world,
suggesting that the modern Middle East began with Napoleon implies
that modernity in the Middle East is a European phenomenon that
arrived once Europeans showed up, especially since Napoleon justified
his conquest with his desire to spread the Enlightenment.

Applying Eurocentric notions of time to Islamic history also over-
shadows internal forces that were at play prior to European dominance.
By tracing modern trends (such as the Usuli movement) that developed
prior to European imperialism we can conclude that modernity in the
Islamic world predates European dominance. It then becomes clear
that Europeans did not simply inscribe or bestow modernity on the
region and that Muslims and Middle Easterners were highly involved
in creating their own paths to modernity. Therefore, the creation of the
modern Middle East and Islamic world involved people, places, and
events "inside" and "outside" the region, a process that began before
the year 1800.

WORLD SYSTEMS AND MULTIPLE MODERNITIES

Scholars in the field of world systems analysis have criticized traditional
Eurocentric narratives by reconstructing modern history on the basis
of global economic trends. World systems analysts often looked to Karl
Marx who famously asserted that "the discovery of gold in America, the
extirpation, enslavement and entombment in mines of the aboriginal
population, the beginning of the conquest and looting of the East-Indies,
the turning of Africa into a warren for the commercial hunting of black-
skins, signalised the rosy dawn of the era of capitalist production."[23] In
other words, Marx argues that modernity began with capitalism, which
was a result of the interaction between Europeans and the world. World
systems analysts, therefore, argue that economics are at the heart of
modern structural changes.

Immanuel Wallerstein, among the most prominent advocates of world
systems theory, suggests that a capitalist world-economy emerged in the
sixteenth century, which divided the world into a core-periphery relationship and "resulted in an unequal exchange favoring those involved

in core-like production processes."[24] The core, Wallerstein explains, originated "in parts of Europe and the Americas" and "expanded over time to cover the whole globe."[25] He further argues that the world-system is not confined to economics since "endless accumulation of capital had generated a need for constant technological change, a constant expansion of frontiers–geographical, psychological, intellectual, scientific."[26] Therefore, Wallerstein concludes that eighteenth-century philosophers and scientists challenged the "millennial claim of religious authorities that they alone had a sure way to know truth," which resulted in the birth of the "modern" university and the social sciences.[27] Although Wallerstein points out that world-systems analysis strongly attacked Eurocentrism, Europe remains at the center of his analysis.[28]

Andre Gunder Frank, in his *ReOrient: Global Economy in the Asian Age*, insists that world systems analysts, including Wallerstein (as well as Marx, Weber, Werner, Sombart, Polanyi, Braudel, and even his own previous work) "(mis)-attributed a central place in their theories to Europe, which it never had in the real world economy," since "Europe was certainly not central to the world economy before 1800."[29] Additionally, Frank argues that the global economic system did not have a single center but possibly a hierarchy of centers in the early modern period.[30] Frank's conclusion is Asia-centric as illustrated by the subtitle of his book and his argument that the Ottoman, Mughal, Safavid, and Ming/Qing Empires were more economically, politically, and militarily advanced than all of Europe.[31] Therefore, Europe was on the periphery in the early modern period when "the West bought itself a third-class seat on the Asian economic train … and only in the nineteenth century managed to displace Asians from the locomotive" as a result of American silver production and the industrial revolution.[32]

Frank's analysis is partially formed on the basis of Janet Abu-Lughod's criticism of Wallerstein and other world systems analysts for treating the "European-dominated world system that formed in the long sixteenth century as if it had appeared de novo."[33] In *Before European Hegemony*, Abu-Lughod maps out a thirteenth-century world system, which spanned the Eurasian continent, but was not centered in Europe or Asia and had multiple centers and peripheries. Her groundbreaking work shows that searching under the non-European streetlight as well as diverse moments in history leads to a fresh, more complex picture of the whole and its parts. As Abu-Lughod concludes, "there were numerous preexistent world economies" before the thirteenth century, when

Europe became an upstart on the periphery of a system in which the Middle East, India, and China formed "the Old World core."[34]

Although world systems analysis is useful in some respects, it often leads to economic determinism, which can prove disastrous when considering social movements. Hopkins and Wallerstein, for example, assume that modern social movements are reactions to capitalism, most of which are nationalist, socialist, or both. Their narrow conclusion is that "today, there is scarcely a movement which is not nationalist, and there are few national movements that are not socialist."[35] Moreover, they argue that the confluence of nationalist/socialist movements is so great that when it does not occur it "is suspect as a fraud to large segments of the world population."[36] This argument, however, ignores Islamic, feminist, and other movements, which are not necessarily socialist and are often transnational.[37]

An alternative to Eurocentric modernity or an attempt to apply world systems theory to culture is that there is not one path to modernity; there are multiple. And the array of cultural systems exists in a single world. As Eisenstadt argues, modernity is "a story of continual constitution and reconstitution of a multiplicity of cultural programs."[38] Attempting to reconcile modernity with the dominant position of European powers, he then suggests that "Western patterns of modernity are not the only 'authentic' modernities, though they enjoy historical precedence and continue to be a basic reference point for others."[39] Similarly, Mitchell argues that "we should talk neither of a singular modernity that defines all other histories in its terms, nor of the easy pluralism of alternative modernities."[40] Although paths to modernity have distinct theoretical underpinnings and emerge in an interconnected world, they are also rooted in the social, political, economic, religious, artistic, cultural, and historical contexts in which they emerge. In other words, modern changes must be contextualized within the traditions in which they are created.

It is for this reason that the Usuli movement must be considered from the contexts of both the eighteenth-century world and the historical Shi'i tradition, which stretches back in time more than a thousand years. Unfortunately, it is difficult to trace the contemporaneous non-Shi'i roots of Usulism because Usuli scholars rarely referenced their non-Shi'i contemporaries. Most references in Usuli texts are to scholars associated with the rationalist tradition within Shi'ism. This is because Usulis were more concerned with representing their ideas as authentically Shi'i than projecting them as "modern" or as responding to contemporary trends.

However, Usulis were certainly influenced by their contemporaries. Ann Lambton, for example, suggests that "consequent upon growing contact with Western Europe, the works of Montesquieu, Rousseau, Mirabeau, John Stuart Mill, and others began to be read," which resulted in discussions of political reform in Iran.[41]

Usulis developed a Shi'i path to modernity in light of the changes around them, as did other intellectuals around the globe. Although there is little direct evidence suggesting that the Enlightenment influenced Usulism per se, some Usulis eventually accepted core elements of the Enlightenment. For example, Usulis played a prominent role in the Iranian constitutional revolution at the turn of the twentieth century and prominent Usuli clerics (especially Sayyid Muhammad Tabataba'i) promoted constitutionalism. As Abdul-Hadi Hairi argues, however, Shi'i clerics in Iran and Iraq were more interested in deposing what they considered a tyrannical shah than adopting "Western" styles of governance.[42] Additionally, Enlightenment ideals, including constitutionalism, were never adopted as core elements of Usulism, and Usulis generally criticized secularism, materialism, and individualism – concepts that define modernity in the West. Usulis were more interested in reinventing Shi'ism than promoting or criticizing Enlightenment ideas. They sought to adapt Islamic and particularly Shi'i sources to the emerging modern world in a time of change.

CREATION OF THE MODERN WORLD

The assumption that modernity originated in Europe is perhaps rooted in the fact that Europeans have dominated much of the modern world economically, militarily, and politically. It has been estimated that European military expansion resulted in the European powers' control of thirty-five percent of the world in the early nineteenth century, sixty-seven percent in 1878, and eighty-four percent by 1914.[43] There is no doubt that European empires were dominant in the nineteenth and twentieth centuries – after the decentralization and collapse of gunpowder empires, which was underway by the eighteenth century. Therefore, "Westernization" was, in fact, pervasive and the majority of the world was influenced by trends that spread from Europe. However, this is not the whole story since Westernization and European dominance were not all-pervasive. Additionally, the so-called rise of the West must be considered in relation to the regions in which Europeans exercised their hegemony.

Historians still do not agree on how Europeans became dominant. However, the eighteenth-century Industrial Revolution, which was rooted in scientific breakthroughs, seems to be at the heart it. As Peter Stearns rightly argues, "no factors even remotely rival industrialization's impact in explaining what has gone on in the [modern] world" since it "affected every aspect of human and social life."[44] Indeed, some historians argue that it was the most important historical change since the agricultural revolution, which provided the very basis for settled societies thousands of years ago.[45] For the first time in history, manufacturing became a greater source of wealth than agriculture for some societies.[46] Additionally, industrialization was the primary cause of urbanization, which is among the most radical social changes in human history. Since the Industrial Revolution, the number of people living in cities has increased from roughly ten percent to ninety percent.

Industrialized countries gained a critical edge in trade and military, which also allowed them to become politically and socially dominant and colonize the non-industrialized world. In general terms, countries that industrialized relatively early, such as England, Germany, France, and Japan, became dominant in the modern world. Those that did not (most of the Middle East, Africa, and Asia) were forced into a position of defensive developmentalism.[47] In terms of economics, this often meant that non-industrialized regions became producers of cash crops, which were traded on the global market at prices linked to the demands of industrialized markets.

Military and economic dominance, which presupposed social dominance was won, therefore, with new industrially produced technology, which created conditions of inequality and differentiated those with and those without it. Therefore, European powers became dominant technologically and then attempted to project their culture, history, and ideals as superior as a result. This is not to say that all socio-political ideals are equal. Some ideas are better than others. However, the ideas promoted by industrial states will be given added weight as they are backed by political and military power.

Aside from developments in science and industry, it is difficult to suggest that Europeans progressed beyond the rest of the world in the modern period. Attempts by scholars to move beyond industrialization as an explanation for European dominance often become problematic.

For example, Edmund Burke points out that Marshall Hodgson's attempt to explain the rise of the West in cultural terms resulted in "a deep tension in Hodgson's thought between his tendency to view modernity as a world historical process and as linked to particular cultural trends deeply rooted in the West."[48] Hodgson, who was otherwise ahead of his time in conceptualizing world history, argues that "the great Western transmutation" was the result of "technicalization," which is "a condition of rationally calculative (and hence innovative) technical specialization."[49] In addition to the science of Brahe and Kepler and the philosophy of Descartes and Kant, Hodgson goes on to suggest that technicalization was reflected in "legally operated social control" associated with the French Revolution. Although philosophy and the French Revolution might be up for debate, Hodgson's attempts to apply his concept of "technicalism" to European society becomes increasingly Eurocentric as he suggests that Europeans are more humane as a result of the "gentling of manners," in which the "better classes were being softened and 'civilized'."[50] In light of the atrocities of World War One and Two alone, it is just as plausible that Europeans were becoming less civilized. Therefore, Hodgson's otherwise insightful commitment to cultural and civilizational studies, results in Eurocentric conclusions as he attempts to explain the rise of the West in cultural terms.

TRADITION AND CHANGE: FROM PRE-MODERN TO MODERN

During what is often referred to as the "Middle Ages" or "Middle Period" of world history (roughly the millennium that preceded the modern period), new empires and civilizations continued to develop on the basis of religious and philosophical traditions. Each major religion was imbedded in its geographical region and enjoyed state sponsorship. Buddhism provided foundations for states in Korea, Japan, and Vietnam; Confucianism in China; Hinduism in India; and Christianity in Europe. Islam was the basis for successive polities in the Middle East, North Africa, West Asia, and Iberia and later spread to East and West Africa as well as Central and South Asia. Confucianism, Buddhism, Greek philosophy, Zoroastrianism, and Judaism originated in the so-called Axial Age (c. 800–200 BCE), while Christianity emerged several hundred years later. Islam, therefore, was the only major religion that emerged after the so-called classical period of world history.

Islamic civilization, therefore, was particularly molded in the post-classical period and became especially influential during the "Dark Ages" of European history. Building on the advances of Persian government, Greek philosophy, Roman law, Chinese inventions, and Indian mathematics, Muslims established one of the most enduring civilizations in world history. Adding to past human achievements, credit is due to Muslims for the invention of science and notable contributions in art, literature, politics, law, and civil rights as evidenced by the discovery of algebra by al-Khwarizmi (d. 850), the medical advances of Ibn Sina (d. 1037), the poetry of Jalal al-Din Rumi (d. 1273), and so on. Although often overlooked by Europeanists and world historians alike, these achievements provided the foundation for modern European scientific and intellectual innovations. For example, translations of Ibn Sina's *Canon of Medicine* were used as textbooks in European medical schools well into the seventeenth century – a full six hundred years after he died! Moreover, European universities were modeled on the Islamic *madrasa* system.

By the thirteenth century, westward migration of Mongols, Turks, and other nomads had transformed the Eurasian continent and the Islamic world along with it. Mongols brutally toppled entire empires as they moved west. The most powerful blow to the Islamic world was the sacking of Baghdad in 1258, which brought an end to the five hundred-year-old Abbasid caliphate (750–1258). As Abu-Lughod argues, the Mongols unified much of Eurasia into a single system, which had previously been fragmented. She points out that the Mongol conquest signals the first moment that Western Europeans made direct contact with East Asia through papal and trade missions (via Marco Polo) as they attempted to establish an alliance with the Mongols against Muslims.[51] Additionally, she argues that Middle Easterners had already known the sailing routes around Africa and to the Americas, which Europeans only discovered during their fifteenth-century "Age of Exploration." Middle Easterners, however, did not make regular use of these circuitous routes because they controlled more direct paths to trade markets.[52] Despite the fact that the great Mongol conqueror Genghis Khan failed to establish an enduring politically unified empire stretching from China to Europe, Abu-Lughod argues that Mongol rule "facilitated the conduct of both trade and diplomacy" in Eurasia. She concludes, therefore, that the

Portuguese, Dutch, and English only began to insert themselves into the "old world system" after the Ming Chinese withdrew its fleet in 1453 and Arab and Indian merchants became overextended in the Indian Ocean. Therefore, "the 'Fall of the East' preceded the 'Rise of the West' and it was this devolution of the preexisting system that facilitated Europe's easy conquest."[53]

Two significant processes developed in the fifteenth century, namely the expansion of centrally organized "gunpowder" empires and further integration of the global economy. For the most part, these states continued on the model of traditional empires, relying on the military conquest of new territory to increase tax income and secure trade. In this pre-industrial age, agricultural surplus and trade in luxury goods made up the bulk of tax revenue. While military might gave rulers power in the eyes of most civilians, it did not give them political legitimacy.

Imperialists relied on religious officials or philosophers to legitimize their right to rule and ensure the maintenance of law and order. Clerics and scholars were generally happy to comply as long as rulers funded religious activities and safeguarded the tradition. The population of notables and subjects were also more likely to throw their weight behind a ruling dynasty that supported their religious values. As leaders of cultural and socio-religious activities, clerics and scholars also had a direct tie to the people, which allowed them to influence public opinion. Therefore, conquerors had to co-opt religious establishments if they hoped to establish long-term rule.

Members of the ruling dynasties of the early modern period maintained a close relationship with religious officials. In specific terms, the Habsburgs, who ruled much of Europe, adopted Catholicism. Russian imperialists established themselves as guardians of the Eastern Orthodox Church, which had been orphaned by the fall of the Byzantine Empire after the Ottomans sacked Constantinople in 1453. The Qing dynasty in China was heir to Confucianism. Sunni Islam was the official religion of the Ottomans and Mughals, and the Safavids adopted Shi'ism. Although these empires were modeled on old imperial practices, early modern political and religious systems continued to change, as illustrated by the Protestant Reformation, *kaozheng* Confucianism, and the Akhbari-Usuli dispute.

The expansion of most gunpowder empires peaked in the seventeenth century after which they decentralized or completely disintegrated, which eventually led to the formation of nation-states. The year 1722 marked the beginning of this process when the Safavid Empire fell. After nearly a century of tribal warfare, the Qajars came to control Iran. As will be discussed in more detail in the following chapter, chaos in Iran reverberated throughout much of the world, including the political fragmentation of the Mughal Empire after 1725, which allowed the British to gradually replace the Mughals as rulers of the Indian subcontinent. The Ottoman Empire also began to decentralize in the eighteenth century, but did not fall until 1918. That European powers did not step into the power vacuum in the Islamic world until the nineteenth century illustrates that they were not global superpowers until after the Industrial Revolution.

As the Islamic world began to wane militarily, it also suffered internal economic weakness as it lost control of trade networks, which Muslims had dominated for over a millennium. Therefore, the Ottomans and Qajars eventually faced the reality of maintaining elaborate military and administrative systems with fewer resources. Additionally, at a time in which European powers were pioneering new technologies, the Islamic world did not always adopt new developments as they once had. Sectarianism also played a role in weakening governmental authority as Christians, Sunnis, Shi'is, and Hindus began asserting their authority in the face of decreased imperial power. Yet even as European control of global trade increased, some local and regional merchants benefited from the new arrangements. European imperialists were often happy to champion independence movements, especially since they weakened their imperial competitors.

As the eighteenth century was a period of monumental change in world history, it was also a watershed in the Islamic world. Describing this change in negative terms, Hodgson argues that whereas "the age of the sixteenth and seventeenth centuries was one of the greatest in Islamdom's history," the period's achievements were "beclouded by the decline of the eighteenth century and the subsequent debacle."[54] More recent historians, however, have rejected this "decline" thesis. Dana Sajdi argues that although the Middle East may have undergone a process of political decentralization, everything associated with Islamic society and culture was not necessarily in a state of free-fall.[55] Reinhard Schulze also argued that the decline thesis was based on Orientalist assumptions.[56] Instead, Schulze suggested that the transformation of the eighteenth-century Islamic world was the beginning of an Islamic Enlightenment. Several scholars, including Bernd Radtke[57] and Rudolph Peters,[58] have rejected Schulze's Enlightenment theory. Additionally, Ali Allawi has added to the debate by questioning whether Islamic civilization will ever recover from the crisis triggered over two hundred years ago with "the expansion of the West into Muslim lands."[59] He concludes that Islam "appears to be at odds with the rest of the modern world"[60] and that "Islamic civilization is now nearly bereft of most of the vital elements that had previously given it coherence and meaning."[61]

As indicated already, I argue that political decentralization and fragmentation of the eighteenth-century Islamic world took place prior to European imperialism and gave rise to new (modern) social, cultural, religious, economic, and political trends. Wahhabism, Usulism, and neo-Sufism are among the socio-religious trends that developed during this period. As John Voll points out, political ineffectiveness, military defeats, and economic difficulties inspired a reconstruction of Islamic society.[62] Islamic reform that began in this period, therefore, has a direct correlation to the decentralization of the gunpowder empires. Islamic learning and scholarship was on the rise in the eighteenth century and the influence of Muslim clerics took a quantum leap throughout much of the Islamic world. Muslim scholars were attempting to provide answers to the challenges of a changing socio-political landscape and even began filling voids in power.

Much of the confusion of associating the term Enlightenment with eighteenth-century Islamic movements is that Enlightenment suggests both the emancipation from tradition and the acceptance of rational sciences, neither of which are universal to the Islamic reformation in the eighteenth century. Many scholars actually embraced a return to tradition and some rejected rational thought altogether. As with changes in Christianity, the terms revival and reform are more apt than Enlightenment, Renaissance, or decline in describing eighteenth-century Islamic trends. After all, every reform-minded Muslim scholar was engaged in reviving and adapting a tradition within Islam.

Eighteenth-century Islamic movements generally did not develop in reaction to the West nor were they attempts to reconcile Islam with Western conceptions of modernity. The reformers' acceptance of rational thought was not necessarily a sign of the adoption of Enlightenment philosophy, as indicated already. Explicit attempts to reconcile Islam with European or Enlightenment ideas did not develop in the Middle East until the nineteenth century, after European imperial incursions into the region.

Western scholars often label modern Muslim scholars as accomodationists or rejectionists in an attempt to position them in relation to
Westernization. For example, Jamal al-Din al-Afghani (1838–97) and
Muhammad 'Abduh (1849–1905) are often called accomodationists,
whereas Ruhullah Khomeini (1902–89) and the Muslim Brotherhood
are labeled rejectionists. Such designations are misleading for late eight-
eenth- and early nineteenth-century scholars (including Bihbihani, Ibn
'Abd al-Wahhab, and Ibn Idris), who were generally unconcerned with
the West. If anything, they ignored the West.[63] Although Ibn Idris was
in Cairo when Napoleon invaded Egypt in 1798, his writings make no
mention of the French invasion or the Enlightenment ideas that Napoleon
was supposedly spreading. This is not to say that Muslim scholars were
unaware of European thought and advancements but rather that they
were overwhelmingly concerned with reviving their own traditions.

As John Esposito puts it, Islamic "revivalism was primarily a response
from within Islam to the internal sociomoral decline of the community."[64]
Indeed, eighteenth-century Muslim reformers perceived clerics within
their own tradition as enemy number one, not Christians or Europeans.
Ibn 'Abd al-Wahhab demonized the Sunni establishment in the Arabian
Peninsula, while Ibn Idris attacked popular Sufism, and Bihbihani
declared that all Akhbari Shi'is were infidels (*kuffar*).

Because the Wahhabi, Usuli, and Idrisi movements were established
on the eve of European dominance, they eventually influenced responses
to Western forms of modernity. More precisely, these Islamic movements
were in a position to respond to the West in the nineteenth and twentieth centuries and are still vastly influential in defining the post-colonial
Islamic world. Heads of the Islamic reform movements were particularly critical of Westernization projects, especially when it meant the
adoption of ideas and institutions that were perceived as "un-Islamic."
We will return to a discussion of these Islamic reform movements in
the final chapter. Now, let us turn to the regional matrix that gave rise
to neo-Usulism.

Chapter 2

Shi'ism and the Emergence of Modern Iran

INTRODUCTION

This chapter and the next focus on the local and regional worlds in which the Usuli movement and modern Shi'ism emerged. Although Iranian, Arab, Indian, and Turkish identities became more pronounced with the development of ethnic and linguistic nationalisms, sectarian identity has often trumped nationalism in the modern Middle East. Therefore, the following emphasizes the transnational, transregional character of Usulism in particular and Shi'ism in general. This chapter discusses the context of modern Iran, while Chapter 3 focuses on Iraq. As Juan Cole has already established, Usulis also developed transregional ties to Shi'is in the principality of Awadh in northern India.[1]

The politically chaotic interregnum in Iran between the Safavid (1501–1722) and Qajar (1785–1925) dynasties resulted in the resettlement of prominent scholarly Shi'i families, who had been based in the Safavid capital of Isfahan. The relatively small diaspora that moved to southern Iraq became highly influential in the creation of Usulism. When the Safavid Empire collapsed, countless families scattered to "Shi'i" towns in Iraq, Iran, and India, creating networks that criss-crossed national and ethnic "boundaries." Scholarly migration will be illustrated in Chapter 4 with the family of Wahid Bihbihani, the founder of the Usuli movement.

SAFAVID CENTRALIZATION OF IRAN (1501–1722)

Modern Shi'ism and Iran emerged with the establishment of the Safavid Empire, founded by Isma'il I (1487–1524) in 1501. The Safavids laid political, religious, economic, and social foundations that still prevail in the Persianate and Shi'i world. Shah Isma'il I's adoption of Shi'ism as Iran's state religion and the subsequent conversion of the majority of Iranians from Sunnism to Shiʻism stand out as the most enduring legacy of the Safavids.

Four major trends of Safavid Shiʻism are discernable. The first phase, which mixed charismatic Sufism and exaggerated (*ghuluww*) Shiʻism, was associated with Shah Ismaʻil I and his Qizilbash supporters. Emphasizing this current, Kathryn Babayan argues that "*ghuluww*, Alid loyalty, and sufism (mysticism)" are the "predominant features" of Safavid Islam.[2] After the death of Ismaʻil I, his son and successor, Shah Tahmasb (1514–76), sought to distance the Safavid regime with the religious tendencies of his father. Therefore, he favored legalistic Usuli Shiʻism as the state ideology, which is the second major current of Safavid Shiʻism. The third trend was the development of the Akhbari movement and the fourth was the rise of the Illuminationist "school of Isfahan." Throughout each phase, the Safavid state was closely associated with the Shiʻi establishment in Iran as illustrated by its funding and appointment of religious officials.

The authority of Shah Ismaʻil I was initially based on his position as the spiritual guide of the Safaviyya Sufi brotherhood, which is where the Safavid state derives its name. Ismaʻil I inherited his position as shaykh of the Safaviyya from his father. By 1501, when Ismaʻil was only fourteen years old, his army sacked Tabriz, the key city in northern Iran. Within a decade, Ismaʻil and his Qizilbash warriors seized control of the Iranian plateau and beyond. The Qizilbash wore special red hats bearing twelve pleats, a symbolic commemoration of the twelve Shiʻi Imams, which is where we get the term "red heads" or *qizilbash*. Although the nature of the Safaviyya commitment to Shiʻism prior to 1501 is difficult to untangle, it appears that they had converted to Shiʻism in the mid-fifteenth century – roughly a century after the brotherhood was founded by Safi al-Din (d. 1334).[3]

In addition to adopting Shiʻism as the state religion, Ismaʻil I took the ancient Persian royal title of *shah* (king) and revived Persianate culture. Therefore, the Safavid political structure was rooted in absolutism based on divine right with a blend of Sufi and Shiʻi culture. To strengthen his claim on Shiʻism and divine rule, Ismaʻil I claimed to be a descendant of the seventh Shiʻi Imam (Musa al-Kazim). Responding to messianic sentiments of the time, Shah Ismaʻil I also claimed to be a return of the Twelfth (or Hidden) Imam, Muhammad al-Mahdi. In his poetry, under the penname of "The Sinner" (*Khatai*), Ismaʻil claimed to be "The Absolute Truth" and states: "My mother is Fatima, my father is

Ali; and I am the *Pir* of the Twelve Imams ... I am the living Khidr and Jesus, son of Mary. I am the Alexander of [my] contemporaries."[4] As Babayan points out, Isma'il drew on the Abrahamic tradition to claim that he was the return of the whole line-up of prophets, including Adam, Noah, Abraham, Moses, Jesus, and Muhammad. He also rooted the Safavid project in Persianate culture by claiming to be the reincarnation of Mazdean kings, including Jamshid, Zahhak, Feraydun, Khusrraw, and Alexander.[5] Finally, he claimed to be the incarnation of God, to which his poetry attests: "In me is prophethood [and] the mystery of Holiness. I am God's eye [or God himself]; come now, O blind man gone astray, to behold the truth I am the Absolute doer of whom they speak. Sun and Moon are in my power."[6] As such, Isma'il's Qizilbash followers apparently believed that he was infallible (*ma'sum*), which made them invincible on the battlefield and prompted some fearless warriors to charge into war weaponless.[7] Each of these claims contributes to the characterization of early Safavid religion as exaggerated (*ghuluww*) Shi'ism, which some scholars have also defined as extremist.

After early Safavid military success and a pro-Safavid Shi'i revolt in Anatolia in 1511, Ottoman forces attacked the Safavid start-ups. The Ottomans executed 40,000 Qizilbash in Anatolia as punishment for the rebellion.[8] With the aid of artillery and firearms, the Ottomans devastated the Qizilbash in northwestern Iran at the famous battle of Chaldiran in 1514.[9] The military loss exposed the myth that Isma'il was all-powerful. Possibly as a result, he never participated in another military campaign. According to Homa Katouzian, the loss at Chaldiran caused Isma'il to sink into a deep depression and spend the end of his life "drinking and debauching in the company of 'rosy-cheeked' youths."[10] As the Ottomans went on to capture key cities in Iraq, Syria, and Egypt, the Qizilbash began making use of gunpowder, which fueled their own expansion. Although the Safavids had been aware of gunpowder technology before Chaldiran, they had rejected it because they believed that the protective power of Shah Isma'il I was a stronger weapon, and gunpowder weapons seemed unmanly to the Qizilbash.

Shah Isma'il's son, Tahmasb (1514–76), was ten years old when he came to power. During the early years of his reign, the power struggle between Turkish and Tajik tribes, which made up the Safavid power base, devolved into civil war (1524–36). To make matters worse, the Ottoman forces of Sultan Suleiman the Magnificent took advantage of the internal struggle by launching an offensive on Iran, which only ended in 1555 with the Amasya treaty. In addition to granting the Iraqi territory of Baghdad and Kurdistan to the Ottomans, the treaty shifted the Safavid center further east as indicated by the fact that the Safavids relocated their capital from Tabriz to Qazvin.[11]

Until Tahmasb came of age, the Qizilbash amirs and their militias controlled the state although they did not necessarily act as a unified group.[12] Shah Tahmasb's followers considered him a divine figure as they did his father, but Tahmasb had no desire to play this role. Indeed, he suppressed *ghuluww* tendencies and attempted to erase his father's legacy as a divine messiah. He even executed a group of Qizilbash who proclaimed him to be the Mahdi.[13] Instead, Tahmasb redefined Shah Isma'il I as a saintly warrior (*ghazi*) who prepared the way for the Hidden Imam.[14] As Babayan illustrates, Tahmasb claimed his own charismatic authority as the friend (*wali*) of Imam 'Ali, instead of the incarnation of the Imam.[15] In fact, Tahmasb's biography cites countless dreams in which 'Ali inspired him, taught him secrets, and helped him in battle.

Shah Tahmasb was convinced that legalistic Islam was useful for the state and attempted to reconcile Qizilbash animism and Sufism with legalistic Shi'ism. Inspired by dreams of the Imams, Shah Tahmasb issued decrees upholding Islamic laws associated with gambling, prostitution, drinking, and music.[16] He also created official court positions for scholars who had been trained in Shi'i law. According to Rula Jurdi Abisaab, Albert Hourani, and others, the Safavids invited Shi'i scholars specifically from the Jabal 'Amil region of southern Lebanon to implement Shi'i legalism, which resulted in a migration of 'Amili scholars to Safavid Iran.[17] Many of these scholars, in fact, were Usulis. Abisaab argues that Safavid shahs supported 'Amili scholars in particular because Jabal 'Amil had established itself as the pre-eminent center of Shi'i learning and because 'Amili scholars made use of *ijtihad* and were versed in Sunni doctrines, which was useful for polemics against the Ottomans.[18] Andrew Newman, however, rejects the notion that a "migration" took place and suggests that the number of scholarly emigrants to Safavid Iran has been overestimated. Instead, he argues that most Shi'i Arab scholars actually rejected the Safavid project, which they claimed was carried out by a few unorthodox Shi'i scholars.[19] Therefore, Newman concludes that during Shah Tahmasb's reign, Safavid religion remained as heterodox as it had been in the early years of Shah Isma'il I.[20]

Although Arab Shi'is may not have been flocking to aid the Safavid government in implementing its Shi'i policies, 'Amili scholars were influential in the Safavid government.[21] The first of these scholars was 'Ali b. 'Abd al-'Ali "Muhaqqiq" al-Karaki (d. 1533).[22] Most Shi'i biographical dictionaries cite Karaki as an Usuli, no doubt because he supported the use of *ijtihad*. Shah Isma'il I had invited him and additional Shi'i scholars to preside over the Shi'ification of Iran. After visiting the court of Shah Isma'il several times, Karaki moved to the Safavid capital toward the end of Shah Isma'il's reign. When Shah Tahmasb came to power, he ordered all officials to obey Karaki in all affairs and bestowed him with the title of "Seal of the *Mujtahids*."[23] Karaki introduced the Usuli idea that Shi'i scholars are, in fact, the deputies (*na'ib*) of the Imams, and Tahmasb relegated religious authority to the Shi'i clerics. In return, Karaki bestowed the title of "just Imam" on the shah.[24]

As the court's favorite *mujtahid*, Karaki was instrumental in implementing legalistic Shi'ism. One of his first orders of business was to encourage the conversion of Iranians from Sunnism to Shi'ism. To this end, he ordered the appointment of prayer leaders throughout the country to teach people the fundamentals of Shi'ism.[25] He was, therefore, one of the first Shi'i clerics to encourage the performance of Friday prayer, which had traditionally been rejected by Shi'is when it was performed in the name of a Sunni sovereign. According to Abisaab, Shah Isma'il had been particularly interested in using the Friday prayer to publicize his sovereignty and was inspired by a dream of Imam 'Ali to station armed soldiers in the mosque in order to discourage Sunnis from resisting.[26]

As a legalistic-minded Usuli jurist, Karaki defined Shi'ism on the basis of scriptural exegesis carried out by *mujtahids* and rejected Islamic mystical and folk traditions, which remained prominent throughout much of the Safavid period. Karaki wrote several treatises directly challenging Sufis and Sunnis, including "Refuting the Criminal Invectives of Sufism" (*Mata'in al-mujrimiyya fi radd al-sufiyya*), and "Breath of Divinity in Cursing Magic and Idolatry" (*Nafahat al-lahut fi la'n al-jibt wa al-taghut*), which was aimed at Sunnism.[27] For roughly a century after Karaki's death, state-sponsored clerics continued to support the Usuli tradition.

Scholars often point to the reign of Shah 'Abbas I the Great (r. 1588–1629) as a high point of Safavid history. When he inherited the throne, the empire was in disarray. With the help of Armenian and Georgian slave-soldiers (*ghulams*), Shah 'Abbas launched a campaign to retake lost territory. Like many empire-builders, Shah 'Abbas paved the way to prosperity with excessive brutality. On suspicion of treason, he ordered the execution of several family members, including one of his sons. Two other sons were blinded. He also massacred 100,000 Georgians and deported over half that many.[28]

Safavid monopoly on the regional silk industry gave Iran a ticket to participate in the expanding global market.[29] Silk revenue allowed Shah 'Abbas to stabilize the empire by rebuilding bureaucratic and military institutions. He also moved the capital from Qazvin to the more central city of Isfahan and transformed it into an impressive capital and global trade center. Therefore, Shah 'Abbas was able to keep Ottoman forces at bay, drive out Portuguese merchants from the Hormuz Strait, and add new territory to the empire.

Strengthening his absolutist rule, Shah 'Abbas suppressed the Qizilbash, Sufism, and exaggerated (*ghuluww*) Shi'ism in favor of a new royal slave (*ghulam*) army and a new Shi'i elite. As Babayan points out, he sought to eradicate the Nuqtavi movement and executed its leaders because they predicted his abdication and possibly his assassination on the basis of astrological readings.[30] In a move to eliminate Qizilbash power and end the second civil war (1576–90), Shah 'Abbas replaced the rebellious governors in the provinces of Fars and Kirman with his slaves (*ghulam*).[31] He then centralized his control over the military, especially after his invasion of Georgia in 1614 when he enslaved more than 300,000 Caucasians, many of whom replaced Qizilbash fighters.[32] In terms of his persecution of Sufi orders, Shah 'Abbas particularly targeted Ni'matu'llahis, who had previously been Safavid allies, causing many to relocate to India.

Shah 'Abbas also lavished wealth on Shi'i scholars and holy sites, including the shrines in Karbala' and Najaf. As a public pronouncement of his Shi'i religiosity, he made the pilgrimage from Isfahan to Mashhad on foot, which was a critical step in developing Mashhad as a pilgrimage center.[33] The shrine of Safi al-Din, the founder of the Safaviyya Sufi order, had previously been considered the holiest place for the Safavids. In addition to building up Mashhad as a place of pilgrimage, Shah 'Abbas constructed several seminary schools in Isfahan, where he encouraged scholars from Jabal 'Amil and Bahrain to study and teach. As a result, Isfahan became the leading center of Shi'i learning in the world, a status that it maintained until the fall of the Safavids.

The concentration of Shi'i scholars in Isfahan and the suppression of popular Sufism resulted in a renaissance in Shi'i studies. This period is especially associated with the revival of Illuminationist scholarship. Several scholars who were mystically and philosophically inclined became *shaykh al-Islam* of Isfahan, including Shaykh Baha'i (d. 1621) and Mir Damad (d. 1631). After Shah 'Abbas died in 1629, it was Mir Damad who presided over the coronation ceremony of his successor (Shah Safi, r. 1629–42) and later accompanied the new shah on pilgrimage to the shrine cities in southern Iraq.

According to the orientalist E. G. Browne, "the greatest philosopher of modern times in Persia" was Mulla Sadra Shirazi, a student of Mir Damad.[34] Indeed, Mulla Sadra is possibly the most celebrated Shi'i philosopher. He laid intellectual foundations for a new school of Shi'i thought, which is often referred to as the School of Isfahan. According to Sajjad Rizvi, he "revolutionised the doctrine of existence in Islamic metaphysics and extended the shift from Aristotelian substance metaphysics to Neoplatonic process metaphysics of change."[35] Needless to say, Shi'i intellectualism flourished during Shah 'Abbas's reign as claims to the divinity of Safavid kings were fading.

By the seventeenth century, scripturalist Shi'i scholars began criticizing the rationalist Usuli establishment, suggesting that they were whittling down the Shi'i tradition. The scripturalists hoped to recover the true spirit of Shi'ism by adhering closer to textual traditions. As indicated already, Muhammad Amin al-Astarabadi (d. 1627) was the first to articulate the traditionist critique and is often referred to as the founder of modern Akhbarism.[36] In his polemical *Fawa'id al-madaniyya*, Astarabadi condemned Usuli scholars for mimicking the Sunni model of jurisprudence. Safavid-era philosophers were found on both sides of the rationalist-scripturalist debate and some, like Mulla Sadra, favored a system of knowledge production and authority that created a synthesis of rational thought, scripture, and mystical inspiration.

Abisaab argues that Safavid officials began to support Akhbarism partially because it encouraged a homogenous interpretation of Shi'ism. Explaining the seventeenth-century shift from rationalism to traditionism she argues: "If interpretive rationalism served the militant expanding empire in the sixteenth century ... then traditionism seemed more suitable for a religiously stable empire with modest military goals and erosion in the power of its monarchs."[37] Although this ebb and flow of rationalism and scripturalism may have been true for the Safavid period, it does not necessarily apply to other periods of Shi'i history. During the early Qajar period, for example, the state did, in fact, support rationalist Usuli scholars. Akhbarism, however, was not revived in the middle Qajar period and has not made a significant comeback to this day. Denis MacEoin seems to argue the opposite of Abisaab by suggesting that "for some time after the Safavid collapse, indeed the Akhbaris offered a more viable system in the absence of a centralized government" and that "it was inevitable that the Usulis would [eventually] win the struggle" with Akhbaris.[38] Because the conditions for the adoption of one school of thought over the other are so complex and there are no clear historical patterns to suggest when Usulism is accepted over Akhbarism and vice versa, it is probably best to consider the changes on a case-by-case basis.

The Akhbarism of Astarabadi was so successful that by the second half of the seventeenth century a chief religious official (*sadr*) of the Safavid court claimed that there were no Iranian or Arab Shi'i *mujtahids* (Usulis) in the world during his time.[39] Although this is possibly an exaggeration, Akhbari influence continued throughout the Safavid period. Akhbaris also became prominent in the Shi'i centers of Iraq in the seventeenth century and were outright hostile to Usulis by the time Wahid Bihbihani came to Karbala' in the late eighteenth century.

Historians have not come to a consensus in terms of when and why the demise of the Safavid Empire began. Andrew Newman, for example, rejects what he calls the "conventional preoccupation with Safavid 'decline'" and instead asks, "why the Safavids endured as long as they did?"[40] Rudi Matthee, however, takes up the challenge of explaining Safavid decline in his *Persia in Crisis*. Matthee argues that the symptoms of weakness in the second century of Safavid history include the ineptitude and debauchery of the shahs, partially as a result of their harem upbringing, agricultural mismanagement, stagnation of silver influx (which led to the debasement of its currency), tribal revolts, and the diminishing of military alertness.[41] In terms of how Shi'ism factored into Safavid "decline," Matthee states that "a diminishing willingness to accommodate and coopt marginal groups as part of a growing emphasis on the Shi'i character of the state alienated the Sunni tribesmen of the borderlands" which resulted in "a series of rebellions and depredations that metastasized into a full-scale invasion."[42] He is careful to point out, however, that the empire was not in free-fall as evidenced by the fact that "Iran's silk and wool exports continued to grow" and that "as late as 1700 no one knew that the Safavid state would collapse a mere two decades later."[43]

It was in the context of weak Safavid rule that Shi'i clerics asserted their authority and began to create a powerbase outside the state. No single cleric is more illustrative of this process than Muhammad Baqir al-Majlisi II (d. 1699), who was appointed head jurist (*mullabashi*) and became the face of a renewed attempt to popularize Shi'ism. He created a direct tie between the clerical establishment and the masses by promoting popular religious practices and Shi'i rituals, such as Ashura – the commemoration of the martyrdom of Imam Husayn. Additionally, Majlisi II completed the victory of legalistic scholars over philosophical, mystical, *ghuluww*, and other forms of Shi'i authority. As Babayan rightly puts it, "With the banning of sufi lodges, Greek philosophy, wine, sodomy, singing, dancing, and clapping, the jurists secured their position among the ranks of the men of religion."[44] Majlisi II, therefore, advocated a militant form of religion, exemplified by his destruction of Sufi lodges and massacre of dervishes.[45]

Majlisi II is especially important to the Usuli-Akhbari debate because he initiated a departure away from the Akhbari school, even if Akhbaris have often claimed that Majlisi II was an Akhbari. Usulis often project Wahid Bihbihani as Majlisi II's successor, largely because Bihbihani was his nephew. There is little doubt that Majlisi II's father and predecessor as head cleric (Muhammad Taqi al-Majlisi I, d. 1660) was an avowed Akhbari like most scholars of his time.[46] Majlisi I confirms that "most people in Najaf and the *'atabat* approved of [Akhbarism] and began to refer to the traditions as their sources."[47] Majlisi II, however, avoided the designation of Usuli or Akhbari and famously claimed to travel the middle way (*tariq al-wusta*) between the two schools, which is evidenced in his works. Therefore, he began the process of swinging the pendulum from Akhbarism to Usulism. On the one hand, his *Bihar al-anwar* is the most extensive modern collection of Shi'i Hadith and he accepted several Akhbari doctrines, including the idea that unbelievers can be transmitters of just Hadith reports.[48] On the other hand, Majlisi II extended the authority of Shi'i clerics, which is central to Usulism.

Although he attempted to reconcile the Akhbari and Usuli schools of Shi'ism, which he hoped to extend to the masses, Majlisi II commissioned the brutal persecution of religious minorities in Iran, especially Sunnis. Largely in response to these oppressive measures, Sunnis in the Safavid realm revolted. Among those who rose up were Ghalza'i Sunni

Afghans, who captured Isfahan in 1722 after the city had suffered from famine and plague. With the sack of Isfahan, the Safavid Empire came crashing down.

DECENTRALIZATION OF IRAN (1722–85)

After the Safavids fell, the Russians, Ottomans, and most importantly regional tribal forces attempted to fill the power void. As Ann Lambton has pointed out, eighteenth-century Iran was marked by a period of ruthless tribal competition between Ghalza's, Baluch, Abdalis, Lurs, Bakhtiaris, Afshars, Zands, and Qajars.[49] Although Ghalza'i Afghans toppled the Safavid capital, they spent twenty-five years unsuccessfully trying to establish their rule. Subsequently, the Afshar and Zand tribes established short-lived control followed by the Qajar dynasty, which came to power by ruthlessly suppressing competing tribes. It was during this chaotic period that descendants of Safavid clerical families forged Usuli ideology into a social movement, semi-independent of a centralized state.

Nadir Shah of the Afshar tribe (r. 1736–47) ousted the would-be Afghan rulers, expanded the territory of Iran, and established his own short-lived Afsharid dynasty by 1736.[50] Michael Axworthy argues that "in the 1740s the army Nadir had created was probably the most powerful military force in the world" and "no Shah of Persia had enjoyed such military success for a thousand years or more."[51] Even though Nadir Shah's officers later founded independent states in central Asia, he failed to bring political stability to Iran. Instead of becoming known as the founder of a prosperous dynasty, Nadir Shah is remembered for his destructive military campaigns, which were comparable to the fourteenth-century conqueror Tamerlane (Timur the Lame). Both military legends laid waste to entire towns, leaving pyramids of decapitated heads in their wake. Indeed, the episode of Nadir Shah is a throwback to the age-old struggle between city dwellers and nomadic tribes. After securing the withdrawal of Ottoman and Russian forces from Iran, Nadir Shah launched an offensive against the Mughal Empire. He took the key cities in Afghanistan and then marched to the Mughal capital of Delhi where his forces massacred 20–30,000 people.[52] The devastating attack hastened the demise of the Mughal dynasty and eased the way for British forces to take control of India. Therefore, Nadir Shah in particular, and the decentralization of Iran in general, played a critical role in the "rise" of Western European powers.

Nadir Shah also attempted to extend his control in the Gulf to reap the benefits of the early modern trade boom. Like the Safavids, Nadir Shah established a cordial relationship with European merchants and even made an attempt to build up his own navy for which he purchased ships and guns from the British East India Company and Arab neighbors. However, starting from his initial mission to Julfar and Oman in 1737, his naval campaigns in the Gulf did not succeed. Years after Nadir Shah died, his two naval ships wasted away in the port of Bandar Abbas, symbolizing Iran's failure to establish a navy in the age of global seaborne trade.[53]

Nadir Shah had been the deputy of Shah Tahmasb II (r. 1722–32), who had assumed the Safavid throne during the Afghan siege of Isfahan. As the shah's deputy, Nadir took on the title of "the slave of Tahmasb" (Tahmasb Quli). However, in 1736 Nadir broke away from the Safavids and proclaimed himself shah, thus putting an official end to the Safavid dynasty. As Ernest Tucker argues, "Nadir's coronation effectively ended the role of the Imami [Shi'i] lineage as a basis of royal legitimacy in Iran," the implications of which have continued down to the present.[54] Therefore, the relationship between the Iranian state and the Shi'i clerical establishment was thrown into question and many clerics associated with the Safavids fled to Iraq, India, and elsewhere.

Nadir Shah's most pressing task, then, was to create a new theory for the legitimacy of his empire, which eventually stretched from India to Iraq and included a diverse mix of populations, including large groups of Sunnis and Shi'is. Although Nadir had previously promoted Safavid legitimacy and devoted himself to the Shi'i cause, he now wanted to undermine Safavid claims to the throne, sign a peace treaty with the Ottomans, and unify his empire. In reference to the latter, Nadir Shah himself is reported to have said: "In my realm there are two areas, Afghanistan and Turkistan, in which they call the Iranians infidels. Infidelity is loathsome and it is not appropriate that there should be in my domains one people who call another infidels."[55] For this reason, Nadir Shah hoped to reverse Safavid policies of promoting Shi'ism at the expense of Sunnis.

In an attempt to reduce sectarian tensions, Nadir Shah proposed that Sunnis would recognize Shi'ism as a fifth Sunni legal school (to be called the "Ja'fari *maddhab*" after the sixth Shi'i Imam, Ja'far al-Sadiq), build a symbolic fifth column in the Ka'ba in Mecca, and appoint an Iranian *amir al-hajj* to accompany Iranian pilgrims to Mecca. In return, Shi'is would no longer engage in practices that were perceived as anti-Sunni, such as renouncing the first three Caliphs. Tucker has convincingly argued that Nadir Shah presented his plan quite differently for domestic and foreign consumption.[56] Nadir Shah presented the Ja'fari *maddhab* to the Ottomans as a school free of all anti-Sunni elements and argued that the "anti-Sunni" practices associated with Shi'ism were in fact inventions of the Safavids, who had corrupted Islam. Domestically, however, Nadir Shah favored a Ja'fari school that retained core elements of Shi'ism, such as visitations to the shrines. To this end, Nadir Shah renovated the shrine of Imam 'Ali in Najaf after his invasion of Iraq in 1743.[57] Because of Nadir Shah's continued support of Shi'ism, Tucker concludes that Shi'i opposition cannot be considered as a reason for Nadir Shah's downfall.[58] Conversely, Nadir Shah's successor ('Adil Shah) assumed that Nadir Shah's abandonment of Shi'ism was the cause of his assassination and therefore sought to restore Shi'ism as the state ideology and adopted the title of "Slave of the King of *vilayat*, [Imam] 'Ali."[59]

In his attempt to reconcile Sunni-Shi'i sectarianism, Nadir Shah made several attempts to persuade Ottoman officials to accept Shi'ism. After Ottoman officials rejected his "Ja'fari *madhhab*" proposal in 1741, Nadir Shah declared war and his troops captured Baghdad. Two years later he arranged a conference in Najaf and requested Ahmad Pasha, the governor of Baghdad, to send a Sunni representative. The governor chose Shaykh 'Abdullah al-Suwaydi (d. 1760), a prominent Sunni scholar from Baghdad. Mulla 'Ali Akbar (Nadir Shah's head cleric) represented the Shi'i position. After a public debate, the Sunni and Shi'i representatives signed four declarations (one of which was written by Nadir Shah himself) stating that Ja'fari Shi'ism was the fifth Islamic legal school. Hamid Algar suggests that Suwaydi only came to the conference as a result of his fear of Nadir Shah, while the Shi'i scholars were exercising dissimulation (*taqiyya*).[60] Although Ottoman officials rejected Nadir Shah's plan, they signed a treaty with him in 1746, shortly before his commanders murdered him. The treaty welcomed Iran as part of the Sunni world and protected the rights of Shi'is to travel in Ottoman territory. Therefore, although Nadir Shah's Ja'fari *maddhab* proposal was not accepted, his attempt to resolve sectarian tensions was not without consequence.

Nadir Shah's ploy to reconcile Shi'ism and Sunnism were generally not welcomed by Shi'i scholars, especially since the shah's policies diminished their authority and threatened their livelihood. In addition to ordering the execution of the last Safavid head jurist (*mullabashi*), Nadir Shah confiscated charitable endowments (sing. *waqf*) from the Shi'i establishment, which included schools and mosques.[61] Moreover, Algar argues that Nadir Shah's position undermined the fundamental Shi'i claim that the Imams were the sole interpreters of Islam, which accounts for the primary difference between Sunnis and Shi'is and is, therefore, not likely to be reconciled.[62]

Although Nadir Shah's ecumenical designs were unacceptable to both Sunni and Shi'i scholars, this episode illustrates that Shi'ism was at a crossroads. On the one hand, Shi'ism had largely taken hold in Iran and the Shi'i clerical establishment had become an integrated part of Iranian society. On the other hand, Nadir Shah illustrated that the fate of Shi'ism was inextricably tied to the state. Therefore, Nadir Shah's attempt to diminish the status of Shi'ism was something of a litmus test for the Shi'i establishment. The fact that many clerical families, including the Bihbihanis, were willing to migrate in order to preserve their status as guardians of Shi'ism, indicates that the Shi'i establishment would survive without state patronage. It also illustrates the transnational nature of Shi'ism.

One of the commanders of Nadir Shah's forces, Karim Khan (1705–79) of the Zand tribe, briefly established control over most of Iran from 1759–79. This is the critical period in the establishment of the neo-Usuli movement in Karbala'. Instead of crowning himself shah, Karim Khan took the title of "deputy of the subjects" (*wakil al-ra'aya*) and "the people's deputy" (*wakil al-kala'iq*).[63] As John Perry points out, Karim Khan viewed students of theology and clerics, who rely on state patronage, as parasites.[64] However, unlike Nadir Shah, he did not directly meddle in religious affairs, which allowed Bihbihani and his Usuli movement to become more independent. Although he attempted to limit the power of Shi'i clerics, Karim Khan demonstrated a conventional commitment to Twelver Shi'ism by including religious sayings (for example, *sahib al-zaman*) on Zand coins and building mosques and shrines. He also appointed a *shaykh al-Islam* in his capital city of Shiraz, but did not designate a head jurist (*mullabashi*). Further, as will be discussed in the next chapter, Karim Khan invaded Iraq on the pretext that the Mamluk rulers were harassing Iranian Shi'is.

Like Nadir Shah, Karim Khan attempted to involve Iran in global seaborne trade by establishing a relationship with English and Dutch merchants and extending his power in the Gulf. The Zands granted permission for French and Dutch merchants to establish themselves on Kharg Island in the Persian Gulf. Although the French did not take advantage of the offer, the Dutch East India Company relocated there from Basra, but eventually left the Gulf altogether after being harassed by pirates. At this point, the British monopolized trade with Iran, which prompted the British East India Company to move its base of operations in the Persian Gulf from Bandar Abbas to Bushihr in 1765.[65]

QAJAR RECENTRALIZATION OF IRAN (1785–1925)

By the end of the eighteenth century, the Qajar tribe brutally asserted its control of Iran and remained in power until after World War One. The Qajars inherited the carcass of Safavid Iran in which only one third of Iranians living in cities survived the devastating effects of nearly a century of warfare, disease, and famine.[66] The Qajar shahs revived absolutist government and adopted fantastical titles, such as "Pivot of the Universe." During the Safavid period, the Qajars had been incorporated into the Qizilbash confederacy. By the time they came to power, they were all that remained of the Qizilbash. The Qajars had also been the fiercest rivals of the Zands.

The founder of the Qajar dynasty was Muhammad Khan (1742–97). He had been castrated by a rival of his father and taken hostage by the Zands, who kept him under house arrest for sixteen years. During the chaos surrounding the death of Karim Khan Zand in 1779, Muhammad Khan made an escape and rallied his tribal forces. A decade later, his army of some 60,000 men brutally suppressed most of Iran and continued to raid territory in Georgia.[67] Qajar brutality is exemplified by its policy of blinding its enemies – by now a political tradition in Iran. After the inhabitants of the city of Kirman failed to stop the Qajar invasion of their town, the soldiers gouged out the eyes of 10,000 inhabitants and took some 20,000 women and children as slaves.[68] The remainder of the adult males were put to death. Apparently, Muhammad Khan was particularly enraged because a crowd of Kirmanis had taunted him by chanting the words "Muhammad Khan the Castrated!"[69]

Muhammad Khan was crowned shah in 1796 and established a new capital in Tehran to be closer to the power base of his tribe. The following spring he marched his forces again to Georgia, but was murdered by slaves whom he had sentenced to death. Qajars eventually found the slaves and carried out their chief's last decree by chopping their bodies into little pieces.[70]

If Muhammad Shah brought the Qajars to power by ferociously suppressing tribal competitors in Iran, it was his nephew and successor, Fath 'Ali Shah (r. 1797–1834), who laid foundations for Qajar rule. Therefore, Fath 'Ali Shah succeeded where the successors of Nadir Shah and Karim Khan failed. The fact that Fath 'Ali Shah ordered the execution of his prime minister (Ibrahim Kalantar) proved that he could be just as brutal as his predecessors. Ibrahim Kalantar had been the mayor of Shiraz during the reign of Karim Khan Zand, but sided with Muhammad Khan, who promoted him to prime minister because he helped deliver southern Iran to the Qajars. When Muhammad Khan died, Ibrahim Kalantar held Qajar forces together and promoted Fath 'Ali as the new shah.[71] Fath 'Ali Shah, however, charged the prime minister with conspiracy and ordered him to be cooked in hot oil. Apparently, he had become too powerful for Fath 'Ali Shah's taste.

Fath 'Ali Shah spent most of his four decades of rule fighting internal and external threats, starting with the rivals within his family. He also worked tirelessly to secure Qajar legitimacy by seeking favor from the Shi'i establishment, which was now dominated by Usulis. Fath 'Ali Shah seemed to have been genuinely interested in supporting the development of culture and learning; he was even an aspiring poet (though not a good one according to his own court poet). As Abbas Amanat states, the shah's court "was frequented by a host of calligraphers, painters, musicians, book illuminators, jewelers, and craftsmen whose magnificent array of productions is a testimony to the artistic enrichment of the period."[72]

By the time Fath 'Ali Shah came to power, the Usuli movement had gained control of the shrine cities in southern Iraq and the most prominent Shi'i scholars in the world were the students of Wahid Bihbihani. Although the relationship between the Qajars and Usulis will be discussed in more detail in Chapter 5, a few words can be said here. The shah offered financial rewards to those clerics willing to promote Qajar rule and many Usulis jumped at the chance to receive government support. Therefore, the Qajars and many Usuli scholars entered a client-patron relationship. The Qajars, however, had little control over the

Shi'i establishment. Prior to the Qajar rise to power, Usulis had learned to survive without state sponsorship. Therefore, the Qajars inherited a clerical establishment that had developed a culture of independence, illustrated by the fact that many of the most prominent Usulis remained in southern Iraq during the Qajar period. Instead of solely relying on state funding, they generated revenue from the Shi'i faithful, profiting from the flow of pilgrims and the desire of Shi'is to be buried near the shrines. Additional revenue came from merchants, landowners, and other wealthy Shi'is who established endowments. The most famous endowment came from the Shi'i principality of Awadh in northern India. After British officials took control of Awadh, they attempted (but largely failed) to disburse the money to clerics who would be favorable to their policies.[73]

Fath 'Ali Shah was in power during the first wave of European incursions into Iran, which were part of the Napoleonic Wars. Therefore, some scholars argue that Fath 'Ali's reign signals the beginning of "modern" Iran.[74] As indicated already, I disagree with this assessment, although European military might had in fact surpassed that of the Qajars by the time Fath 'Ali Shah came to power. Russian expansion into northern Iran and British military success in the Persian Gulf gave the imperial powers the economic and political upper hand in their dealings with the Qajars. Moreover, the British-Russian rivalry in the region paradoxically ensured Qajar longevity and Iran's lack of development.

Although Iran was not formally colonized, Britain and Russia competed for economic, political, and military hegemony in what historians often refer to as the "Great Game." The two European powers increased their economic control over Iran during the course of the nineteenth century and almost completely dominated Iran's foreign trade by 1914.[75] The Qajars maintained themselves in power by balancing the interests of the imperialists, tribes, and provinces. They also sold and bestowed government assets and functions to the highest bidders and farmed out tax collection and mintage of coins. Therefore, large land holdings became the private property of merchants, government officials, and Shi'i clerics.[76]

The history of Qajar capitulations to European powers began with Russian expansion into northern Iran. Concerned that France and Russia had set their sights on India, Britain signed a treaty with Fath 'Ali Shah in 1801. The Russian annexation of Georgia, which had been part of Iran during the Safavid period, led to the first Russo-Persian war

(1804–13). As will be discussed in Chapter 5, Usulis supported the war against Russia by issuing declarations of *jihad* against Russia. Despite Britain's aid and military training, Russia badly defeated the Qajars. In the Treaty of Gulistan, which was negotiated by British officials, the Qajars lost much of their northern territory, granted Russia exclusive military access to the Caspian Sea, and set the Russian trade tariff at a low five percent.[77] The second Russo-Persian war (1826–7) ended with a similarly devastating Treaty of Turkmanchai, which gave Russia more territory and required Iran to pay the enormous indemnity of twenty million roubles (five million tomans). Although the Russo-Persian balance of trade was in Iran's favor during the first half of the nineteenth century, Russia dominated trade in the second half of the century. By the early twentieth century Russian economic interests in Iran outpaced that of Britain; Russia had industrialized and penetrated key industries in Iran, including banking and roads. In 1890 Russia secured an agreement with the Qajars, which ensured that railroads would not be built in Iran, making it more difficult for British goods to find their way to Iranian markets.[78] The absence of railroads also ensured Iran's lack of development.

Hoping to compensate for its losses in the Russo-Persian wars, Iran turned eastward and launched several failed attempts to retake Herat in western Afghanistan starting in 1833. Partially in fear of Russian influence in Iran, the British supported the emerging Afghan state in hopes that an independent Afghanistan would become a buffer zone between Russia and India. Britain also took the opportunity to strengthen its position in the Persian Gulf and by 1857 the British navy occupied Kharg Island and Bushihr.[79] British officials used the victory to force the Qajars to grant Britain "most favored nation" status, which meant that British merchants, like Russians, only paid a five percent tax on trade. By mid-century Britain controlled half of Iran's foreign trade.[80]

During the second half of the nineteenth century, the Qajars granted a series of concessions to Britons and other foreigners, which led to the further exploitation of Iran's resources.[81] Nasir al-Din Shah (r. 1831–96) granted the most wide-reaching concession in 1872 for the control of banking, factories, mining, and other industries to Baron Paul de Reuter (1899), who incidentally was the founder of Reuters news agency. According to Lord Curzon, the Reuter concession was "the most complete and extraordinary surrender of the entire industrial resources of a kingdom into foreign hands that has probably ever been dreamed of, much less accomplished, in history."[82] Although popular outcry forced the shah to cancel the concession, his attempts to sell Iran's resources continued.[83]

It was the tobacco concession granted by Nasir al-Din Shah in 1890 that forced the hand of Usuli clerics to cast aside their pious aloofness from politics and involve themselves in worldly affairs. The "Tobacco Revolt" ended after Ayatollah Mirza Hasan Shirazi (d. 1895) issued a *fatwa* from Iraq stating that "the use of ... tobacco in any form is reckoned as war against the Imam of the Age" and that *jihad* would be declared if the concession was not cancelled.[84] The success of Shi'i clerical involvement in the Tobacco Revolt would later convince many Usuli clerics to throw their weight behind the Constitutional Revolution a decade and a half later. Although the Reuter and tobacco concessions were cancelled by the shah, the British Anglo-Persian Oil Company (later renamed BP), retained control of its concession for oil, which was granted in 1901. Two decades later Winston Churchill estimated that British revenue from Iranian oil was forty million pounds, while Iran had earned a mere two million pounds.[85]

CONCLUSION

The Safavid adoption of Shi'ism as the state religion transformed not only the religion of Iran, but its socio-cultural identity. The four trends of *ghuluww*, Usulism, Illuminationism, and Akhbarism defined Safavid Shi'ism. After the Safavid Empire fell, Shi'i scholars had to learn to survive in the absence of state support. They also navigated the reality that the influence of Shi'ism in Iran had been directly tied to the state, which could be undone by Nadir Shah or any other head of state that was not fully committed to the Shi'i cause. Prior to the rise of the Qajar dynasty, which supported Shi'ism, some Shi'i scholars moved to southern Iraq, where they revitalized the cities of Karbala' and Najaf and turned Usulism into a powerful transnational Shi'i movement. The following chapter focuses on the conditions in Iraq, which is the birthplace of neo-Usulism. In many respects, southern Iraq remained the center of the international Shi'i community throughout the Qajar period.

Chapter 3

Shi'ism and the Emergence of Modern Iraq

INTRODUCTION

Although Shi'ism was not the state religion of Iraq as it was in Iran, the influence of Shi'ism in Iraq increased dramatically during the eighteenth and nineteenth centuries, which is evidenced by the mass conversion of southern Iraqi tribes from Sunnism to Shi'ism. The conversion of the majority of southern Iraqis to Shi'ism occurred in or near Karbala' and Najaf, partially as a result of the Usuli movement. The two Shi'i cities became the epicenter of global Shi'ism after the fall of the Safavids and were located on the periphery of power centers within Iraq. And Iraq itself was located on the periphery of the Ottoman Empire. Therefore, southern Iraq was a frontier within a frontier, which allowed Usulis to expand their influence beyond the shrine cities.

During the early modern period of Sunni Ottoman rule, Arab tribes comprised the majority of the population of Iraq, and as late as 1867 half of Iraq's population was nomadic.[1] Furthermore, the population of tribesmen in southern Iraq increased over the course of the eighteenth and nineteenth centuries, largely as a result of tribal migration from the Arabian Peninsula. After tribal conversion, Shi'is made up more than fifty percent of Iraq's population and became the overwhelming majority in southern Iraq by the mid-nineteenth century.[2] Given that Sunni Islam was the state religion of the Ottomans, how could such mass conversion have taken place? As will be clear in what follows, the Shi'i strongholds of Najaf and Karbala', which were revived after the fall of the Safavids, attracted the allegiance of Arab tribes that settled in southern Iraq to engage in agriculture. The sedentarization of the tribes was, in turn, linked to Iraq's incorporation into the global market as an exporter of agricultural goods.

Throughout much of the modern period, Iraq was a porous frontier, buffer zone, linking region, and veritable interstitial space between

Ottoman and Iranian territory. As Hala Fattah and Thabit Abdullah have clearly demonstrated, southern Iraq was oriented towards the Gulf and the Indian Ocean at least as much as it was to the Ottoman center.[3] Fattah, therefore, warns against imposing barriers on the region and instead emphasizes the Gulf's "fluidity, permeability, access, acculturation," and impermanency, which is "the natural by-product of societies constantly in the throes of formation, making and remaking themselves to suit the particular circumstances of the moment."[4] According to Hanna Batatu, although economics linked Iraqi towns to the broader region, "eighteenth-century Iraq was composed of plural relatively isolated, and often virtually autonomous city-states and tribal confederations" in which "urban class ties tended to be in essence local ties rather than ties on the scale of the whole country."[5] Therefore, southern Iraq was part of several worlds at once. It was oriented politically toward Baghdad and the Ottoman Empire; religiously, toward Iran; and economically, toward the Gulf. Simultaneously, southern Iraq was quite localized and semi-autonomous from each of these regions.

OTTOMAN AND MAMLUK RULE IN IRAQ

Iraq became the frontline between the Ottoman and Safavid empires after the Ottomans conquered Iraq in the mid-sixteenth century when the Safavid state was in its incipient stage. After conquering Iraq, the Ottoman Sultan Suleiman the Magnificent (r. 1520–66) stationed 32,000 troops in Iraq and focused infrastructural development on building fortresses and defensive walls.[6] Additionally, the Ottomans improved religious buildings and irrigation, including the Shi'i shrines in Najaf and Karbala' and the Husayniyya canal, which brought water to Karbala'. Such gestures, however, did not stop the Safavids from invading. Shah 'Abbas I successfully conquered much of Iraq in 1623 and particularly attacked Sunnis and Sunni holy places.

The Ottomans then retook Iraq after fifteen years of Safavid rule, which prompted Sultan Murad IV (r. 1623–40) to order the massacre of Iranian Shi'i residents. Surely, his aim was to retaliate against Shah 'Abbas's attack on Sunnis and eliminate what was perceived as a potential fifth column. Realizing the financial potential of Shi'i pilgrims from Iran to Najaf and Karbala', however, Ottomans eventually settled on the policy of allowing the safe passage of Shi'is to the shrine cities. This was made official in the Ottoman-Safavid Treaty of Zuhab (1639) in which the Safavids formally granted the territory of Iraq to the Ottomans. The Treaty of Zuhab remained in force for most of the remainder of Ottoman history. Iraq itself remained part of the Ottoman Empire until it became a British mandate after World War One.

Under Ottoman rule, governors, commanders of the Janissaries, chief judges (*qadi*), and other key officials initially came from Istanbul and were appointed by the central government of the Sublime Porte. Ottoman centralization, however, was not to be found prior to the mid-nineteenth century. The political instability of Iraq is illustrated by the fact that between 1638 and 1704, Baghdad had twenty-four different Ottoman governors, roughly half of whom died violent deaths as a result of political intrigue.[7] Ottomans generally did not heavily invest in Iraq economically or politically because of its distance from Istanbul and its status as a border zone.[8] Iraq's frontier status is illustrated by the fact that it took nearly two hundred days for the military to travel from Istanbul to Baghdad prior to the introduction of steam ships in the nineteenth century, which reduced the voyage to just over a month.[9] Because of its perceived remoteness, Baghdad was considered by some Ottomans to be a place of banishment.[10] Tom Nieuwenhuis, however, argues that Iraq's remoteness and strategic location as a buffer zone and trade center "provided good conditions for ambitious and capable governors to build up their own power."[11]

The Ottomans ruled the territory associated with contemporary Iraq as three separate provinces: Mosul in the north, Baghdad in the center, and Basra in the south. The three provinces were then combined as part of the British mandate. Ottomans encouraged decentralization in hopes that dividing the region into smaller provinces would limit the potential of local governors to assert their independence and power. Mosul became a key city in the Kurdish region, which extends west into Turkey and east into Iran. Baghdad was a military post that boasted sixteen gunpowder factories by the late eighteenth century and was responsible for repelling attacks from Iran.[12] Finally, Basra was a port city, which the Ottomans also attempted to use as a naval base.[13] Additionally, southern Iraq was prime real estate for farming and home to the Shi'i shrine cities.

During the early Ottoman and Mamluk periods, southern Iraq was oriented toward the Gulf, which is primarily indicated by Basra's trade patterns. Basra was Iraq's only port city, often the largest port in the Gulf in the early modern period, and the key city in southern Iraq aside from the Shi'i shrine cities. The city is strategically located on the Shatt al-Arab waterway at the mouth of the Tigris and Euphrates rivers, connecting much of Iraq and Syria with the Indian Ocean region. Therefore, it was one of the most important ports in classical Islamic history, supplying the Abbasid (750–1258) capital of Baghdad with luxurious spices and silks. In the early modern golden age of seaborne trade, Basra experienced rebirth as a port city, especially after Afrasiyab (d. 1624) created a relatively prosperous semi-autonomous local dynasty (1596–1668) attached to the Ottoman Empire. During this period, Basra increased its trade with European merchants, especially the British, Dutch, and Portuguese. The port city was also a meeting place for Arabs and Iranians making the pilgrimage to Mecca and Medina and it became a center of communication between India and Europe, which meant that it was of special interest to the British.[14] Rudi Matthee argues that Safavid Iran was nearly as influential in Basra as the Ottomans during this period.[15] However, after the Ottomans signed the Treaty of Karlowitz with European powers in 1699, they dispatched troops from Baghdad to bring Basra under Ottoman control. Trade continued as Basrans exported dates and horses in return for Yemeni coffee, Indian spices, sugar, and textiles.

Although Iraq was historically one of the most agriculturally productive regions on the planet, crop production in early Ottoman Iraq was relatively low. To make matters worse, Ottomans auctioned off the right to collect taxes in the practice known as tax farming (*iltizam*), which eventually became inheritable. Ebubekir Ceylan suggests that economic and agricultural decline was primarily a political phenomenon caused by Ottoman wars with Iran, tribal rebellions, state ownership of the land, and high taxation.[16] Since the majority of land belonged to the state, peasants were restricted from planting trees or building houses and therefore did not develop a sense of ownership over the land. In addition to these political issues, Nieuwenhuis focuses primarily on environmental problems, arguing that recurrent changes in the course of the Tigris and Euphrates as well as flooding, silting, and salinization made large irrigation projects difficult.[17]

In southern Iraq, flooding resulted in vast marshes and severe plagues, which occurred nearly once every generation during the early modern period. Nieuwenhuis concludes, therefore, that "tribal forms of social organization were an adaptation to this situation."[18] Ottoman and

Mamluk militaries particularly struggled with subduing tribes that had adapted to the marsh region, which proved difficult for armies to navigate. This prompted one governor of Baghdad, Rashid Pasha (1852–7), to build 200 riverboats in an attempt to enhance his army's ability to defeat tribes who took shelter in the marshes.[19] Without a centrally organized irrigation infrastructure, tribes often used land for grazing instead of engaging in agriculture. It was not until the 1858 Land Code that Ottomans encouraged agriculture, which they did by forcing tribes to settle and outlawing tribal ownership of land.[20]

Throughout the eighteenth century, the Mamluk dynasty (1704–1831) controlled most of present-day Iraq, which illustrates the decentralization of the Ottoman Empire, but the centralization of Iraq.[21] Mamluks were generally tolerant of Shi'is in the shrine cities although they did persecute Shi'is in Baghdad and Basra. One visitor to Iraq recalls that Mamluks would spit on Shi'is outside Karbala' and Najaf because they "could not stand the sight of Shi'is."[22] However, they were careful not to provoke Shi'is in the shrine cities. Although the Mamluks never formally broke away from the Ottoman Empire, they asserted their economic and political independence.

The Mamluk dynasty started with the Ottoman governor (*pasha*) of Baghdad, Hasan Pasha (r. 1704–23), who had been educated in Istanbul. Hasan Pasha built a new military primarily composed of Georgian slaves (*mamluks*) in an attempt to check tribal forces, curb the independence of Janissary militias, and provide security for merchants. In addition to military instruction, the Mamluks received training at the palace and took on administrative positions.[23] The Mamluk army quickly gained control of Ottoman Iraq, aside from the region around Mosul where Hasan Pasha's son and successor, Ahmad Pasha (d. 1747), exiled Janissaries. Taking advantage of the disorder in Iran after the Afghan invasion, Hasan Pasha also captured the Iranian city of Kirmanshah in 1723, which was followed up by a campaign led by Ahmad Pasha that added more Iranian territory to Iraq.

Ahmad Pasha gained the support of notables, merchants, and religious officials in Iraq, partially by reducing the taxes they paid to the Ottomans. After Ahmad Pasha died in 1747 (the same year as Nadir Shah), the Ottomans attempted to reassert control over Iraq by appointed governors from the capital.[24] However, Baghdad elites were unwilling to accept non-local governors for fear that the Sublime Porte would increase their taxes and lack the ability to check tribal power.[25]

By 1750, Ahmad Pasha's former slave and son-in-law, Sulayman Abu Layla ("Night Raider," r. 1750–62), became the first Mamluk governor of Iraq. When Ahmad Pasha died, Sulayman, who had been governor of Basra, marched his forces to Baghdad and overthrew the new Ottoman-appointed governor.

Although the Ottomans made several attempts to oust the Mamluks, officials from Istanbul were often murdered before arriving in Baghdad. Partly because they were distracted with operations in Europe, Ottomans settled on recognizing a succession of Mamluk governors. Although local nobles generally retained their religious and judicial positions, Mamluks often replaced the political elite in Baghdad in administrative offices and tax farms.[26]

During the reign of Umar Pasha (1762–76), bubonic plague broke out in Moldova in 1770 during the Russo-Ottoman war (1768–74) and spread throughout much of Russia and the Middle East. After the plague hit the Gulf region in 1772, Basra suffered tremendously, losing a third of its population of roughly fifty thousand inhabitants.[27] The plague also killed a total of fifty thousand people in Moscow.[28] Shortly after the plague, the Banu Ka'b tribal confederation added insult to injury by plundering Basra.

Karim Khan Zand also took advantage by attacking Basra just as the plague came to an end in the summer of 1773.[29] He dispatched his brother Sadiq to besiege Basra and sent an additional force to take Mosul in 1775. Karim Khan justified his attempt to occupy southern Iraq on the basis of the anti-Shi'i policies of the Mamluk governor, Umar Pasha, who had imposed a new toll on Shi'i pilgrims and deported Iranian Shi'is living in Baghdad. Even though Sadiq gathered a massive army of roughly forty thousand men, it still took the Zands more than a year to occupy Basra.[30] Once they successfully barricaded the city, Sadiq refused to allow Basrans to leave the city and his men looted.[31] More concerned about the attack on Kurdistan, Ottomans did not send support to Basra.

When Karim Khan Zand died in 1779, Sadiq rushed back to Shiraz to take part in the succession. He left Basra in the hands of 'Ali Muhammad Zand the "Lion Slayer" (*shirkush*), who savagely continued to attack Basrans. Particularly atrocious was his abduction and rape of young girls and married women. Although Karim Khan had instructed his officers to treat the people of Basra well, 'Ali Muhammad murdered a British East India Company employee in a drunken rage.[32] Having subdued the shrinking population of Basra, 'Ali Muhammad turned his attention elsewhere. He made peace with the Muntafiq tribe that inhabited lower Iraq, and after swearing on the Qur'an to grant their safety, he viciously attacked them.[33] In retaliation, the Muntafiq destroyed Basra's levees, flooding the desert. The Muntafiq then ambushed 'Ali Muhammad's army, killing him in the process. Although the Muntafiq could have seized Basra, they instead heisted several tons of dates and abandoned the city.[34]

In the wake of the plague, the Mamluk governor, Sulayman the Great (1780–1802), reunified Iraq with a standing army of some 12,500 slave-soldiers in addition to part-time armed forces.[35] With Basra devastated, Sulayman shifted Mamluk attention to the north, which left Najaf and Karbala' with unprecedented independence. In an attempt to appease Shi'is and show his authority, Sulayman made the pilgrimage to the shrine cities and by the end of his reign, the cities did not pay taxes to Baghdad.[36] Such freedom led to the rise of the Usuli movement and exposed southern Iraq to attacks from Saudi Wahhabis. In addition to the territory previously dominated by the Mamluks, Sulayman extended his rule into the northern Kurdish region. In 1784, he and his son established the city of Sulaymaniyya, which still bears his name and is a cultural and economic center of northern Iraq. By the end of Sulayman's reign, the British opened a consulate in Baghdad, which increased their political influence. Sulayman authorized the British navy to protect trade in Basra, which was now a ghost town that did not recover for several generations. Merchants, including the British, moved to other ports in the Gulf, especially Kuwait, which traces its rise to this point in time.

The last Mamluk ruler in Iraq, Dawud Pasha (r. 1816–31), attempted to completely break away from the Ottoman Empire. Like his contemporaries, Muhammad 'Ali (r. 1805–48) in Egypt and Fath 'Ali Shah in Iran, Dawud Pasha began the process of defensive development in Iraq. Working with European advisors, he increased his standing army to twenty thousand troops and advanced Iraq's military industry.[37] According to Stephen Longrigg, no officers or army recruits came from outside Iraq by this time. Instead, the Janissaries, which were eventually enrolled in the new Nizamiyya Army, were "locally raised" and "locally paid."[38] Dawud Pasha's administration also boosted agricultural output and developed textile factories.

Mamluk rule ended abruptly, however, after a plague hit Baghdad in 1831 and the Tigris River flooded, which prompted thieves to loot the city.[39] According to Abdullah, fifteen hundred people were dying per day at the height of the disaster.[40] Just before tragedy hit, Dawud Pasha strangled an Ottoman envoy (Sadiq Effendi) who had demanded his resignation.[41] Although Dawud was preparing for war with the Ottomans, he willingly stepped down after the plague hit Iraq, allowing the Ottomans to reassert direct control over Iraq for the first time in over a century.

Shortly after regaining control of Iraq, the Sublime Porte initiated an empire-wide reform project known as the *Tanzimat* (1839–76), which took several decades before it reached Iraq.[42] Political and economic reform are evidenced in the 1858 Land Code and the 1864 Provincial (*Vilayet*) Law, which aimed to centralize Ottoman control over Iraq.[43] During this period, new developments associated with modern technology flooded into Iraq, including a telegraph line between Istanbul and Baghdad, and the proliferation of printing houses, newspapers, steamboats, and factories.

Ottoman centralization was associated with Iraq's "transition from a subsistence to an exporting economy" and its incorporation into the world market, as Marion Farouk-Sluglett and Peter Sluglett have argued.[44] Especially after the Suez Canal opened in 1869, Iraq became a major exporter of grain to the Gulf and India. Therefore, the percentage of cultivators increased from forty-one percent to sixty-eight percent between 1867 and 1930, and the number of nomads steadily declined from thirty-five percent to seven percent during the same period.[45] As Robert Fernea notes, the settlement of tribes ended a history of tribal autonomy in southern Iraq, which lasted for nearly half a millennium.[46]

The Ottoman attempt to settle Iraqi tribes was rooted in its desire to increase agricultural production and incorporate the tribes into the Ottoman state. Such were the aims of the *Tanzimat* reforms. As noted above, the 1858 Land Code outlawed tribal ownership of land and encouraged tribal settlement, which also facilitated de-tribalization. Landowners were required to register their land in return for a title deed. However, legitimate claimants were discouraged from registering their land because they feared that it might facilitate military conscription and they did not see the advantage of claiming what was already theirs.[47] Although the Ottomans eventually abandoned the Land Code, the overwhelming majority of Iraqi tribes were settled by the early 1900s.[48] However, the state still retained ownership of eighty percent of land in Iraq.[49] Like the Land Code, the Provincial Law of 1864 was designed to extend the Ottoman administration to the tribes and contributed to both de-tribalization and sedentarization.[50] Because the Ottomans lacked a military option to enforce the Land Code and Provincial Law, they implemented these policies through a "divide and rule" strategy in which Ottomans exploited tribal rivalries and undermined the authority of tribal shaykhs who resisted government control.[51]

SHI'ISM AND ARAB TRIBES IN SOUTHERN IRAQ

The Shi'i strongholds in southern Iraq (Najaf and Karbala') have a long history of maintaining their independence from imperial powers. The relationship between these cities and the Ottomans and Mamluks is no different. Although the Mamluks in Baghdad seem to have successfully appointed Sunni Mamluks as local administrators in Karbala' and Najaf, Shi'is maintained a high level of control over the cities. Nieuwenhuis notes that although soldiers stationed in Najaf were paid by the Mamluks, the Shi'i holy places were guarded by Iranian troops.[52] After the Saudi-Wahhabi attack on Karbala' in 1801, Fath 'Ali Shah sent several hundred Baluchi families to defend the city.[53] In 1815, Najafis rebelled against the Mamluk governor and declared their independence. The city later descended into chaos as rival clans (Shumurt and Zuqurt) erupted into violence to the extent that police checkpoints were stationed at the city gates.[54] Despite Ottoman re-centralization of Iraq in the mid-nineteenth century, Shi'is increased their control of the cities. Ceylan even notes that "Ottoman governors would not dare enter" Karbala' in fear for their lives.[55] Najaf similarly rejected Ottoman rule in the nineteenth century and it took Ottomans two years to re-establish control after the city rebelled in 1852.

The independence of Najaf and Karbala' was enhanced by the conversion of Iraq's southern tribes, who also have a long history of maintaining their independence from imperial power. In the eighteenth century, the tribes contended with the Mamluks, who constantly campaigned to subdue the tribes in hopes of asserting their own political and economic control over the country. In fact, the Bani Lam, Khaza'il, and Muntafiq tribes were major obstacles in the way of Mamluk hegemony in Iraq. The Bani Lam were especially challenging to the Mamluks because they disrupted the security of trade by plundering caravans. Additionally, the Khaza'il tribe attempted to create its own state. Hasan Pasha's

Mamluk forces successfully campaigned against both tribes. Possibly to counter Shiʿism, Mamluks used religion to justify military action against the tribes. In fact, Mamluks required tribal shaykhs to take an oath of allegiance by pledging to "enter into the Muslim community" and "live in peace under Islam."[56] When the Ottomans attempted to curb the power of southern tribes and confiscate their land during and after the *Tanzimat* period, the tribes often revolted. In the second half of the nineteenth century, at least seven rebellions occurred in reaction to taxation, attempts to reclaim land deeds, and military conscription.[57]

In the late eighteenth and early nineteenth centuries, Arab tribes (including the Zafir, Anaza, Harb, and Shammar Jarba) migrated from Najd, the central region of the Arabian Peninsula.[58] As Uwaidah al-Juhany argues, migration was caused by Saudi-Wahhabi military campaigns in Najd as well as ecological reasons, including droughts, plagues, and crop failures.[59] By the nineteenth century, Saudi-Wahhabis carved out a regional state in the Arabian Peninsula in which expansion by *jihad* was justified by the Wahhabi notion that many of the inhabitants of the Arabian Peninsula and beyond were not true Muslims. Wahhabi jurists declared infidelity (*takfir*) on those who worshiped idols, saints, or at shrines – including Shiʿis and Sufis. Therefore, Saudi forces especially targeted Karbalaʾ and Najaf in an attempt to subdue Shiʿism. The most severe attack on Shiʿis occurred in 1801, when Wahhabis looted the shrine of Husayn and killed several thousand inhabitants, including one of the prominent students of Wahid Bihbihani – ʿAbd al-Samad Hamadani.[60] Saudi-Wahhabis attempted to gain control of regional trade routes and engaged in plunder, which brought them into direct competition with Arab tribes and market towns in the Gulf region.

Southern Iraqi tribes were the first line of defense against Saudi-Wahhabi attacks on the Shiʿi centers, causing an alliance between the tribes and Shiʿi officials. Therefore, the development of the Saudi-Wahhabi state and its expansionist policy seems to have made the southern Iraqi tribes and Usuli Shiʿis natural allies. In addition to the Shiʿi shrine cities, Saudi forces directly targeted their attacks on tribes in southern Iraq, including the powerful Muntafiq and Khazaʾil. These attacks were part of a cycle of violence as tribes in southern Iraq struck back in the heart of Wahhabi territory. Therefore, Yitzhak Nakash argues that "the Wahhabi attacks of Najaf and Karbala reinforced the sectarian identity of the Shiʿi *ʿulamaʾ* and increased their motivation to convert the tribes."[61] Although Meir Litvak emphasizes the fact that the process of conversion had begun before Wahhabis began raiding in southern Iraq, he does agree that Wahhabi attacks "may have reinforced the 'ulama''s resolve to convert the tribes."[62] If the Wahhabi attacks were not the only major cause of conversion, then what was?

Like most major historical changes, southern Iraqi tribes converted to Shi'ism for a variety of complex reasons. Conversion was made possible because the Ottomans exercised little authority outside Iraq's cities and therefore had little coercive power over mobile tribes in the countryside.[63] Although the Ottomans and Mamluks restricted Shi'is from exercising religious freedom in Baghdad and even Basra, as the eighteenth-century traveler Carsten Niebuhr observed, Shi'is were relatively free in Najaf, Karbala', and among the tribes.[64] Additionally, several scholars have argued that the tribes were attracted to Shi'ism because of their shared disdain for the authority of the central government in general and the Sunni Ottomans in particular.[65]

An additional major cause of conversion is the fact that the Shi'i strongholds of Najaf and Karbala' were a magnet for newly settled tribes. The markets in Najaf and Karbala' attracted tribesmen to the cities, which exposed them to the influence of Shi'ism. Nakash argues that "the transition of the tribes from nomadic life to agricultural activity disrupted tribal order and created a major crisis among the tribesmen," which was partially resolved by conversion to Shi'ism.[66] Additionally, Shi'i worship of Imam Husayn seems to have corresponded to tribal values, such as heroism, pride, honor, and courage.[67]

Karbala' and Najaf became successful market towns as a result of the Husayniyya and Hindiyya canals, which brought water to the two respective towns.[68] As noted already, the Husayniyya was repaired during the early Ottoman period, which prompted a revival of Karbala'. Therefore, Shi'i refugees primarily fled to Karbala' instead of Najaf after the fall of the Safavid empire. Najaf became more habitable after Usuli clerics secured funds for the Hindiyya canal from the chief minister of the Shi'i state of Awadh in northern India in 1790.[69] The canals changed the course of water flow in southern Iraq and tribes began to settle and cultivate crops near the canals. So much water was channeled into Najaf by the Hindiyya that the Euphrates River dried up by the late 1800s.[70]

The tribes that converted to Shi'ism were almost entirely those that settled into an agricultural life. Therefore, nomadic tribesmen in Iraq remained Sunnis.[71] Conversion of tribes, then, largely depended on geography, which is exemplified by the fact that branches of the same tribe living in the "Sunni zone" north of Baghdad have remained Sunnis, whereas those in the "Shi'i zone" south of Baghdad converted to Shi'ism.[72] Once tribes settled near the fertile land near Najaf and Karbala', Usulis sent out missionaries to preach among the tribespeople. The tribal-Shi'i alliance is attested by marriage links between Shi'i officials and tribal shaykhs. For example, an influential Usuli scholar, Shaykh Ja'far al-Najafi "Kashif al-Ghita'" (1743–1812), married the daughter of a shaykh from the Banu Jaliha tribe.[73]

Usuli officials seem to have been motivated to convert the tribes for socio-religious reasons, as Litvak has already suggested.[74] Indeed, Usuli *mujtahids* attempted to replace tribal law with Islamic law, even if conversion did not necessarily entail a rejection of tribal ethics.[75] Litvak concludes, therefore, that the primary motiving force behind the missionary work was "the entrenched sect-like mentality of the Shi'i 'ulama'" that urged the persecuted minority to proselytize among the dominant majority and "conquer it from within."[76] Additionally, Usulis may have hoped that the tribes would assist Shi'is with the protection of the shrine cities and Shi'i pilgrims from Ottomans, Mamluks, Wahhabis, and other tribes. Although Litvak rejects the economic motive for conversion given that most of the tribesmen were poor, Shi'i clerics may have considered conversion as a means to increase the number of contributors, as Nakash suggests.[77]

As Shi'i influence in Iraq continued to increase over the course of the nineteenth century, Sunnism seems to have diminished. This is partially a result of the fact that the Ottomans decreased Sunni endowments (*waqf*) as part of the *Tanzimat* reforms.[78] By the late 1880s, the reversal of Sunni and Shi'i fortunes in Iraq alarmed the Ottoman Sultan Abdulhamid (r. 1876–1909). An Ottoman report laments that "while the Sublime Sultanate worked to devastate and throw back the angry flood of Christianity, and always tried to attach the Muslims of India and China to the Supreme Caliphate, Shiism intervened like a vast uncrossable sea ... Thus millions of Muslims are enslaved by the infidels. The memory of this treachery will endure as long as human kind."[79] Well known for his support of Islamic unity (*ittihad-i Islam*), Abdulhamid solicited the support of the famed Jamal al-Din al-Afghani (1838–97) and others to eliminate sectarian differences between Sunnis and Shi'is throughout the Islamic world. However, Abdulhamid clearly distrusted Iranian Shi'is, who, he claimed, "constantly maintain their heretical beliefs in order to live separately from the Ottoman government, and have endeavored to convert the Sunnis to their sect by deceiving ignorant people in Iraq and Baghdad."[80] The Sultan was especially concerned after he learned that Shi'is made up an integral part of the Ottoman Sixth Army stationed in Baghdad, which prompted him to transfer the Shi'i soldiers so that the entire Sixth Army would be composed of Sunnis.[81] Additionally, Abdulhamid made a feeble attempt to convert Iraqi Shi'is to Sunnism, which was partially inspired by American Protestant missionaries working in Armenia. Abdulhamid ordered that students from Shi'i cities in Iraq be sent to Istanbul for religious instruction in Sunnism, so they could correct their "superstitious belief" and return as Sunni missionaries. However, as Gokhan Cetinsaya points out, this project and Abudlhamid's future endeavors never produced the desired results.[82]

CONCLUSION

During the early modern period southern Iraq was connected to several different worlds at once, including the Ottoman Empire, Iran, the Gulf, and the Arabian Peninsula. Although the Ottomans ruled Iraq as three separate provinces, the Mamluk dynasty brought the region together during the long eighteenth century as the Ottoman Empire decentralized. However, Iraq remained quite localized, especially as a result of tribal autonomy, several bouts of the plague and flooding, invasions from the Zands and Saudi-Wahhabis, and sectarianism. The Shi'i shrine cities in particular enjoyed a high degree of autonomy. Such were the conditions in which Shi'i scholars reinvented themselves after the fall of the Safavid Empire. Karbala' and Najaf were revitalized with investments from abroad, which allowed the cities to become the new religious centers of the Shi'i world as well as regional economic centers. As Arab tribes settled near the shrine cities, they converted to Shi'ism, which, in turn, bolstered the Usuli movement. No other individual was more influential in crystallizing the authority of the clerical elite in this context than Wahid Bihbihani, who is the subject of the following chapter.

Chapter 4

Wahid Bihbihani: Shi'i Reviver and Reformer

INTRODUCTION

Western-language scholarship has generally adopted the Shi'i tradition that Wahid Bihbihani single-handedly put an end to the Akhbari-Usuli dispute. Shi'i biographical dictionaries unanimously describe him as the person who liberated Shi'ism from the stifling Akhbari school of thought that was dominant for much of the eighteenth century. Indeed, he played a central role in deciding the outcome of the Usuli-Akhbari dispute, which had been hundreds of years in the making. Bihbihani reports that when he entered Karbala' in the 1760s, Akhbaris were so dominant that those who were caught with Usuli texts ran the risk of being beaten. However, by the time he died, less than thirty years later, Akhbaris were driven out of the city and the Akhbari school was almost completely defunct. In its place, Bihbihani and his followers established the dominance of the rationalist Usuli school of thought, not only in Karbala', but in the other Iraqi shrine cities, throughout much of Iran, and the rest of the Shi'i world.

Prior to Bihbihani, the Usuli-Akhbari dispute had not resulted in violence and was primarily an intellectual debate. Bihbihani, however, revived the practice of declaring infidelity (*takfir*) on non-Usulis, which became a tool for Usulis to enforce orthodoxy and cast out those who challenged their authority. This was a departure from the Safavid Shi'i establishment, which was willing to accept a broader spectrum of views.[1] The "orthodox" position that Usulis put forward was that individual *mujtahids* were the supreme sources of living knowledge and authority for all members of the Shi'i community, who were required to emulate their rulings. By the mid-nineteenth century this sentiment evolved into the institution of "the source of emulation" (*marja' al-taqlid*), who was to be the deputy of the Hidden Imam, chief legal expert, and supreme exemplar for the Shi'i world. As I have argued elsewhere, Shaykh Murtada Ansari (1799–1864) became the prototypical *marja' al-taqlid*. Indeed, he redefined the theoretical and practical underpinnings of Shiʿi law and leadership as the first universally recognized *marjaʿ* in Shiʿi history.[2]

The most important long-term consequence of the Usuli victory, therefore, was that clerics henceforth played a more central role in Shiʿi society, and the clerical hierarchy became more stratified. Bihbihani's movement initiated a revival of scholarly output that rivals any other period of Shiʿi history and the Usuli victory prompted the proliferation of *mujtahids* at an unprecedented rate.[3] During the early Qajar period (first half of the nineteenth century), Bihbihani's network of clerics dominated Shiʿi centers in Iran and Iraq and amassed religious, social, and economic power as never before. The Usuli interpretation of Shiʿism and the powerful position of Shiʿi clerics have continued to the present. Iran's attempts at secularization in the twentieth century seemed to have restrained the Usuli establishment. However, the movement re-emerged in the 1979 Islamic revolution in Iran, which brought Usuli clerics to power.

Although Wahid Bihbihani laid the foundations for modern Shiʿism and promoted the school of thought that is unquestionably the most dominant force in Shiʿi Islam, he has received little scholarly attention, often ignored not only by Western scholars but Shiʿis as well.[4] Therefore, it is not immediately clear how Bihbihani, apparently single-handedly, caused such a monumental shift in Shiʿi leadership in such a short time. The following, then, will examine the extent to which socio-historical factors played a role in Bihbihani's overthrow of the Akhbari establishment. I argue that the victory won by Usulis was a pragmatic one. Bihbihani's success was a result of his ability to marshal financial and political resources and train a cadre of disciples who spread his school of thought throughout the Shiʿi world. He also benefited from the timely death of Yusuf al-Bahrani, the most prominent Akhbari scholar during Bihbihani's lifetime, in 1772. As noted in the previous chapter, the Usuli movement simultaneously benefited from tribal support, political decentralization, and the plague that hit Iraq in 1772.

A fair account of Bihbihani's biography is difficult to write because of the dearth of verifiable information about him. Nearly everything we know about Bihbihani was passed down by his students and descendants who were interested in projecting him in the best possible light. Therefore, most of the vignettes about Bihbihani were written for the purpose of showing his piety, impeccable knowledge, and leadership qualities. Nevertheless, these sources give us an understanding of how the Shiʿi tradition views Bihbihani. Although Shiʿi biographical dictionaries (*tabaqat*) written in the nineteenth century are largely hagiographical and heresiographical accounts of Shi'i scholars, they are invaluable sources because they contribute significantly to the formation of popular Shi'i opinion.

REVIVER OF THE EIGHTEENTH CENTURY

Wahid Bihbihani is universally hailed in Shi'i sources as the "reviver" (*mujaddid*) of Shi'i Islam in the twelfth Islamic century (eighteenth century CE) or the founder (*mu'assis*) of the thirteenth century.[5] According to a poem by 'Abdullah Mamaqani, "Bihbihani is the teacher of mankind, and the renewer of the Usuli school in the twelfth century."[6] A student of Bihbihani claimed that he was "the founder of the nation of the Prince of mankind at the beginning of the thirteenth century."[7] Bihbihani's qualification as a reviver was that he attacked Akhbarism and established Usulism as the most influential Shi'i school of thought. As Muhammad Baqir Khwansari explains, Bihbihani's greatness is a result of his elimination of the opinions of Akhbaris, which were the same as those in the age of ignorance (*jahiliyya*).[8] Likewise, Muhammad Tunikabuni states that the very reason Bihbihani is considered as the reviver of the twelfth Islamic century is that he defeated the Akhbaris, who were extremist, excessive, and widespread.[9]

The concept of renewal (*tajdid*) is rooted in the Prophetic report (*khabar*), which says that "God sends at the turn of each century a man who renovates for this community the matters of its religion."[10] In a similar tradition, the Prophet is reported to have said, "righteous men ('*udul*) shall bear this religion in every century, who shall cast out from it the interpretation of the false, the corruption of the extremists, and the arrogation of the ignorant, just as bellows remove the dross from the iron."[11] The Shi'i concept of renewal is also based on a report attributed to the seventh Imam, Ja'far al-Sadiq, which says that "the religion will be carried in every century by an upright person through whom the invalid interpretations will be nullified and the deviation of the extremists and false claims of the ignorant persons (*jahilin*) will be refuted."[12] Similarly, Bihbihani himself explains that a Shi'i renewer comes every one hundred years during the occultation of the Hidden Imam in order to promote the true religion.[13] Theoretically, the importance of renewers in Shi'ism is second only to the Imams. In practical terms, *tajdid* became a method for justifying reform and has been used by scholars to prove the legitimacy of periodic change in Islam, often associated with *ijtihad*. No method of electing a *mujaddid* developed and it never became an official position; instead it has remained an honorific title.[14]

Since Bihbihani was the nephew of the above-mentioned Muhammad Baqir al-Majlisi II, Shi'i historians often present Bihbihani as the successor of Majlisi II.[15] Indeed, the interrelated Majlisi, Bihbihani, and Tabataba'i families played a critical role in the formation of the Usuli movement. Merchants in these families provided funding for the movement and high-ranking clerics, especially in the first several generations of neo-Usulism, were often from these families or were linked to them by marriage. As Arjomand rightly argues, "kinship performed the crucial function of substituting for the state-dependent institutional ties."[16] As discussed above, Majlisi II was arguably the most important Shi'i scholar of the late Safavid period and is considered a renewer (*mujaddid*) of the eleventh Islamic century because he popularized Shi'ism in Iran. As Denis MacEoin points out, Usuli scholars often ignore scholars working in the period between Majlisi II and Bihbihani. Indeed, Khwansari states that this was a "period of the absence of the *'ulama'*."[17]

Shi'i historians, then, have compiled lists of the renewers of each century. Such lists appear in *Firdus al-tawarikh* and *Jam' al-usul*, which were both written after Bihbihani's time.[18] The following is a combined list from these two books in chronological order. The first two renewers were Imams and Bihbihani appears as the twelfth renewer on both lists.

1. Imam Muhammad al-Baqir (d. 733)
2. Imam 'Ali al-Riza (d. 819)
3. Muhammad al-Kulayni (d. 940)
4. Shaykh al-Mufid (d. 1022)
5. Ibn Shahrashub Mazandarani (d. 1192)
6. Ibn Idris al-Hilli (d. 1202)
7. 'Allama al-Hilli (d. 1325)
8. Shahid al-Awwal (b. 1384)
9. Muhaqqiq al-Karaki (d. 1533)
10. Mulla 'Abdalla Shushtari (d. 1612) or Muhammad Taqi al-Majlisi I (d. 1660)
11. Muhammad Baqir al-Majlisi II (d. 1699)
12. Wahid Bihbihani (d. 1792)
13. Murtada Ansari (d. 1864)

Bihbihani's biographer, 'Ali Davani, suggests that Bihbihani is also a descendant of Shaykh al-Mufid (948–1022), who is cited as a renewer of the fourth Islamic century as a result of his leading role in establishing the rationalist approach to Shi'ism. Davani, however, does not provide a firm basis for this claim. As Davani himself points out, there are no indications from Bihbihani's own writings, including the licenses (*ijazas*) he wrote for his students, that his family tree includes Shaykh al-Mufid.[19] Why then is there an insistence that Bihbihani was his descendant? First, Shaykh al-Mufid was an outstanding scholar. In addition to his contributions in Islamic theology (*kalam*), he developed the field of Shi'i rationalism and is often considered the founder of the Usuli school of thought.[20] Like his alleged predecessor, Bihbihani endeavored to promote Usulism at a time when traditionists dominated Shi'i learning. Therefore, the assertion that Bihbihani was a descendant of Shaykh al-Mufid suggests that his knowledge was passed down through successive generations by the founder of the Usuli school.

BIHBIHANI'S EARLY LIFE

Wahid Bihbihani was born in the early eighteenth century (either 1704 or 1706) in Isfahan when the city was still the bastion of Shi'i learning and capital of the Safavid Empire. His father named him Muhammad Baqir, apparently after his own teacher, Muhammad Baqir al-Majlisi II. Wahid is a title that Bihbihani acquired later in life, which means "unique." He acquired the name Bihbihani after his family moved to Bihbihan, a small town in southern Iran. He first traveled to Bihbihan and southern Iraq as a teenager with his father after the Afghan invasion of Isfahan in 1722. Bihbihan became his adopted hometown and many of Bihbihani's relatives moved there.

Bihbihani received his early religious education from his father. According to one of his students, Bihbihani studied the traditions (*akhbar*) with his father and therefore knew more about Akhbari teachings than about Usulism in his early life.[21] Surely, Bihbihani's father imparted the knowledge he had learned from Majlisi II, who was a famous Hadith collector. For this reason, MacEoin argues that Bihbihani represents "a link between the late Safavid and early Qajar periods."[22] Although this may be a simplified version of the truth, later scholars, including Aqa Buzurg Tihrani (d. 1970), traced their chain (*isnad*) of authority back to Bihbihani and Majlisi II.[23] Another scholar argues that if there was no link connecting Bihbihani to Majlisi II, there may have been a break in the chain of transmission of Shi'i learning.[24]

Bihbihani moved to southern Iraq after his father died. He studied Usuli thought with his older cousin and scholar, Sayyid Muhammad Tabataba'i Burujirdi,[25] whose daughter Bihbihani later married. Bihbihani's first son, Muhammad 'Ali Bihbihani, was from this wife and was born in 1732.[26] Bihbihani also studied Hadith with Sayyid Sadr al-Din al-Qummi, who apparently persuaded him to adopt the Akhbari school.[27] According to his grandson, Bihbihani became passionate about Akhbarism and worked hard to learn as much as he could about Akhbari teachings.[28] A student of Bihbihani explains that after a complete study of both schools of thought, he became enlightened. Once Bihbihani realized the invalidity of Akhbarism, he chose the path of Usulism and dedicated his life to fighting Akhbari doctrines and spreading Usuli teachings.[29] Bihbihani's grandson simply says that he chose the way of *ijtihad* (Usulism) and started promoting it as a result of his steadfastness.[30] It is clear from Bihbihani's writings that he rejected Akhbarism because of what he perceived as rigid literalism. For example, he argued that if the Hadith said that a sick person could be healed by cold water, Akhbaris would believe it.[31]

BIHBIHANI IN BIHBIHAN

Nadir Shah's invasion of the Shi'i cities of southern Iraq in 1732 caused the displacement of many Shi'i families. At this point, Bihbihani's family moved back to Bihbihan, where they stayed for the next three decades. In a politically tumultuous time, Bihbihan was off the map of competing forces. In the 1730s, it was the stronghold for the Kuhgilu tribe, which allied with Nadir Shah against Muhammad Khan Baluch but was largely autonomous.[32] The city was also on a trade route connected to the port of Daylam.

By the time Bihbihani moved to southern Iran, he was in his late twenties. He had received roughly ten years of scholarly training in southern Iraq and was ready to begin a career as a teacher-cleric. According to Davani, Bihbihani moved to southern Iran for the very purpose of opposing Akhbarism, which had already been promoted in Bihbihan by Yusuf al-Bahrani.[33] The reality is that Bihbihani's family network was already in Bihbihan, including one of his cousins who taught there.[34]

Bihbihan proved to be fruitful ground for Bihbihani. Although the majority of Shi'is in Bihbihan were Akhbaris, Bihbihani began to attract followers and made powerful alliances, which certainly enhanced his prestige as a scholar and eventual leader of a social movement. The city of Bihbihan was divided into two major neighborhoods, Qanavat and Bihbihan. Initially Bihbihani had settled in Qanavat, which was the poorer of the two areas. However, people from both neighborhoods began claiming that Bihbihani was from their side, which seems to indicate his popularity as a teacher.[35] Bihbihani's grandson recalls his charismatic qualities, saying that he was a great speaker and storyteller and that people would often retell his stories.[36]

Bihbihani established economic, political, and religious alliances through marriages. As noted above, his first wife (the daughter of Sayyid Muhammad Tabataba'i Burujirdi) linked him to the Shi'i establishment in Iraq. He made another marriage alliance after a merchant and family member (Hajji Sharafa Bihbihani) invited him to teach and live in the wealthier part of Bihbihan.[37] Bihbihani later married the merchant's daughter.[38] An additional alliance was made after the village leader (*kadkhoda*) of Bihbihan offered his daughter to Bihbihani.[39] These alliances with powerful families in Bihbihan were crucial for Bihbihani's movement as they strengthened his base of support and emboldened his Usuli activities.

Not surprisingly, Bihbihani began writing pro-Usuli, anti-Akhbari tracts in Bihbihan, which became the ideological basis for his movement. These texts include "Treatises on the Principles of Exemption" (*al-Risalat usalat al-bara'a*), "Treatises on Analogy" (*Risalat al-qiyas*), "Treatises on the Probativity of Consensus" (*Risalat hujjiyyat al-ijma'*), and his most famous anti-Akhbari work titled "Treatises on *ijtihad* and *akhbar*" (*Risalat al-ijtihad wa al-akhbar*).

USULI-AKHBARI DISPUTE IN KARBALA'

After cultivating a base of support in southern Iran, Bihbihani moved to Karbala' sometime in the early 1760s, roughly a decade before the plague of 1772. Bihbihani was now an established scholar in his late fifties. According to Davani, the reason that Bihbihani decided to move out of Bihbihan is that he had a confrontation with his father-in-law, the village chief of Bihbihan, who told him that it was he, not Bihbihani, who commanded the people gathered at prayer time.[40] As Litvak has suggested, Bihbihani probably also realized that the Usuli-Akhbari dispute would be settled in the shrine cities of Iraq.[41]

Bihbihani's return to Karbala' is portrayed in Shiʿi biographical literature as an epic moment of triumph. Bihbihani is depicted as the savior of Karbala', Najaf, and Shiʿism as a whole because he was able to rid the cities of Akhbaris. According to one of Bihbihani's students, "The cities of Iraq, especially Karbala' and Najaf, were full of Akhbari *ʿulama'* before Aqa [Bihbihani] came from Bihbihan."[42] Akhbaris who wanted to touch Usuli books would use a handkerchief so their hands would not become impure (*najis*).[43] The famous biographical dictionary *Nujum al-sama'* says that prior to Bihbihani's time, *usul al-fiqh* was not practiced widely by Shiʿi scholars – meaning that they were not using Usuli methodology. According to the tradition therefore, Usulism only grew in popularity because of the work of the great, erudite Bihbihani.[44]

The greatness attributed to Bihbihani in Shiʿi literature is almost solely based on the fact that he ended Akhbari supremacy in the shrine cities. As Khwansari puts it, "the dust of the Akhbaris' opinions," which were eliminated by the blessing of Bihbihani's firm precepts, "were the same as the whims of the ignorant (*jahiliyya*) before them."[45] Three of the biographical dictionaries even elevate Bihbihani's status to an instrument of God, suggesting that "God emptied the land of [Akhbaris] by the blessing of his arrival."[46]

Davani suggests that as soon as Bihbihani came to Iraq, he gained a following because Shiʿis had become aware of the wrongdoings of the Akhbaris and were already looking for someone to fix the problems that the Akhbaris were causing.[47] In reality, however, Bihbihani did not receive a rapturous reception in Karbala'. In fact, he considered leaving Karbala' shortly after he arrived because of his troubles with the Shiʿi community. He only decided to stay after Imam Husayn appeared to him in a dream requesting him to remain there.[48] As a result of the dream, Bihbihani apparently realized that his destiny was to stay and fight Akhbaris on behalf of the Imam.

An additional story indicates that Bihbihani faced challenges gaining followers when he first came to Karbala'. Apparently, he had been preaching that Shiʿis should not question why the Hidden Imam had not appeared. Some interpreted this to mean that he did not want the Hidden Imam to return. ʿAli Akbar Nahavardi relates the story that a follower came to Bihbihani's door and said that he realized he had been praying on Bihbihani's rug in the mosque and therefore his prayers were invalid. Bihbihani took the rug and closed the door. Later the follower came back, asked for forgiveness, and kissed Bihbihani's feet.[49] This vignette seems to illustrate Bihbihani's overall experience in Karbala'. He was initially rejected, but eventually gained support.

The fact that Bihbihani's son, Muhammad 'Ali Bihbihani, received a teaching license (*ijaza*) from the famous Akhbari scholar, Yusuf al-Bahrani, is also indicative of the fact Bihbihani did not dominate scholarly circles in Karbala' as soon as he arrived. According to Bihbihani's grandson, Muhammad 'Ali continuously contradicted Yusuf al-Bahrani and his Akhbari teachings, which caused Muhammad 'Ali to leave Karbala'.[50] He then went on pilgrimage to Mecca, where he also studied and came into contact with Wahhabi ideology.

Wahid Bihbihani gradually recruited students in Karbala'. Initially, his study circle was made up of his younger relatives, including Sayyid Muhammad Mahdi Tabataba'i (1742–96), who was his grandnephew, and Sayyid 'Ali Tabataba'i (1748–1815), his sister's son.[51] In fear of Akhbaris, Bihbihani and his students had to study in his basement because anyone caught with Usuli texts risked being beaten by Akhbari allies.[52]

In the absence of central rule in southern Iraq, landowning Sayyids, urban gangs, and the leading clerics filled the power vacuum.[53] As Juan Cole and Moojan Momen explain, Shi'i scholars often allied themselves with urban gangs in Karbala' in the absence of Ottoman political control.[54] Algar also argues that this phenomenon extended into the Qajar period, when *mujtahids* had "private armies," initially made up of brigands (*lutis*) but later replaced with students of the *mujtahids*.[55] Therefore, urban toughs enforced Akhbari dominance and intimidated their Usuli rivals. Although explicit evidence linking Bihbihani to the leader of a specific gang or tribe has not been found, he certainly worked inside the power structure of Karbala'. As he had allied himself with the political establishment in Bihbihan, he likely created alliances with urban gang leaders in Karbala'. He also employed strongmen to enforce his judgments, as indicated below.

In addition to his marriage alliances, Bihbihani had merchant contacts through his half-brothers in Isfahan and Shiraz.[56] The Bihbihani family was also connected to wealthy Bengali civil servants through marriage.[57] These civil servants were descendants of the Majlisi family, but from a different branch than the Bihbihanis. These contacts enhanced

Bihbihani's power and authority and were a necessary source of funds for his survival and the stipends of his students.

Once Bihbihani gained ample socio-religious, political, and economic support, he challenged Yusuf al-Bahrani for his students and his position as the most prominent Shi'i leader in Karbala'. Bihbihani is reported to have stood up at a meeting and declared, "I am the proof of God (*hujjat Allah*)."[58] According to Shi'i teachings, the world cannot exist without a proof (*hujja*), which is associated with the knowledge possessed by the Imams. Apparently not rejecting his claim to be the proof of God, those present asked what he wanted. At this point, he requested to take over the pulpit (*minbar*) of Yusuf al-Bahrani as well as his students. According to Mamaqani, Bahrani consented to allow Bihbihani to lead prayers in his place and teach his students because he was quarrelling with local Akhbaris. As a result, Usuli reports suggest that Bihbihani converted two-thirds of Bahrani's students to Usulism, which brought Bahrani great joy.[59] In reality, it is unlikely that Bahrani was happy to lose students. However, Bahrani does seem to have taken a conciliatory approach to Bihbihani. Bahrani reportedly said that if one prays behind Bihbihani his prayer is valid.[60] Additionally, Bihbihani did start to attract Bahrani's students, including Bahr al-'Ulum and Mirza Muhammad Mahdi Shahristani, both of whom became leading *mujtahids* after Bihbihani's death.

As Bahrani seems to have capitulated to Bihbihani, the latter wholeheartedly rejected Bahrani's leadership. Bihbihani issued a judgment against Bahrani as a prayer leader, indicating that any prayers said behind Bahrani would be invalid. Bihbihani then forced his students to stay away from Bahrani's classes, which explains why his nephew is reported to have snuck out in the middle of the night to see what Bahrani was teaching.[61] Tunikabuni even says that one of Bihbihani's students felt disgusted at the mention of Bahrani's most famous book (*al-Hada'iq al-nadira*) because Bihbihani did not allow his students to mix with Akhbaris.[62]

Usuli sources indicate that Bihbihani eventually made amends with Bahrani. Tunikabuni recounts a story in which Bihbihani went to Bahrani's house one night and told him:

> "Tonight the Imam Husayn came to me in a dream and told me 'cut your nails.' Then I woke up. I interpret this as meaning that I should repel the enmity of the Akhbaris and discuss and argue with them. I have come now so that I might discuss the matter with you."[63]

In other words, Bihbihani realized that he had to defeat Bahrani through debate, instead of by force. In fact, Bihbihani and Bahrani did engage in a number of debates. One report depicts the two talking on the veranda of the mosque during the early morning call to prayer after having been up all night discussing their differences.[64]

When Yusuf al-Bahrani died in 1772, Bihbihani led the prayers at his funeral, indicating that he would succeed Bahrani as the leading scholar in Karbala'. This was the moment that Usulism began to overturn Akhbari dominance of the Shi'i world. Bihbihani had established himself as the most powerful Usuli scholar in Karbala' and Akhbaris were not in a position to challenge him.

The dissonance between Yusuf al-Bahrani's scholarly commitment to Akhbarism and his support for Bihbihani raised questions about how Bahrani fits into the Akhbari-Usuli conflict. Much of the Shi'i biographical literature paints Bahrani as a reformed Akhbari, as Robert Gleave argues.[65] In other words, Usulis often argue that Bahrani was once a strict Akhbari, but he returned to the middle way after his encounter with Bihbihani. *Qisas al-'ulama'*, however, considers Bahrani an Akhbari (not a reformed Akhbari), but one who was accepted by Bihbihani.[66]

Bahrani himself also seems to have been conflicted over the Akhbari-Usuli dispute. On one hand his theoretical work is distinctively Akhbari and shows a lifetime commitment to the Akhbari doctrine.[67] On the other, however, Bahrani attempted to resolve the Usuli-Akhbari conflict. Both in his *al-Durar al-najafiyya* and in *al-Hada'iq al-nadira*, he clearly argues that the Usuli-Akhbari conflict should be put to rest because it had divided the Shi'i community. He even attacked the founder of the Akhbari movement (Muhammad Amin al-Astarabadi) for the bitter tone he had introduced to the debate.[68] While 'Abdullah Samahiji and other Akhbaris emphasized the differences between Akhbarism and Usulism, Bahrani sought to minimize them and even conceded that Akhbaris use *ijtihad* as much as Usulis, which is often cited as the primary difference between the two schools.[69] Additionally, Bahrani emphasized that Akhbaris and Usulis are all followers of the Imams.

The contradictions in Bahrani's writings must be understood in historical context. The Shi'i establishment was under attack after the fall of the Safavids and the loss of state sponsorship. Additionally, because Nadir Shah and Saudi-Wahhabis posed a serious threat to Shi'ism, Bahrani wished to present a unified front.[70] If Bahrani felt that Usulis posed a danger to him, he could have also been engaging in dissimulation (*taqiyya*).

The Usuli position was also bolstered when the plague spread throughout Iraq in 1772, prompting Bihbihani to command his students to leave Iraq. He sent his son, Muhammad 'Ali Bihbihani, to Kirmanshah in Iran. Although Muhammad 'Ali was reluctant to leave, he emphasized his duty to flee in the following poem: "Go, go … if you don't go, how disobedient."[71] Another student of Bihbihani, Sayyid Muhammad Mahdi Tabataba'i (1742–96), fled Karbala' for Mashhad. He returned in 1779 and had already issued licenses (*ijazas*) to his own students in Isfahan and Khurasan.[72] Another scholar, Bahr al-'Ulum, even composed a treatise on the obligation for believers to flee from plagues. Bihbihani's students who fled Iraq survived to lead the Usuli movement. Furthermore, those who fanned out to Iranian cities and elsewhere contributed to the spread of Usulism and the creation of a transnational network of supporters. Clerical families outside Bihbihani's network do not seem to have been as successful in fleeing the plague. For example, the above-mentioned Sunni cleric 'Abdullah al-Suwaydi returned to Baghdad from Kuwait to find that all of his one thousand students had perished.[73]

The death of Yusuf al-Bahrani and the plague created a power vacuum in the clerical establishment of Karbala', which Bihbihani's network quickly filled. In an attempt to put the last nail in the coffin of Akhbarism, Bihbihani declared that all Akhbaris were infidels (sing. *kafir*). Similar to Akhbaris before him, he enforced his proclamation with the support of mafia-type ruffians. One of his students, Shaykh Ja'far al-Najafi "Kashif al-Ghita'" (1743–1812), remembers that executioners (sing. *mirghadab*) regularly accompanied Bihbihani.[74] Apparently, the executioners slayed Akhbaris who resisted his movement. This helps to explain why few Shi'is claimed to be Akhbaris in Iraq by the time Bihbihani died. One of Bihbihani's prominent successors, Mirza Muhammad Mahdi Shahristani (d. 1800–1), maintained an approach to Islamic law that was closer to Akhbarism than Usulism, which indicates that the intellectual side of the Usuli-Akhbari debate would survive. However, Bihbihani and his supporters had dealt a serious blow to the Akhbari movement.

The Historical and Mythical Bihbihani

By overthrowing the Akhbari establishment, Bihbihani altered mainstream Shi'ism. Unlike Safavid Shi'ism, neo-Usulis were unwilling to accept alternative interpretations of Islam. Bihbihani set the stage for the widespread acceptance of an Usuli interpretation of Shi'i knowledge and authority at a critical moment in history. He trained a new generation of clerics and, by the time of his death in 1791, he had ushered in a new era of Shi'ism. The Shi'i community was much more unified ideologically and Bihbihani's disciples were widely recognized as the pre-eminent leaders of the Shi'i world. Although no formal hierarchy emerged in the Shi'i establishment at this point, Usulism contributed to the stratification of the Shi'i establishment. The Usuli movement was ready-made for its adoption by the incipient Qajar dynasty, which will be discussed in the following chapter.

Usuli ideology allowed these scholars to assume duties that Akhbaris argued were prerogatives only to be carried out by Imams. Usuli clerics and Shi'i merchants established a direct relationship, free from the control of a centralized state. The merchant-cleric relationship was mutually beneficial as clerics provided legal-religious support to merchants, who, in turn, financed Usuli clerics.

As the founder of the Usuli movement, then, it is no wonder that Wahid Bihbihani has been held posthumously in such high esteem. Additionally, Usulis were the only ones left to write the history of modern Shi'ism. Tunikabuni takes the art of praising Bihbihani to new heights in his *Qisas al-'ulama'*. He tells the story of one of Bihbihani's students who attended class in a state of ritual impurity (*najis*). Without being told, Bihbihani realized that the student was *najis* and decided to cancel class as a result. After dismissing the student's classmates, he gave the student money to go wash himself, which amazed the student because he realized that Bihbihani was aware of all things.[75] This story is supposed to demonstrate that Bihbihani had innate knowledge of and complete control over his students. Tunikabuni also describes Bihbihani's pious performance of rituals at the Imams' tombs to show his reverence for the Imams.[76] An additional story in *Qisas al-'ulama'* tells how Bihbihani cut the sleeve of his robe for a poor man who needed a headdress to cover his cold head, which shows Bihbihani's great generosity and care for the poor.[77]

Although the nineteenth-century Shi'i biographical dictionaries unanimously praise Bihbihani's leadership of the Usuli movement, they become apologetic when discussing his scholarship. According to al-Shahid al-Thalith (Hajji Mulla Muhammad Taqi), when Bihbihani's book, *al-Fawa'id al-ha'iriyya* reached Isfahan, Shi'i scholars mocked the book by saying that it seemed as if the book was written by someone who had studied under a woman.[78] Tunikabuni attempts to cover up the insult by saying that Bihbihani did, in fact, study under his father's sister.[79] Immediately following this story, Tunikabuni switches the subject and explains how knowledgeable Bihbihani's students were and that each of them were specialists in different subjects. Coming back to Bihbihani, Tunikabuni says that because his students were specialists in different fields, Bihbihani must have mastered each of the sciences. Further, Tunikabuni is amazed that Bihbihani's contemporaries criticized him for only being versed in matters of worship (*'ibadat*). He then concedes that Bihbihani did write a lot on the subject of worship, but explains that he was also versed in other subjects.[80] Muhammad 'Ali Kashmiri's *Nujum al-sama'* also claims that Bihbihani was the teacher of all (*ustad al-kull*) because all of the famous Shi'i scholars after him can trace their chain (*silsila*) of learning back to him.[81]

Although Usulis later persecuted Shaykhis, in part, for making claims to intuitive revelation (*kashf*), Bihbihani claimed that his knowledge was divinely inspired by dreams that usually featured Imam Husayn.[82] According to one of his students (Sayyid Muhammad Hasan Zunuzi), Bihbihani would recount his dreams at large gatherings.[83] In one such dream, Bihbihani saw his own relatives (who were in fact bothering him at the time) torturing Imam Husayn. When Bihbihani stopped his relatives, Husayn gave Bihbihani a scroll that contained the principles of Islam. Bihbihani later wrote his *Sharh mafatih al-shara'i* on the basis of the scroll.[84] An additional dream depicts Bihbihani visiting the shrine cities of Iraq when he was a young man. Years later, when he arrived in Karbala' for the first time, he found the shrines to be the same as in his dream.[85] In yet another dream, Bihbihani asked Imam Husayn whether people buried next to him are free from the wrath of angels. Husayn rhetorically replied: "which angel dares bother anyone buried next to me?" Bihbihani then asked Imam Husayn about the nature of Sufism to which Husayn replied, "they are people who want to destroy Islam!"[86] More than representing the ideas of the Imam, these dreams were a way for Bihbihani to claim that his ideas were rooted in the tradition and were sanctioned by the Imams.

Although Bihbihani's greatness is well cited in the Shi'i tradition, none of his works became standards in the Shi'i seminaries. What explains this dissonance? Although an unknown number of Bihbihani's books that were in the library of the Friday prayer leader (*imam jum'a*) of Kirmanshah were burned when his library caught fire (probably in the early nineteenth century), many of Bihbihani's texts are extant.[87] Most accounts attribute at least sixty titles to him and Davani has counted seventy-two.[88] Among those that survived, most have not been published. As Gleave points out, Bihbihani's most important work on Shi'i jurisprudence (*al-Fawa'id al-ha'iriyya*) is unorganized and seems more like random comments on unmentioned questions than a systematic work of *fiqh*.[89] Rather than a manifesto of Usulism, the book is a refutation of Yusuf al-Bahrani's *al-Hada'iq al-nadira*. The polemical nature of Bihbihani's work indicates that he was more interested in overcoming the Akhbari establishment than producing standard works of scholarship.

Bihbihani, therefore, fostered a network of students to propagate his Usuli movement. Bihbihani's work is not studied partly because the scholarship of his students and later scholars has overshadowed his own. However, as the instructor of those students, Bihbihani's thought is still critical to the historical development of Shi'ism. Although Bihbihani's scholarship is no longer current, his importance to Shi'i history was not an invention of Shi'i hagiographers. Because Bihbihani's hagiographers have cast him as a great scholar, they must include accolades for his writings in their evaluations. Yet, there is no doubt that Bihbihani's most important role was as a great teacher who was able to attract some of the brightest students of his time whose intellectual output became fundamental to the course of Usulism. This seems to indicate that Bihbihani was a well-respected teacher during his lifetime who supported his pupils intellectually and financially. Therefore, many of the great Shi'i scholars, such as Bahr al-'Ulum and Murtada al-Ansari refer to him as "the greatest teacher" (*al-ustad al-akbar*), "the teacher of all" (*ustad al-kull*), and "the verifier" (*al-muhaqqiq*).[90]

Conclusion: Why Usulism Prevailed

It has been the aim of this and preceding chapters to consider, why, against significant odds, Usulism overcame Akhbarism at this particular historical moment. What made Bihbihani and his followers reject the Akhbari school that they had previously adopted, when doing so was a potential risk to their lives? Like most historical changes, the success of Usulism was a result of both rational and non-rational factors. As time passes, members of a tradition are bound to re-evaluate the application of the tradition, whose origins are in the past. For example, the Shi'i tradition was formed during the period of the Prophet Muhammad and the Imams. Once the formative period ended and questions arose that were not answerable within the traditional framework, a measure of interpretation, even if not admitted, was necessary to bridge the gap. However, those who feel that innovation threatens the fundamentals of that tradition, may attempt to revert back to the fundamentals. In the Shi'i tradition, Astarabadi filled this role in the seventeenth century, which resulted in the revival of Hadith collections by Shi'i scholars. Again, when the traditional account (albeit reinterpreted for a new era) runs its course, the pendulum may swing back to favor change – indicated by the rise of the Usuli movement. Bihbihani and his disciples adopted rationalist Usuli methodology in an attempt to adapt the Shi'i tradition to the changing conditions of the late eighteenth century.

The downfall of the Safavid dynasty and the invasions of Nadir Shah and Saudi-Wahhabis threatened the Shi'i establishment. Clerics, like Wahid Bihbihani, were forced to survive independent of state sponsorship. The Shi'i establishment responded by expanding the influence of clerics and cultivating strong transnational networks that provided socio-religious, economic, and political support for the Usuli movement. In addition to allying himself with political elites, Bihbihani also maintained economic ties to his family members in India and Iran.

Although the triumph of Usulism was by no means inevitable, the right mix of historical conditions made it possible. When Yusuf al-Bahrani died, Bihbihani had more than a decade to consolidate his control over Karbala'. His network of followers also survived the plague. Additionally, as indicated in the previous chapter, the Usuli movement emerged at a moment in the history of southern Iraq in which the Shi'i cities had unprecedented freedom, allowing Usulis to create alliances with Arab tribes, eventually leading to the conversion of the majority of Iraqis to Shi'ism. Finally, the timing of the establishment of the Qajar dynasty simultaneous to the rise of Usulism contributed to the survival of the Usuli movement.[91] The continuation of Usuli preeminence after the death of Bihbihani would have been less likely had he not cultivated a large network of students, which is the subject to which we now turn.

Chapter 5

Wahid Bihbihani's Usuli Network In Iraq And Iran

INTRODUCTION

Bihbihani focused much of his energy in Iraq on training a network of students, who became leaders of the new Usuli-based Shi'i establishment in Iraq and Iran. Therefore, the first generation of modern Usuli scholars was comprised of Bihbihani's disciples, most of whom fostered an alliance with the Qajars. In addition to discussing the nature of the Usuli-Qajar alliance, this chapter, then, is a prosopographical study of Bihbihani's students as they came to dominate religion in Iran and southern Iraq. The figures who came to control the Usuli movement in Iraq were Sayyid Muhammad Mahdi Tabataba'i "Bahr al-'Ulum" (1742–97), Shaykh Ja'far al-Najafi "Kashif al-Ghita'" (1743–1812), Mirza Muhammad Mahdi Shahristani (d. 1800–1), and Sayyid 'Ali Tabataba'i (1748–1815). The prominent leaders who moved to Iran were Mirza Abu al-Qasim Qummi (1739–1817), Mulla Ahmad Naraqi (1771–1829), Muhammad Ibrahim Kalbasi (1766–1845), and Muhammad Baqir Shafti (1761–1844). Each of these figures became heads of long-lasting clerical dynasties, which have produced numerous prominent *mujtahids* over the past two hundred years.

After Bihbihani's death, the Usuli movement was dominated by individual *mujtahids* who had come together around the common ideology of Usulism. Although the Usuli movement was stratified on the basis of those who could perform *ijtihad* and those who could not, singular headship in modern Usulism has been rare because of the "theoretical equality of the *mujtahid*," as Arjomand puts it.[1] Also because a method of selecting a single *mujtahid* never developed, the Usuli movement often remained decentralized, which has had both divisive and democratizing influences. The divisiveness of the system is prevalent in that *mujtahids* engaged in antagonistic competition for authority, patronage, power, students, and followers. The geographical locations of *mujtahids* also tilted toward the decentralization of Usulism as Bihbihani's successors established *mujtahid*-networks and competing centers of learning in Isfahan, Qum, Kashan, Karbala', Najaf, and elsewhere.

Although Shi'is are supposed to emulate the rulings of a *mujtahid*, individual believers were free to choose which scholar to emulate, leading to democratization within the Usuli establishment, which vehemently rejected non-Usuli interpretations of Shi'ism. In practice, there were often multiple high-ranking *mujtahids* (*marja's*, Ayatollahs) at any given time. Periodically, however, a single *mujtahid* did gain a following throughout much of the Shi'i world. After Bihbihani, for example, leadership became centralized in the mid-nineteenth century around Murtada Ansari. According to Cole, therefore, "The Shi'i religious institution attained the ability to alternate between a Roman Catholic-type model wherein there was one supreme, recognized authority, and a more Eastern Orthodox model, wherein there were several almost coequal regional leaders."[2]

By consolidating Shi'i leadership in the first half of the nineteenth century, Bihbihani's students ensured that Usulism would be at the forefront of socio-religious developments in Iran and southern Iraq for centuries to come. Although Shi'is maintained some autonomy in southern Iraq after Ottoman recentralization in the nineteenth century, they did not play a central role in Iraqi politics. In Iran, however, Shi'i fortunes played out quite differently.

USULI-QAJAR ALLIANCE

As already noted, Bihbihani's death coincided with the rise of the Qajar dynasty in Iran. Several years before his coronation, the founder of the dynasty, Muhammad Khan Qajar, invited Bihbihani's son, Muhammad 'Ali, to the capital. According to Arjomand, this act "marked the beginning of the *rapprochement* between the Qajar state and the Shi'ite hierocracy, and decisively sealed the fate of the office of the *Mulla-bashi*," which had developed under the Safavids.[3] The foundations for Qajar society were established during the long reign of Fath 'Ali Shah (r. 1797–1834), who came to power five years after Bihbihani died. Continuing where his father left off, the shah supported the Usuli movement and assisted Usulis in their persecution of non-Usulis. In fact, Muhammad 'Ali Bihbihani convinced Fath 'Ali Shah to banish all Sufi dervishes from the Qajar capital. In cooperation with Bihbihani's disciples, the shah used state funds to repair the Shi'i shrines in Iran and Iraq.[4] He also financially supported Bihbihani's students and built or rebuilt Shi'i seminaries for them, including the Madrasa Faydiyya in Qum, which later became a center of protest during the 1979 Iranian revolution. Fath 'Ali Shah contributed to the emergence of a religious center in Qum, where he commissioned a tomb for himself and exempted townspeople from taxation.[5]

Many Usuli scholars, therefore, moved to Iran, partially reversing the migration of scholarly families who had emigrated to southern Iraq after the fall of the Safavid Empire. Several of Bihbihani's most influential disciples, however, remained in Iraq, and Iranian seminary students continued to study in Karbala' and Najaf. Usuli scholars in Iraq and Iran exerted their influence on the Qajar state and it was not until the mid-twentieth century that the locus of Shi'i leadership returned to Iran with the emergence of Qum as the leading center.

Desperate to legitimize Qajar rule, Fath 'Ali Shah invited Usulis to be collaborators in the establishment of the new state and proclaimed that he considered his kingship to be "exercised on behalf of (*ba niyabat*) the *mujtahids* of the age."[6] Initially, Fath 'Ali Shah devoted himself to Bihbihani's most outstanding disciple, Bahr al-'Ulum, and is reported to have "obeyed him in all matters."[7] After Bahr al-'Ulum died, the shah pledged his allegiance to a second student of Bihbihani, Kashif al-Ghita', who announced that Fath 'Ali Shah was permitted to reign on his behalf and that he had appointed the monarch as his deputy.[8] Both scholars lived in Iraq and Bahr al-'Ulum apparently never visited Iran.[9]

Most Usulis recognized Fath 'Ali Shah as "the shadow of God (*zill Allah*) on earth."[10] Whether this means that the *mujtahids* granted legitimacy to the Qajar government is debatable and, in fact, quite complex. The short answer is that although Usuli jurists did not grant the Qajar government with legitimacy according to Shi'i legal and theological norms, they did legitimize and support specific actions of the Qajars, which often created the appearance of legitimacy. So, although Usulis referred to Fath 'Ali Shah as the "shadow of God," the meaning of the title was up for debate. Mirza Abu al-Qasim Qummi, for example, argued that since God has no form, he has no shadow and therefore the shah has no claim to divinity. Instead, Qummi suggests that a king who exercises divine justice is like shade, which protects people from the oppression of the hot sun.[11] Kashif al-Ghita' complicated matters by arguing that "what is meant by kingship is not real kingship but apparent kingship, which is as a loan."[12]

The reticence of Usulis in granting Qajar legitimacy partially stemmed from the established Shi'i doctrine that all states are illegitimate in the absence of the awaited Imam. Bihbihani's successors increasingly believed that in the Imam's absence, real legitimacy belonged to the *mujtahids*. Mulla Ahmad Naraqi, for example, advanced the theory of the "guardianship of the jurist" (*wilayat al-faqih*) in which *mujtahids* "are the Imam's deputies and rulers during the absence of the Imam" and that "the superiority of the jurists over common man is like that of the Prophet over the lowest member of the community."[13] Although the concept of vicegerency created friction between the Usuli movement and the Qajar state, Ahmad Kazemi Moussavi argues that the concept of vicegerency was not initially aimed at decreasing the power of the Qajars, but was part of the struggle for charismatic authority with Akhbaris, Sufis, and Shaykhis. Therefore, Usulis "enhanced their doctrine of vicegerency to exclude unqualified claimants to the authority of the Imam."[14]

Nevertheless, after Fath 'Ali Shah's reign, the relationship between the Iranian state and Usuli *mujtahids* became strained, which continued off and on until the 1979 revolution. One constant cause of Usuli-Qajar conflict was the Iranian justice system, which was divided between religious law (*shar'*) administered by the *'ulama'* and the state-run common law (*'urf*) court.[15] A second cause of concern for Usulis was the Qajar turn towards Sufism. Although Usulis already dominated popular religion in Iran by this time, Sufism became associated with the aristocracy, which resulted in a class-based religious bifurcation in Iran.[16] Therefore, when Fath 'Ali Shah's successor, Muhammad Shah (1834–48), aligned himself with Sufis, Usuli control over the Qajars diminished, which meant that they could only rely on the coercive power of the state if their interests were aligned. Usulis, then, had to wait for Muhammad Shah's successor, Nasir al-Din Shah (1848–96), for the state to take decisive action against the Babi movement, which directly challenged the supremacy of Shi'i *mujtahids*. Therefore, it was not until 1850 that the founder of the Babi movement (the Bab) was executed.

Despite tensions in the Qajar-Usuli relationship, Usulis relied on Qajar military and governmental support when they declared infidelity (*takfir*) on Akhbaris, Sufis, Shaykhis, Babis, and Baha'is. With the coercive power of the state, therefore, Usulis were able to narrow the field of religious orthodoxy. As MacEoin argues, "attempts to redefine orthodoxy will lead to the identification or emergence of heterodoxy, particularly in the context of an established church system like that which began to reappear in Iran under the Qajars."[17] In other words, the Usuli-Qajar alliance fostered the reconstruction of religious orthodoxy, heterodoxy, and heresy.

During Fath 'Ali Shah's reign, Usuli clerics relied on the Qajars to enforce their declarations of *jihad* against Russia, which led to the first Russo-Persian war (1804–13).[18] The declarations of *jihad* against Russia have sparked debate among historians regarding the question of Qajar legitimacy. Lambton and Arjomand, for example, suggest that the *mujtahids* who issued the declarations of *jihad* did, in fact, view Qajar rule as legitimate. In Lambton's words, the declarations gave "validity, or at least temporary validity, to the rule of a shah whom they appointed to engage in *jihad*."[19] According to Arjomand, "the twin functions of the imamate – supreme political and religious leadership of the community," the so-called pen and sword, "became divided between the ulama and the rulers," the vicegerents of the Imam.[20]

More recently, however, Gleave has convincingly presented a more nuanced view by suggesting that although *mujtahids* legitimized the Qajar war against Russia, they simultaneously maintained the Shi'i principle of illegitimacy of government during the absence of the Imam. Gleave's argument makes a distinction between "the right to declare a *jihad*, and the right to lead it," which, he argues, is "crucial for an evaluation of views of the religious legitimacy of the early Qajar state."[21] Qummi, for example, did not consider the war against Russia a *jihad*, but rather a defensive war. The declaration of *jihad* by Kashif al-Ghita' explains that Fath 'Ali Shah was authorized to wage war on behalf of the *mujtahids'* collective office of the general deputyship (*niyaba 'amma*) of the Hidden Imam. Therefore, Gleave concludes that although some clerics gave de facto legitimacy to the Qajar state by approving their military action against Russia, they "maintained the *de jure* illegitimacy of government during the occultation."[22]

It is also important to bear in mind here that Shi'i scholars might make one claim in a work on Islamic legal theory and a completely different claim in a work on political theory, mysticism, and so on. For example, in his *Mi'raj al-sa'da*, Mulla Ahmad Naraqi argues that Fath

'Ali Shah was divinely appointed, yet in a work on mysticism he claims to despise being associated with the Qajars. Therefore, scholars such as Naraqi appear to be schizophrenic when comparing their works from different genres. As Gleave insightfully argues, such inconsistencies are the result of "the powerful generic boundaries which exist in the Muslim literary tradition."[23]

BIHBIHANI'S STUDENTS IN IRAQ

Before considering the Usuli scholars who established centers of learning in Iran, let us first discuss Bihbihani's most influential successors who remained in Iraq. After Bihbihani died, leadership of the Usuli movement passed to Bahr al-'Ulum and Kashif al-Ghita', and the pre-eminent center of Shi'ism moved with them from Karbala' to Najaf. Leadership in Karbala' then passed to Shahristani and Tabataba'i. Each of these scholars will be addressed in what follows.

Bahr al-'Ulum (Najaf)

The *mujtahid* recognized as Wahid Bihbihani's primary successor was his long-time student Sayyid Muhammad Mahdi Tabataba'i (1742–97), better known as "Bahr al-'Ulum" after the title of his book "The Ocean of Sciences" (*Bahr al-'Ulum*). Bahr al-'Ulum married Bihbihani's aunt and as a member of the Tabataba'i family, he was also related to the Majlisi family. Bihbihani repeatedly called him "my spiritual son" and considered him the most knowledgeable of his students, largely because he mastered multiple scholarly fields.[24] He was born and raised in Karbala', where he attended the classes of the Akhbari scholar Yusuf al-Bahrani for five years.[25] Fleeing the plague in 1772, Bahr al-'Ulum stayed in Mecca for several years before returning to Karbala' to study with Bihbihani. Largely because he was the most prominent scholar after Bihbihani's death, the primary center of Shi'i learning shifted with him to Najaf when he moved there.

Bahr al-'Ulum developed a reputation for converting non-Shi'is by teaching and debating with them. Tunikabuni devotes much of his entry on Bahr al-'Ulum to his stay in Mecca, where he is said to have become an expert in Sunnism and converted the Friday prayer leader (*imam jum'a*) of Mecca to Shi'ism after Bahr al-'Ulum taught him about Ja'far al-Sadiq (the seventh Shi'i Imam).[26] Additionally, Bahr al-'Ulum reportedly converted three thousand Jews after debating with them in Dhu'l-Kifl, a small town located between Najaf and Karbala'. The town is home to a shrine which is supposed to contain the remains of Dhu'l-Kifl, the biblical Ezekiel, who is venerated by Muslims as well as Jews, who have, at times, controlled the shrine.[27]

Although not all high-ranking *'ulama'* were subordinates of Bahr al-'Ulum, most clerics in Iran and Iraq respected his superiority. The chief Akhbari opponent of Usulis in the early nineteenth century (Mirza Muhammad Akhbari) even studied under Bahr al-'Ulum because he thought it was a rare opportunity and because "the entire community was in agreement" on Bahr al-'Ulum's leadership.[28] Similarly, Kashif al-Ghita', who was already a senior *mujtahid*, attended Bahr al-'Ulum's classes in order to receive the blessings for doing so.[29] In this way, Bahr al-'Ulum inherited Wahid Bihbihani's disciples as his own.

With such support, Bahr al-'Ulum created a loose hierarchy under his leadership by assigning the *'ulama'* around him with specific roles.[30] As Litvak has pointed out, Kashif al-Ghita', for example, was assigned to *fatwas*, emulation (*taqlid*), and organization, while others were appointed as prayer leaders, judges, and Bahr al-'Ulum's personal representatives.[31] Although it seemed that a nascent bureaucracy was developing, institutionalization of Usulism did not occur, which underscores the tendency of decentralization in modern Shi'i leadership. Nonetheless, Usuli *mujtahids* have often replicated elements of Bahr al-'Ulum's model in which representatives are appointed for different tasks.

Like Bihbihani and other Usulis, Bahr al-'Ulum appealed to the authority of intuitive illumination (*kashf*) and was more interested in philosophy, mysticism, and theology than Bihbihani's other students, who primarily emphasized the legalistic approach to Shi'ism. Bahr al-'Ulum is said to have reached the highest stage of mystical experience, or annihilation in God (*fana'*), and received mysteries from the Hidden Imam, who revealed himself to Bahr al-'Ulum.[32] One of his students argued that if Bahr al-'Ulum claimed infallibility (*'isma*) nobody would have disputed it.[33] However, given that Shi'is only attribute infallibility to the Prophet Muhammad and the Imams, Bahr al-'Ulum would have had to proclaim himself the Hidden Imam, which would certainly not have gone unquestioned. At any rate, Bahr al-'Ulum's emphasis on *kashf* was famously continued by the founder of the Shaykhi movement,

Shaykh Ahmad al-Ahsa'i, who was one of Bahr al-'Ulum's students. Although Ahsa'i became one of the most respected Shi'i scholars in the early nineteenth century, Usulis eventually declared infidelity (*takfir*) on his Shaykhi movement – also referred to as Kashfiyya.

Illustrative of the penchant for Usulis to make use of *takfir*, Bahr al-'Ulum declared infidelity (*takfir*) on Sufis after Usulis in Karbala' requested it, even though Bahr al-'Ulum himself was a mystic. Although he arranged for Sufis to leave the shrine cities unharmed, his declaration of *takfir* is telling of an age in which most Usulis were not willing to accommodate non-Usuli interpretations of Shi'ism. Sufism, therefore, was relegated to a position of heresy in its relation to the Usuli establishment as Bahr al-'Ulum and his Usuli colleagues rejected the authority of Sufi shaykhs.

Shaykh Ja'far al-Najafi "Kashif al-Ghita'" (Najaf)

Shaykh Ja'far al-Najafi (1743–1812), known as "Kashif al-Ghita'" (lit. "Remover of the Veil"), was one of Bihbihani's most illustrious students. After the passing of Bihbihani, Kashif al-Ghita' became Bahr al-'Ulum's favorite student. Therefore, when Bahr al-'Ulum died in 1797, Kashif al-Ghita' became head of the Shi'i establishment in Najaf. Kashif al-Ghita' was certainly aware of his own prominence as he was heard mumbling the following to himself by one of his students: "First you were Ja'far, then Shaykh Ja'far, after that the shaykh of Iraq, then the shaykh of Muslim shaykhs."[34] As the leading Shi'i scholar in Najaf, Kashif al-Ghita' also inherited the most prominent students of Bihbihani and Bahr al-'Ulum as his own disciples.[35]

The honorific "Kashif al-Ghita'" was derived from the title of his most prominent work: *Removing the Veil from the Obscurities of the Distinguished Shari'a* (*Kashf al-ghita' 'an mubhamat al-shari'at al-gharra'*). This book stands out as one of the most famous Shi'i legal texts of the entire Qajar period and is a prime example of anti-Akhbari literature, which became a standard in Usuli methodology. In this book, Kashif al-Ghita' attempted to develop Shi'i leadership by expanding the concept of "general deputyship" (*niyaba 'amma*). While he was alive, Kashif al-Ghita' was referred to as the "deputy of the Imam" (*na'ib al-Imam*) by his students and Fath 'Ali Shah.[36] Kashif al-Ghita's theory of deputyship was that the *'ulama'* were collectively responsible to rule on behalf of the Imam in his absence, and that a single *mujtahid* should have supreme authority among them. Since the Imam is hidden, it is impossible (unless by supernatural means) to determine which *mujtahid* the Imam prefers to fulfill this role. Therefore, Kashif al-Ghita' suggested that the supreme *mujtahid* should be the most learned (*a'lamiyya*) and the most just (*afdal*). Although he did not outline a method for selecting the most knowledgeable scholar, in practice *mujtahids* have generally displayed their knowledge in their books and legal judgments. Kashif al-Ghita', for example, started calling himself the "paramount Shaykh of all Muslims" after he wrote his *Kashf al-Ghita'* and received considerable acclaim for it. Kashif al-Ghita's formulation of *a'lamiyya* and the idea that *mujtahids* should exercise the Hidden Imam's complete authority became integral parts of the theory that a single *mujtahid* should be chosen as the source of emulation (*marja' al-taqlid*) for Shi'is.[37]

Kashif al-Ghita' established close relationships with political figures in Iraq and Iran. He acted as an official representative of the governor of Baghdad to negotiate a peace settlement with the Qajar Army.[38] In Iran, the Qajar government was all too happy to endorse the authority that Kashif al-Ghita' arrogated to himself since he gave his blessing to Fath 'Ali's rule, as indicated above.

Kashif al-Ghita' used his declaration of *jihad* against Russia as a way to advertise his concept of "general deputyship." Indeed, he required the shah to ensure that a prayer leader was appointed to each brigade of the army and that troops listened to a preacher once a week.[39] In his declaration, Kashif al-Ghita' explains that Fath 'Ali Shah was authorized to wage war on behalf of the Imam. He then claimed that the shah's authority to carry out the *jihad* was based on the *mujtahids'* collective office of the general deputyship (*niyaba 'amma*). Further, Kashif al-Ghita' claimed that his own power rested in his position as the deputy of the *mujtahids*. The declaration of *jihad*, however, did not mean that the Qajars were legitimate. In fact, Kashif al-Ghita' considered the shah to be nothing more than a servant carrying out the command of his master.[40] Therefore, the shah's legitimacy only extended to acts carried out on behalf of the *mujtahids*.

In addition to the *jihad* against Russia, Kashif al-Ghita' led a defensive war against Saudi-Wahhabi forces when they attacked Najaf in the early 1800s. According to Ahmad Bihbihani (who was a student of Kashif al-Ghita' and grandson of Wahid Bihbihani), Kashif al-Ghita' stockpiled weapons at his house and wore armor as he went into battle.[41] Kashif al-Ghita' also organized the construction of a protective wall that was built around Najaf. In addition to defending Shi'ism militarily, Kashif al-Ghita' wrote a treatise in response to the Wahhabi declaration that Shi'is were heretics.[42] The treatise was sent to the Wahhabi leader Amir 'Abd al-'Aziz bin Saud (d. 1803) along with gifts requesting that the declaration of infidelity (*takfir*) be removed, but to no avail.[43]

In addition to Qajar support, Kashif al-Ghita' carved out a greater sphere of influence for himself and the Usuli movement by collecting funds directly from his followers. Although he was not fluent in Persian, he regularly traveled to Iran to collect *khums* and absolution payments, which ensured financial autonomy for his network of students and supporters. He was so emboldened that he considered those who withheld payment as rebels.[44] Since he thought he was the deputy of the Hidden Imam, he assumed that obedience to him was equivalent to obeying the Hidden Imam. Therefore, those who did not pay him their *khums* were defying the infallible Imam. Kashif al-Ghita' enforced his legal judgments with the help of one of the two urban gangs in Najaf – the Zuqurt who were rivals of the Shumurt gang. Najaf devolved into civil war after Kashif al-Ghita' sentenced a prominent member of the Milali family (allies of the Shumurt) to death for not appearing in his court.[45]

Kashif al-Ghita' continued the Usuli tradition of narrowing Shi'i orthodoxy by declaring infidelity on Mirza Muhammad Akhbari, who is often referred to as "the last Akhbari." Although Mirza Muhammad had studied with Bahr al-'Ulum as noted above, he attempted to revive Akhbarism in Iran after Kashif al-Ghita' declared him an infidel. Fleeing Najaf, Mirza Muhammad sought the protection of Fath 'Ali Shah. Kashif al-Ghita' warned the shah of Mirza Muhammad's dangerous doctrines and supplied the monarch with one of his anti-Akhbari tracts to prove it.[46] However, during the first Russo-Persian war, Mirza Muhammad promised the shah to use his supernatural powers to obtain the head of Pavel Tsitsianov, a Russian general who had led violent campaigns in northern Iran. In return, Fath 'Ali Shah supposedly agreed to make the Akhbari school the official doctrine of the state.[47] When Tsitsianov's head was, in fact, presented, the shah did not honor the agreement and instead exiled Mirza Muhammad to Iraq. Avoiding the Shi'i strongholds, Mirza Muhammad moved to Baghdad, where he made a bid for governor, but was later murdered after one of the gubernatorial candidates incited a mob to attack his house.[48]

Kashif al-Ghita's death in 1812 marked the end of a short period in Najaf in which Usuli Shi'i authority was centered on a single figure.

Kashif al-Ghita' did groom his son Musa to succeed him, but his son-in-law (Asadallah b. Isma'il Tustari) challenged Musa and neither of them achieved universal recognition. Like the Bahr al-'Ulum clan, the Kashif al-Ghita' family has been a continuous force in the Shi'i establishment and has produced well-known scholars in nearly every generation since Kashif al-Ghita's death.

Mirza Muhammad Mahdi Shahristani (Karbala')

Mirza Muhammad Mahdi Shahristani (d. 1800–1) was the most influential *mujtahid* in Karbala' after Bihbihani died. Like Bihbihani, Shahristani was a descendant of a clerical family that was prominent during the Safavid dynasty and his family moved to Karbala' from Isfahan after the Afghan invasion. Shahristani was the oldest student of both Yusuf al-Bahrani and Bihbihani and was one of the first students to join Bihbihani's classes.[49] The two families eventually entered a marriage alliance when Shahristani's son, Sayyid Muhammad Husayn Mussawi Shahristani, married Wahid Bihbihani's granddaughter (the daughter of Muhammad 'Ali Bihbihani).

Although Shahristani received a license (*ijaza*) from Bihbihani, his approach to *fiqh* remained close to his former teacher, Yusuf al-Bahrani, as indicated by his book, *Sharh al-lam'a wa qawa'id al-'ulama'*, which is primarily concerned with Hadith. That Shahristani was from a leading Isfahani clerical family and that he continued with his Akhbari leanings, as a student of Wahid Bihbihani no less, supports the idea that Iranian emigrants from Isfahan were not simply reverting to the Usulism of their forefathers.

Shahristani's status as the leading cleric in Karbala' was enhanced when he became a recipient of the so-called Indian money (*pul-e Hindi*) from the rulers of the Shi'i kingdom of Awadh in India. Between 1786 and 1844, an estimated one million rupees flowed to the shrine cities from Awadh. As a result, clerics in Karbala' received more money from India than from Iran during this period. Shahristani was the recipient of half the total amount given during the first half of the nineteenth century (500,000 rupees).[50] According to Cole, Shi'is of Awadh became strongly connected to Karbala' after a member of the community, Sayyid Dildar 'Ali Nasirabadi, studied with Wahid Bihbihani and then with Shahristani, who granted the student an *ijaza*.[51] Additionally, Shahristani visited Awadh in the 1780s, after which he remained in contact with the Shi'i community in India through pilgrims and students. The "Indian money" was granted to Karbala' by Assaf al-Dawla (the Nawwab of Awadh) for the construction of the Hindiyya canal, which brought water to Najaf and Karbala' from the Middle Euphrates.[52]

Sayyid 'Ali Tabataba'i (Karbala')

Sayyid 'Ali Tabataba'i (1748–1815) was the nephew and son-in-law of Wahid Bihbihani. He became known as "Sahib al-Riyad" after the title of his book, *Riyad al-masa'il.* As a teenager, Tabataba'i was among the early students of Bihbihani in Karbala' who met in secret in fear of Akhbaris. When Shahristani died, Sayyid 'Ali Tabataba'i inherited Shi'i leadership in Karbala' and became the recipient of the "Indian money," which he used to establish endowments for his students.[53] However, Kashif al-Ghita' enjoyed more support than did Tabataba'i, which meant that Tabataba'i's pre-eminence was not recognized in Najaf until after Kashif al-Ghita' died. Apparently tension between the two scholars developed because Kashif al-Ghita' viewed Tabataba'i with contempt. Litvak argues that the division between Sayyids and non-Sayyids as well as the Karbala'-Najaf rivalry were to blame for the rift.[54] Additionally, *mujtahids* in Iran did not necessarily accept Tabataba'i's authority, even though he had a fairly large following in Iraq and India.[55] Tabataba'i's death in 1815 signaled the end of the leadership of Bihbihani's immediate disciples in the shrine cities of Iraq.

Like Kashif al-Ghita' in Najaf, Sayyid 'Ali Tabataba'i was the leading cleric of Karbala' when Saudi-Wahhabis attacked. According to *Rawdat al-jannat,* the assailants attempted to kill Tabataba'i in 1802 on Laylat al-Qadr (the anniversary of the night that the first verse of the Qur'an was revealed to Muhammad). When the attackers arrived, Tabataba'i was in his house with an infant and hid upstairs behind a pile of wood, praying. The Wahhabi attackers entered the house, yelling for him. They came upstairs and began removing pieces of the wood that hid him, but they left before finding him. Tabataba'i lived to tell the story that God miraculously blinded the assailants so they would not see him and kept the child from crying.[56] As other Usulis, therefore, Tabataba'i claimed to be divinely inspired. Shortly after the raid, Tabataba'i received funds from Awadh to build a protective wall around Karbala'.

BIHBIHANI'S STUDENTS IN IRAN

Bihbihani's most prominent successors in Iran were Mirza Abu al-Qasim Qummi, who established Qum as a new center of Shi'i learning; Mulla Ahmad Naraqi, who moved to Kashan, and Muhammad Ibrahim Kalbasi and Muhammad Baqir Shafti, who both moved to Isfahan. Although Qum eventually became the primary center, Shi'i learning in Iran remained geographically decentralized during much of the nineteenth century, as indicated by these scholars.

Mirza Abu al-Qasim Qummi (Qum)

Mirza Abu al-Qasim Qummi (1739–1817) was a prolific scholar and became the leading disciple of Bihbihani in Iran. Prior to joining the circle of Bihbihani in Karbala', Qummi had studied in Iran with his father (Mulla Muhammad Hasan Gilani) and Sayyid Husayn Khwansari, who taught *fiqh* and *usul*. Qummi, therefore, was conversant with Usuli methodology when he arrived in Karbala'. After studying in Iraq, Qummi moved back to Iran and settled in a village called Japulaq, where he lived an austere lifestyle. According to Tunikabuni, Qummi later moved to Qum because the ignorant *mullas* and people of Japulaq harassed him.[57] Qummi established several marriage alliances with the most important families in Qum. One of his daughters married his student, Mirza Abu Talib Qummi, a member of one of Qum's most influential families. Qummi's other daughters married into powerful clerical dynasties, including the Burujirdi, Naraqi, and Bahrani families.

Qummi established a strong relationship with Fath 'Ali Shah and became one of the main beneficiaries of the shah, who spent large sums on developing the infrastructure for Shi'i holy sites and learning centers in Qum. With state funding, therefore, Qummi established Qum as a center of learning and attracted countless students (including Muhammad Baqir Shafti and Muhammad Ibrahim Kalbasi).

Qummi produced a Shi'i political theory that justified Qajar rule, at least in outward appearance.[58] As noted above, Qummi recognized Fath 'Ali Shah as the "shadow of God on earth" and explains that kings are God's divinely appointed lieutenants. Qummi takes great care to emphasize that kings are not divine as the Safavids had claimed. Instead, he suggests that the legitimacy of kings depends on their justice. Therefore, the king's rule is a trial and God will punish him for any errors he commits.[59] Additionally, Qummi separated the duties of the king from that of *mujtahids*, saying that "God has appointed the kings to safeguard the worldly affairs of the people and to protect them ... and God has appointed the *ulama* to safeguard the religion."[60] Therefore, kings and religious officials are in need of each other. According to Abdul-Hadi Hairi, towards the end of his life, Qummi seems to have believed that the Qajars were "oppressive rulers" devoid of legitimacy, even though he had cooperated with them throughout his life.[61] In a letter to Fath 'Ali Shah, Qummi also warns the monarch against following Sufism, "which is worse than Sunnism."[62] Qummi made it clear that oppressive rulers cannot legally collect taxes – in the form of religious or land taxes – unless they have permission from a just *mujtahid*. Although it is possible that Qummi turned his back on the Qajars late in his life, he may have wanted to warn the shah that Usulis would withdraw their support if the Qajars continued to welcome Sufi advances. As already noted, Qummi's apparent schizophrenic relationship to the Qajars might be explained by the fact that Usulis never completely authorized Qajar rule as well as the different genres of his writings.

In addition to his political theories, Qummi wrote on a wide range of subjects. His book, *Qawanin al-usul*, is one of the most important works on *usul al-fiqh* in the Qajar period since it laid much of the groundwork for neo-Usuli ideology. *Qawanin* became a textbook for students and portions of it were used in the Shi'i seminaries long after Qummi died.[63] Like Kashif al-Ghita', Qummi stressed the importance of emulating (*taqlid*) a superior *mujtahid* in doctrine and practice, which contributed to the evolution of a Shi'i hierarchy. Qummi also argued that only living *mujtahids* can be emulated since they represent the continuation of the proof (*hujja*) of God, the Hidden Imam.[64] In Qummi's words, "The proof (*hujja*) of God, after the Imams is the so called *mujtahid* who can infer God's ruling from the proper sources."[65] As the idea developed that the emulation (*taqlid*) of a *mujtahid* was a requirement, Qummi established the principle of the freedom (*tarkhis*) for Shi'is to choose which *mujtahid* they would follow.[66] According to Moussavi, Qummi revived the effectiveness of consensus (*ijma'*), which had not been utilized during the Safavid period.[67] Qummi specifically developed the concept of consciously following (*mutaba'a*) the prevalent view (*al-qawl al-mashhur*) of the *mujtahids* or the ruling of the single most superior *mujtahid* and argued that the consensus of *mujtahids* implies the consent of the Imam.[68]

Mulla Ahmad Naraqi (Kashan)

Mulla Ahmad Naraqi (1771–1829) returned to Iran after his father passed away in 1794, and took his position as the most influential cleric in the city of Kashan. As Qummi had done in Qum, Naraqi's prominence made Kashan a center of Shiʻi learning. Although Kashan never achieved the status of Qum, Isfahan, Karbala', or Najaf, the fact that the city became a center of learning at all was because of the Naraqi family. Mulla Ahmad Naraqi was one of the few polymaths among Bihbihani's students; he wrote poetry and had a keen interest in philosophy, math, and comparative religions. His apologetic book, *Sayf al-ʻamma*, made use of Jewish and Christian sources to respond to the Christian missionary Henry Martin. He also translated a work on ethics for Fath ʻAli Shah.

Like Qummi, Naraqi's written work appears to be schizophrenic in relation to Qajar legitimacy. Naraqi dedicated his *Miʻraj al-saʻada* to Fath ʻAli Shah, whom he refers to as the "shadow of God" and the "fighter for God's cause." In this work, Naraqi argues that kings are divinely appointed to protect people's property and guard them from oppression.[69] Concerning obedience to the shah, he cites a Hadith report that warns Shiʻis not to disobey the king because their righteousness depends on the righteousness of the king.[70] According to Hairi, Naraqi argues that the legitimacy of Qajar rule was proven by astrological signs.[71] However, in a work on Islamic law (*ʻAwa'id al-ayyam*), Naraqi argues that, in the absence of the Imams, *mujtahids* are the only ones authorized to exercise sovereign power over others and that they are "the trustees of the Prophet and will not be tied up with the kings."[72] In yet another work, on mysticism, Naraqi seems to despise the Qajars, claiming that, "I disdain to be associated with the royal crown and throne."[73] Although Hairi argues that Naraqi wished to distance himself from the Qajars as he got older and "regretted his past activities," the variation of Naraqi's claims in his different works may have resulted from the difference in genres, as suggested above.[74] Additionally, Naraqi, like other Usulis, seems to have thought that the Qajars were subservient to *mujtahids*.

According to Naraqi's theory of the "guardianship of the jurist" (*wilayat al-faqih*), *mujtahids*, not kings, have the complete authority (*al-wilaya al-'amma*) of the Prophet and the Imams. As such, Naraqi argued that the emulation (*taqlid*) of a living *mujtahid* was a requirement for lay Shi'is.[75] Naraqi clearly states that the *mujtahid* is "the best creature of God after the prophets and the Imams" and therefore "his mandate is certain."[76] Naraqi's conception of *wilayat al-faqih* caused vigorous debate. Murtada Ansari, for example, rejected it because it did not have enough support from the Hadith. Ayatollah Khomeini, however, revived the theory of *wilayat al-faqih* and made it a fundamental part of his political theory, which has become the basis for the Islamic Republic of Iran.[77] As Moussavi points out, most *mujtahids* prior to Khomeini rejected "Naraqi's straightforward method of authorizing the 'ulama' with the Imam's privilege" and instead promoted the idea of *marja' al-taqlid*, which "entails no less authority" but with different means than the *wilayat al-faqih*.[78] Central to these debates on the authority of *mujtahids* was whether the jurists were authorized to make judgments related to Islamic law or if they had political authority as well.

Regardless of his political theories, Naraqi cooperated with Fath 'Ali Shah and exerted immense influence over the government, which will be illustrated here by two episodes. After Naraqi forced the governor of Kashan out of office, an angry Fath 'Ali Shah called Naraqi to Tehran to reproach him. However, it was apparently Naraqi who chastised the shah, saying, "O God! This unjust king appointed an unjust governor over the people. I put an end to his oppression; and now this oppressor is angry with me."[79] The shah then backed down and appointed a new governor, indicating that his relationship with Naraqi was more important than that of his governor. After issuing his declaration of *jihad* against Russia, Naraqi is said to have forced the hand of Fath 'Ali Shah into declaring war on Russia by traveling to the shah's camp with a group of religious officials. Naraqi is reported to have arrived at the camp wearing a shroud, indicating that he was ready to participate in the *jihad* himself and become a martyr for the cause.[80]

Muhammad Ibrahim Kalbasi (Isfahan)

As Qum and Kashan became key centers of Shi'i learning and leadership, Muhammad Ibrahim Kalbasi (1766–1845) and Muhammad Baqir

Shafti ("Hujjat al-Islam"), attempted to re-establish the prominence of Isfahan. The two were the most powerful scholars in the city during the first half of the nineteenth century. They had studied together in Iraq and remained good friends throughout their lives. The marriage between Kalbasi's son and Shafti's daughter solidified their alliance, and after finishing his studies, Shafti moved to Isfahan and stayed with Kalbasi. Although they shared the leadership of Isfahan, Shafti had much more social, economic, and political influence than Kalbasi.

Kalbasi was born in Isfahan, but moved to Karbala' where he joined the study circles of Bihbihani and Bahr al-'Ulum. Kalbasi also spent time in Qum and Kashan studying with Mirza Abu al-Qasim Qummi and Mulla Ahmad Naraqi. Like his colleagues, Kalbasi became influential over Fath 'Ali Shah and even dismissed a governor that he found unacceptable. Perhaps Kalbasi did not become more influential as a scholar because his writings were abstruse and he was overshadowed by Shafti. Although Kalbasi worked on his magnum opus, *Isharat al-Usul*, for thirty years, the book apparently never became a standard in the seminaries because the average student cannot understand the eloquent language in which it is written.[81]

Muhammad Baqir Shafti (Isfahan)

Like Bihbihani, who claimed to be "the Proof of God," Muhammad Baqir Shafti (1761–1844) came to be known by the title of the "Proof of Islam" (*hujjat al-Islam*).[82] Although one Shi'i source refers to Shafti as the "manifestation of God's power," Shafti is best known for his massive accumulation of wealth.[83] Instead of detracting from his piousness, Shafti's wealth only added to his prestige as a religious figure and some of his followers believed that he had unearthed an ancient treasure or that he discovered the mystery of alchemy.[84] With his massive fortune, Shafti cultivated a network of supporters and dependants in Iran, Iraq, and India and openly challenged the supremacy of the leading *mujtahids* in Karbala' and Najaf. Additionally, Shafti was less willing than his Usulis colleagues to cooperate with Fath 'Ali Shah.

Although Shafti came from a poor family and was penniless when he arrived in Isfahan after studying in Iraq, he became more powerful than the local government and used his position as *shaykh al-Islam* to become extremely wealthy. Indeed, he became one of the richest men in Iran and politicians and merchants were often indebted to him. According to one account, Shafti owned four thousand shops, entire villages in various parts of Iran, and four hundred caravanserais.[85] Furthermore, Shi'is from near and far regularly sent him money to distribute among the poor. In addition to receiving land grants and cash gifts from Fath 'Ali Shah, Moussavi implies that Shafti used his implementation of Islamic law as a pretext to acquire property.[86] Shafti is also reported to have confiscated property with the help of gangs (*lutis*), who served as his executors.[87] A semi-official Ottoman report suggests that, "The easiest thing in Iran is to become rich by joining the ranks of the *mullahs* ... Once a poor man has joined the learned profession and performed the pilgrimage to the holy shrines on foot, there receiving a diploma (*icazet*), in a few years he will be the owner of villages and farms."[88] It is quite likely that this was a direct reference to Shafti. Although the report is exaggerated and a bit tongue-in-cheek, the wealth of Usuli *mujtahids* made a lasting impression, even outside Iran.

Shafti exercised his judicial role as a *mujtahid* to the fullest extent and like his colleagues and Bihbihani before them, he enforced his judgments. Shafti reportedly sentenced upwards of one hundred people to death, for which he dedicated a graveyard near his house.[89] He issued his first death sentence for homosexuality, but was unable to convince anyone to enforce his judgment until after he attempted to carry out the execution himself. Failing to deal the death blow, someone else had to finish what Shafti had started. While leading the funeral prayers for the executed man, Shafti was so overcome with emotion that he fainted. Shafti was clearly an emotional man; his biographers tell us that he regularly spent his nights weeping and beating himself on the chest and head to the extent that his doctors advised him to stop after he became ill with a hernia.[90]

Instead of concerning himself with theoretical works on the principles of jurisprudence (*usul al-fiqh*) like most of Bihbihani's students, Shafti was primarily concerned with *fiqh* and wrote a treatise on the necessity of *mujtahids* to implement punishments for crimes (*hudud*) on behalf of the Hidden Imam.[91] Therefore, Shafti is better understood as a judge than a theorist. In fact, his role in enforcing the law exemplifies the influence that Usulis claimed over the court system in Iran. According to Arjomand, the courts of Usuli *mujtahids* virtually replaced the state-appointed judges (*qadis*) and represents the completion of "the institutional translation of the Shi'ite religious system."[92]

Belittling his colleagues in Najaf and Karbala', Shafti claimed that he learned more in six months studying in Qum with Abu al-Qasim Qummi than during his entire stay in Iraq. Shafti also distanced himself from the leading *mujtahids* in Iraq after Kashif al-Ghita' tried to convince Shafti and Kalbasi to follow his son-in-law (Muhammad 'Ali Hizarjaribi).[93] Ultimately, Shafti failed to return Isfahan to its former status as the primary center of Shi'ism. However, he proved that although more reverence was shown to *mujtahids* in the shrine cities of Iraq, those in Iran were in a better position to amass political and economic power.

Contrary to his colleagues, Shafti also had little interest in cooperating with Fath 'Ali Shah's government. Prior to Shafti's rise to fame, Fath 'Ali Shah attempted to appoint him as the prayer leader of the congregational mosque in Tehran, but Shafti refused to take the post.[94] When the two met, Shafti requested that the shah's royal music house (*naqareh khaneh*) be banned, which angered the shah since it was an integral part of royal ceremonies.[95] Fath 'Ali Shah later offered to relieve Shafti of the taxes he paid on one of his villages, but Shafti rejected the proposition. Asserting his piety, Shafti claimed that he did not want others to be forced to make up the amount. More probable is that he did not want to appear to be colluding with the government. Regardless of his reasoning, it would not have made much of a difference in his vast wealth.

Shafti also undermined the Qajar government by backing the failed attempt of the governor of the province of Fars, Husayn 'Ali Mirza Farmanfarma (d. 1835), to succeed Fath 'Ali Shah. With the support of Fath 'Ali Shah's minister ('Abdallah Khan Amin ad-Dawla) and others, Farmanfarma launched an armed rebellion and had coins struck in his name. Some mosques also recognized him as the new shah.[96] However, Farmanfarma was eventually arrested and brought to Tehran, where he died shortly after his arrival.

Shafti apparently supported Farmanfarma because Fath 'Ali Shah's successor (Muhammad Shah) was a Sufi. In the midst of the succession, Isfahan erupted into anarchy as the city was overrun by gangs (sing. *luti*), who murdered, robbed, and raped without consequence. Shafti helped organize the *lutis* into a militia and allowed them to store their loot in the congregational mosque of Isfahan. Additionally, Shafti provided the *lutis* with sanctuary (*bast*) in his house and employed them as executors of his judgments.[97]

Muhammad Shah (1834–48), the new Qajar monarch, was alarmed at the scene in Isfahan as he feared that a tripartite alliance between *lutis*, high-ranking Usuli clerics, and descendants of the Safavids could prove fatal to the Qajar dynasty, then only four decades old. Therefore, in 1836 the new shah dispatched soldiers to apprehend *lutis* and chop off their hands as punishment. Muhammad Shah's forces also confiscated religious endowments (sing. *waqf*) administered by Shafti, which encouraged Shafti to continue his opposition. In 1837, Shafti and the Friday prayer leader of Isfahan (Mir Muhammad Mahdi) led a revolt against the governor of Isfahan (Khusraw Khan), who had apparently attempted to curb the power of Shi'i officials. Instead of bowing to the governor, Shafti extended his activities with the *lutis* until a Qajar army arrived from Tehran. Over 150 *lutis* were executed and more were exiled.[98] Shafti and Muhammad Shah were now archenemies, but the shah did not dare punish a *mujtahid*, even for treachery. In fact, when Muhammad Shah came to Isfahan to meet him, a Qur'an chanter preceded Shafti's entourage reciting the verse: "We sent a Prophet to the Pharaoh and the Pharaoh rebelled against the Prophet." The shah's soldiers reportedly rushed to meet Shafti and some even kissed his hands and the hooves of his mule.[99]

Additional Students of Bihbihani

In addition to the above-mentioned scholars, countless others studied with Bihbihani. Muhammad 'Ali Habibabadi lists more than forty who became prominent.[100] Davani dedicates roughly a quarter of his biography on Bihbihani to descriptions of thirty-one of Bihbihani's outstanding pupils.[101] The following is Davani's list of Bihbihani's students, including those mentioned above.[102]

1.   Aqa Sayyid Jawad 'Amili
2.   Hajj Mulla Muhammad Astarabadi
3.   Sayyid Ahmad 'Atar Baghdadi
4.   Muhammad 'Ali b. Muhammad Baqir Bihbihani ("*sufi-kush*")
5.   'Abd al-Husayn Bihbihani
6.   Shams al-Din b. Jamal al-Din Bihbihani
7.   Shaykh Abu 'Ali Ha'iri
8.   Sayyid Dildar 'Ali Nasir Abadi Hindi
9.   Mulla Muhammad Hizarjarabi
10.   Muhammad Baqir Shafti "Hujjat al-Islam"

11. Mir Hasan Isfahani
12. Shaykh Muhammad Taqi Isfahani
13. Muhammad Ibrahim Kalbasi
14. Sayyid Mohsen A'raji Kazimayni
15. Shaykh Asadullah Kazimi
16. Mirza Mahdi Khurasani
17. Sayyid Muhammad Qasir Khurasani
18. Shaykh Muhammad Khurasani
19. Mulla 'Abd al-Jalil Kirmanshahi
20. Sayyid Ahmad Tabataba'i
21. Shaykh Ja'far al-Najafi "Kashif al-Ghita'"
22. Mulla Ahmad Naraqi
23. Mirza Muhammad Taqi Qadi
24. Hajj Mirza Muhammad Hasan Qazvini
25. Mirza Abu al-Qasim Qummi
26. Mirza Muhammad Mahdi Shahristani
27. Sayyid Muhammad Shafi' Shushtari
28. Sayyid Muhammad Mahdi Tabataba'i "Bahr al-'Ulum"
29. Sayyid 'Ali Tabataba'i "Sahib al-Riyad"
30. Hajj Mirza Yusuf Tabrizi
31. Sayyid Muhammad Hasan Zunuzi

CONCLUSION

By the turn of the nineteenth century, Bihbihani and his disciples had established the supremacy of Usulism in Iraq and Iran and presented themselves as the Hidden Imam's ultra-spiritual vicegerents. Fath 'Ali Shah and Bihbihani's successors wedded the Qajar state to the Usuli movement. In addition to providing Usulis with state funds, Fath 'Ali Shah dismissed governors with whom the *mujtahids* were not pleased. However, when the shah died, the Qajar-Usuli marriage was thrown into question. Shafti even threw his weight behind a challenger to Muhammad Shah Qajar, who did not support Usulism as enthusiastically as his predecessor. Even though the Usuli movement benefited tremendously from Qajar support and relied on the state to enforce their declarations of *jihad* and *takfir*, they never fully supported Qajar legitimacy. Theoretically, Usuli *mujtahids* arrogated authority in the absence of the Hidden Imam to themselves. In practice, they retained their independence from the state by creating their own networks of followers and supporters. Shafti included *lutis* in his network and used his authority as a judge to confiscate property, while Kashif al-Ghita' considered those who did not pay their *khums* as dissenters. Therefore, Qajar leverage on Usuli clerics was limited and the state had little say in the religious affairs of the highest echelon of Shi'i leadership.

Bihbihani's disciples contributed to the development of a hierarchy in the Shi'i order as *mujtahids* claimed leadership over more than one Shi'i center and delegated their clerical duties. Although some *mujtahids* gained a wide following, leadership has often remained decentralized around multiple scholars. The first neo-Usuli scholars elaborated on principles that justified their authority, including "guardianship of the jurist" (*wilayat al-faqih*), "general deputyship" (*niyaba 'amma*), and the necessity of following the most knowledgeable (*a'lamiyya*) *mujtahid*. These concepts are rooted in the tradition of Islamic law, which Bihbihani and his successors revived and reformed both in theory and in practice. The following chapter focuses on Bihbihani's approach to Islamic legal theory.

Chapter 6

Wahid Bihbihani's Conception of Islamic Law

INTRODUCTION

S ince the majority of this book is concerned with the origins and development of neo-Usulism associated with Wahid Bihbihani, his thought must be considered. Although Bihbihani is the founder of the most dominant trend in modern Shi'ism, he has not received the scholarly attention that one might expect. As a catalyst of the shift towards Usulism, however, a greater understanding of his thought is crucial. For legalistic Muslim scholars (like Bihbihani and his Akhbari counterparts), knowledge and authority belong to the domain of law.

As a result of Bihbihani's desire to overthrow the Akhbari establishment, his writings are primarily concerned with the authority of jurists and the principles of Islamic law (*usul al-fiqh*), which were at the center of the Usuli-Akhbari dispute. Bihbihani presents the Akhbari school as simplistic and unscholarly, when compared to Usulism. Given that Muslims assert Islamic law as a comprehensive system that permeates social, political, and economic life, the implications of the neo-Usuli victory have been immense. Any tectonic shift in Islamic legal thought of this magnitude would have significant consequences.

In what follows, I outline Bihbihani's approach to knowledge and authority, and his methodology of interpreting the foundational texts (i.e. Qur'an and Hadith), and his rationalist approach to the law. Robert Gleave is the only Western scholar who has discussed Bihbihani's thought in any detail. His *Inevitable Doubt* compares the thought of Bihbihani with his chief Akhbari rival, Yusuf al-Bahrani.

Bihbihani wrote a number of works on Islamic law, the most important of which is *al-Fawa'id al-ha'iriyya*. Like other works in the field of jurisprudence (*usul al-fiqh*), Bihbihani wrote *Fawa'id* for the purpose of establishing and exploring authoritative sources of knowledge and authority. Also considered here are Bihbihani's "Treatise on *Akhbar* and *Ijtihad*" (*al-Risala al-akhbar wa al-ijtihad*), "Treatises on Principles of Law" (*al-Risa'il al-usuliyya*), and "Treatises on Legal Understanding" (*al-Risa'il al-fiqhiyya*), each of which were written for the purpose of undermining the Akhbari approach and promoting Usulism. While Bihbihani reaffirms the primacy of the Qur'an and Hadith, he also questions the authority of many Hadith reports, which serves to undermine the authority of Akhbaris, who claim to rely almost exclusively on the texts. Bihbihani also rejects literal readings of the Qur'an and Hadith, which he argues is the method of Akhbaris. Instead, he insists that the texts should be understood within their original contexts in regard to language (*lugha*) and common usage (*'urf*). Therefore, Bihbihani suggests that *mujtahids* must rely on the consensus (*ijma'*) of the early Arab Muslim community.

Bihbihani's Legalistic Conception of Knowledge

Bihbihani makes a critical distinction between knowledge (*'ilm*) and reality (*haqiqa, waqi'*). He clearly states that "knowledge is not what conforms to reality."[1] To clarify, he explains that Jews "know" that Muhammad is not a prophet and polytheists "know" that there is more than one god.[2] In other words, knowledge is relative to the one who possesses it. Reality (*haqiqa*), however, is the ultimate, non-relative truth; it is the truth according to God, the Lawgiver. At first glance, Bihbihani's view of knowledge may seem to conform to the postmodern notion of relativism. However, considering his cosmology, Bihbihani clearly believes that his (Usuli Shi'i) knowledge is superior to that of Jews, polytheists, and so on because it is more likely to conform to the divine reality. Through what means does he have access to this superior knowledge? Although Bihbihani does not include intuitive illumination (*kashf*) in his theoretical framework for deriving knowledge, he claimed intuitive guidance from the Imams as a result of a dream in which he received a scroll from Imam Husayn. Usulis generally reject claims to intuitive illumination as part of the legalistic framework for making judgments, even if Usulis utilized claims to intuitive knowledge as a tool to reinforce the authority of their knowledge. So, if not through mystical means, where does Bihbihani's perfect, or relatively perfect, knowledge come from?

Like other Shi'i Muslims, Bihbihani's link to God's reality is the word of God as found in the Qur'an as well as the Sunna of the Prophet Muhammad and the Hadith reports of the infallible (*ma'sum*) Imams. Since Sunni Muslims reject the legitimacy of the Imams as Muhammad's successors and possessors of perfect knowledge, they are deprived of access to ultimate reality (from a Shi'i perspective). But, Bihbihani did not believe that Shi'is always attain the Truth (*haqiqa*) of divine reality. In fact, he attacked Akhbaris because they did not interpret the texts properly. Therefore, Bihbihani's Usuli methodology of interpreting the texts and applying them to judgments is his basis for claiming that his knowledge is more likely to conform to Reality than that of Sunnis, Akhbaris, Sufis, Shaykhis, and others.

Bihbihani rejects the notion that the "gate of knowledge" (*bab al-'ilm*) was ever closed, which is a response to scholars who assumed that the gate of *ijtihad* was closed several hundred years after the origins of Islam. Such scholars believed that after the gate of *ijtihad* was closed, establishing new rulings through *ijtihad* was no longer permissible. Instead, scholars were supposed to emulate (*taqlid*) rulings that had already been set as precedence.[3] Bihbihani argues that knowledge has always been accessible through "the gate of evidence, the gate of Hadith reports, and the gate of the conjecture (*zann*) of a *mujtahid*."[4] Through these "gates," Bihbihani suggests that it is possible to produce indicators or arguments (sing. *dalil*) that lead to knowledge. An indicator, for example, might be a Hadith report from which a ruling is derived. The acceptance of the conjecture of a *mujtahid* is based on the admission that certainty (*qat'*) is not always possible. Since Akhbaris rejected the issuance of rulings on cases that did not achieve certainty, the acceptance of the conjecture of a *mujtahid* is a distinguishing feature that separates Usulis from Akhbaris. The ability of issuing judgments on the basis of conjecture also enhances the authority of Usuli jurists.

Bihbihani begins *al-Fawa'id al-ha'iriyya* by explaining the high stakes and grave dangers of interpreting Islamic law because of its complexity and long-term impact. He compares law to medicine, explaining that both doctors of law and medicine have the power of authorization. Therefore, they both must use extreme caution because false theories can be disastrous and lead to eternal damnation.[5] However, Bihbihani claims that errors in law are far more dangerous than in medicine because mistakes in medicine can only lead to bodily harm, whereas errors in law affect social and economic relations. Even worse, the misguidance of a legal scholar can have calamitous results in matters of faith.[6] In Bihbihani's mind, social well-being and eternal salvation depend on the wise guidance of doctors of Islamic law (*mujtahids*), not on medical doctors, politicians, or any other professionals. If a *mujtahid* rules incorrectly, he might authorize the death penalty for innocent persons, forbid a permissible marriage, or take money from its rightful owner. Further, according to Bihbihani, the impact of medicine, whether good or bad, is short-term and at most can last a lifetime. However, the all-encompassing influence of Islamic law transcends generations and can even last until the end of time. In other words, Bihbihani accepts the eternality of the influence of *mujtahids*, which makes them the most important members of society.

Bihbihani argues that arriving at absolute knowledge in law is far more difficult than in medicine and the natural sciences. Physicians can use trial and error and other scientific methods in order to prove or disprove their theories, but legal scholars do not have such a luxury. Therefore, as Bihbihani asserts, science does not require great effort because it does not contain contradictions.[7] In Bihbihani's mind, then, the natural world is perfectly rational and therefore predictable. Conversely, contradictions are found in the sources on which Islamic law is based (i.e., Qur'an and Hadith), which require reconciliation. According to Bihbihani, the difference between science and Islamic law is that science is based on a rational world, whereas Islamic law is based on textual sources, which contain incongruous statements.

Does this mean that Bihbihani rejects the idea that God is perfectly rational? If God is the supreme rational being, as Bihbihani asserts, why do the texts that He sent down contain contradictions? Bihbihani reconciles these questions by explaining that all textual contradictions are a result of human errors. As the texts have been passed down through the ages, they have been subject to copyist mistakes. Additionally, dissimulation (*taqiyya*) of the Imams also created incongruous statements in Hadith reports. Finally, the texts contain allegorical statements, which cannot be understood literally. Therefore, the true intention of God can only become evident through the wise interpretations of *mujtahids*, who have been trained in textual exegesis.[8]

Bihbihani puts the onus of resolving textual uncertainties on *mujtahids*, who are the only agency capable of uncovering God's will. Even after the *mujtahid* undertakes the great effort of discerning truth from falsehood, it is possible that doubt will remain. In fact, Bihbihani clearly states that "all *fiqh* is theory or assumption," which is initially located in the realm of confusion, doubt, or even hallucination.[9] Like scientific theories, Islamic law must be tested and stand the test of time. If a theorem remains uncontested, it must be true. Thus, the only way to be sure that a *mujtahid's* legal judgment did, in fact, produce certainty is its widespread acceptance and longevity. Therefore, if scholars accept a *mujtahid's* judgment, it must conform to the Truth of the divine lawgiver. As will be discussed further, this illustrates the importance that Bihbihani places on the legal principle of consensus (*ijma'*). Once a judgment achieves consensus, it becomes absolutely imperative for Muslims to follow it.

Bihbihani states that if a physician is incapable or imperfect, he will be considered the enemy of the flesh. However, if a jurist commits an error, he will become the enemy of Islam.[10] This position seems to go against the widely accepted premise that a *mujtahid* who engages in *ijtihad* will receive one reward if he is wrong, simply for his effort, and two if he is right.[11] However, Bihbihani's argument must be interpreted within the polemical milieu in which he was writing. In effect, he is saying that Usulis have the authority to produce correct legal judgments because their approach is rational, whereas Akhbaris are the enemies of religion because they have rejected the Usuli method. For this reason, Bihbihani felt it necessary to declare infidelity (*takfir*) on Akhbaris. In his mind, they were incapable jurists, and thus enemies of Islam. Citing the Qur'anic verse that says "Whosoever judges not according to what God has sent down – they are the ungodly,"[12] Bihbihani explains that one must look at this verse until he realizes that "whoever rules unjustly becomes an infidel (*kafir*)."[13] Following this line of argumentation, he suggests that Akhbaris are ungodly infidels because they produce unjust rulings as a result of their unsound methods.

Although Bihbihani initially seems to argue that knowledge is relative, he rejects any semblance of pluralism. Bihbihani attempts to narrow the field of Shi'i orthodoxy by arguing that the Akhbari approach to Islamic law is not simply wrong but results in infidelity (*takfir*), even if Usuli methodology sometimes only results in conjecture (*zann*), which may not coincide with divine reality. Arguing that Akhbaris were infidels based on their interpretation of Islamic law had tremendous social, economic, and political implications. It allowed Usulis to establish themselves as the leaders of mainstream Shi'ism, persecute non-Usulis, and therefore monopolize the religio-economic and religio-political spheres in Iran and southern Iraq.

FOUR OR FIVE SOURCES OF USULI SHI'I LAW?

Bihbihani's theoretical approach to Shi'i law is best understood within the context of the tradition of Shi'i rationalism. He does not argue in favor of unbridled reason, nor does he call for an uncritical adoption of all textual sources. In descending order, Bihbihani (similar to the majority of Usulis) argued that the following four sources are the basis of Islamic law, the principles of jurisprudence (*usul al-fiqh*): Qur'an, Hadith, consensus (*ijma'*), and reason (*'aql*). Bihbihani formally and theoretically rejected analogy (*qiyas*) as a fifth source. However, in practice, he makes use of analogical reasoning without calling it *qiyas*. Instead, he argues in favor of the "transference" (*ta'diyya*) of existing judgments to new cases. Analogy, in fact, is one of the methods of transference he accepts, although he differentiates it from the Sunni conception of *qiyas*. Because the hairsplitting difference between his methods of "transference" and the Sunni conception of analogy is minute, it seems that Bihbihani only rejected *qiyas* as part of the ongoing sectarian debate.

1. The Qur'an

The foundation of knowledge for Bihbihani, as for most Muslims, is text-based (*naql*). Textual sources are the only direct connection to absolute truth because God sent the Qur'an directly to Muhammad. Like the Qur'an, the Hadith reports of Muhammad and the Imams are infallible interpretations of God's word. The only proof of God's knowledge is what He says through Muhammad and the Imams. Additional sources are methods of understanding and interpreting the texts, such as reason (*'aql*), which, according to Bihbihani, can be used independently of the texts. Reason as an independent source can only be considered on cases that are not explicitly clear in the texts or have not achieved consensus (*qiyas*).

Like most Muslims, Bihbihani views the Qur'an as the most authoritative source of knowledge. It is the word of God and the supreme source of God's reality and law. Since the Qur'an is the revealed intention of God, the Lawgiver, it is imperative for all to be obedient to its commands and not to question or speculate on the truth found within it.[14] In other words, reason or interpretation cannot be applied to the Qur'an when its intention is clear. To illustrate this point, Bihbihani states that even a child can understand the intention of the Qur'anic verse "Do not come nigh to adultery."[15] Because this statement is clear, interpretation is unnecessary. Further, Bihbihani claims that whoever does not obey the commandments in the Qur'an, does not revere God's speech in it, and is not satisfied with it. Therefore, he is an infidel.[16]

The main argument that Bihbihani makes in regard to the Qur'an is that it has probative force (*hujjiyya*), which produces certainty.[17] This means that jurists are not bound to accept interpretations of the Qur'an found in Hadith reports. He charges that "Akhbaris forbid this completely, which is very surprising because the probative force (*hujja*) [of the Qur'an] is the word of God."[18] Supporting his claim, he says that the Hadith reports which suggest that the Qur'an cannot be interpreted are not widespread and therefore dubious.

Although Bihbihani vehemently argues that the Qur'an is the pre-eminent independent source of law, he acknowledges that Qur'anic verses are not always clear and do not always produce an indicator (*dalil*) of sure knowledge. In fact, he accepts three general categories of Qur'anic indicators, namely definite (*qat'*), strong conjecture (*al-zann al-qawi*), and conjecture (*zann*).[19] Like many Shi'i scholars before and after him, Bihbihani also accepts that some Qur'anic verses (especially those that support Shi'i claims) were not included in the canonized Qur'an.[20] However, he suggests that Shi'is should read one of the known seven versions of the Qur'an based on the Imami Hadith: "read as the people read during the time of the Qa'im."[21] He also concedes that not all Qur'anic verses are necessarily clear to the intellect. However, even if the meaning of a Qur'anic verse is unclear, it still overrules Hadith reports and is subject to the conjectural (*zanni*) ruling of a *mujtahid*.[22]

2. Traditions (Hadith)

For Bihbihani and most Muslims, Hadith reports are the second most authoritative source of law, though Sunnis and Shi'is disagree as to which Hadiths are valid. While both accept Prophetic Hadiths (i.e. Muhammad's Sunna), Sunnis reject the Imams' Hadith reports. Like most Shi'is, Bihbihani justifies the Shi'i position with the Prophetic Hadith in which Muhammad says he has left two things for the community: his book and his family (i.e. the Qur'an and the Imams).[23]

In Bihbihani's view, the Imams provided infallible interpretations of the laws already revealed by God through Muhammad. Therefore, the Imams' rulings cannot be outside the purview of the Qur'an. Bihbihani explains that Hadith reports are a "witness" or supporting evidence (*shahadan*) for the Qur'an and that the original intention of Hadith reports was to explain the manner (*kayfiyyat*) of proper practice.[24] In other words, Hadith reports illustrate the method of carrying out what has been commanded in the Qur'an. According to Bihbihani, therefore, clear Hadith reports are legally binding.[25]

Bihbihani's critique on the manner in which Hadith reports were collected is illustrative of his attack on the Akhbari school. Because of his polemical stance, Bihbihani's approach to the Hadith may seem a bit schizophrenic. On one hand, Bihbihani praises the Hadith as the second most important source of knowledge. On the other, he emphasizes the pitfalls of extracting knowledge from them as a way to undermine the authority of Akhbaris. While he finds that most reports (*akhbar*) are authoritative, he warns that many reports did not survive and many of those that did were not properly examined by Hadith collectors. Moreover, among the reports that were examined, he explains, it is difficult to distinguish between the words of the collector, narrator, and the original Hadith text. Since it is difficult to determine the Prophet's, and therefore, God's original intentions, it is often impossible to extrapolate his commands from individual Hadith reports.[26] Further, Bihbihani claims that the clashing of scholarly opinions over the interpretation of the Hadith (as well as many verses from the Qur'an) often produced opposing viewpoints.[27]

Additionally, Bihbihani argues that copyist errors, misspellings, misplacement of diacritical marks, and other additions or deletions further marred the Hadith.[28] In Bihbihani's mind, the net result was that the original ruling was changed and what is now "known" from the Hadith is not what the Imams intended.[29] However, for Usulis and indeed for Bihbihani, this does not mean that all Hadith reports should be thrown out. It simply means that there must be a system in place to differentiate between sound and dubious reports.

Thus Bihbihani, like most Usulis, adopted a more complex system for using Hadiths than did Akhbaris. As he did with Qur'anic verses, he accepted a hierarchical scale for the Hadith, which includes sound (*sahih*), fair (*hasan*), transmitted (*marsal*), documented (*mawthiq*), and weak (*da'if*).[30] He only accepted widespread (*mutawatir*) reports as authoritative and thus capable of producing sure knowledge (*'ilm*) without the use of reason or other exegetical tools. Since Akhbari thought is primarily based on the texts, Akhbaris sought to maximize the number of acceptable Hadith reports, while Bihbihani minimized the number of acceptable reports in an effort to undermine Akhbari authority.

Given his hierarchy of authority, Bihbihani argues that any Hadith report which contradicts a Qur'anic verse is unsound and cites the following reports in support of his position: "Any Hadith which disagrees with the Qur'an should be thrown against the wall," "we never disagree with the Qur'an," and "what is found in the Hadith is a witness to the Qur'an."[31] Bihbihani concludes, therefore, that it is never acceptable to disagree with the Qur'an.[32]

Given that Bihbihani rejects the ability of many Hadith reports to produce certainty, he is baffled that Akhbaris would even consider accepting a report if it contradicts a Qur'anic verse. Dumbfounded, he wonders how Akhbaris can possibly accept a report as a proof of absolute knowledge, but not a verse from the Qur'an.[33] In this way, Bihbihani exaggerates the position of Akhbaris by suggesting that they reject the Qur'an in favor of the Hadith. He characterizes the Akhbari system of law as almost entirely relying on one imperfect source of knowledge and authority – the Hadith. The implication for Bihbihani is that the Akhbari school is simplistic and unscholarly, whereas his Usuli system is complex, combining textual exegesis, rational thought, and other precise methods. Bihbihani seeks to make it obvious that Usulism, not the primitive Akhbari school, is the high-minded school that better reflects the high stakes of Islamic law.

Many Shi'i scholars have argued that Hadith reports which contradict each other are the result of dissimulation (*taqiyya*) or fabrications by dissenting groups seeking to support their positions. The distance between the issuance of a report and the time of its collection is also cited as a common reason for textual contradictions. Bihbihani argues that intra-Hadith conflicts *cannot* be explained by dissimulation. However, he claims that all contradictions that are found between the Qur'an and Hadith *are* a result of dissimulation. In fact, he claims that dissimulation can only be identified if a report contradicts the Qur'an or agrees with Sunnis.[34]

An additional problem that Hadith scholars are faced with is the fact that some Hadith reports are only reported by one transmitter (*akhbar al-ahad*). Bihbihani dedicates an immense amount of attention to this problem since it is a source of contention between Akhbaris and Usulis.

Unlike most Akhbaris and some Usulis, Bihbihani generally rejects *akhbar al-ahad*, unless they are in agreement with the consensus (*ijma'*) of the companions of the Prophet and Imams, other well-known reports, or a Qur'anic verse.[35] In practice, then, *akhbar al-ahad* are only useful to Bihbihani when they support established judgments. Even if *akhbar al-ahad* do not contradict other acceptable reports, consensus, or the Qur'an, they only have the power to produce probable (*zanni*) knowledge. In Bihbihani's words:

> A singular Hadith report (*khabar wahid*) produces conjectural (*zanni*) knowledge because of its chain of transmitters (*sanad*), text (*matn*), and proofs (*hujjat*), and such conjecture only exists if the report is not opposed to other reports (*akhbar*), Qur'anic verses, or conjectural consensus (*ijma' zanni*).[36]

3. Consensus (ijma')

Bihbihani argues that it is impossible to understand a ruling based on the Hadith without the aid of consensus (*ijma'*).[37] Aside from the Qur'an and widespread (*mutawatir*) Hadith reports, therefore, consensus is the most important source in Bihbihani's methodology of Islamic law. For him, the most valid consensus is the agreement of the companions of the Prophet Muhammad and the Imams. Bihbihani claims, then, that his own methodology is from the sum of the companions.[38] But he also accepts the consensus of Shi'i scholars as a complementary source of authority.

Bihbihani explains the necessity of consensus in very practical terms. He says that although Hadith reports are transmitted from one generation to the next and contain prophetic decrees, the exact intention or spirit of the injunction is not necessarily clear to someone reading it now. However, the believers who originally received the texts understood the intention behind them and thus formulated the correct practice correlated to the textual command.[39] As an example, Bihbihani suggests that a survey of the companions of the Imams clarifies how ablutions before prayer are to be carried out.[40] He further explains that all Muslims agree on the five daily obligatory prayers and the call to prayer because it was established by the head of the religion and, thus, became unanimously accepted by the companions.[41] Especially since Hadith reports from the

Imams support consensus (*ijma'*), Bihbihani suggests that there is no disagreement among Shi'is on the ability of consensus to act as a proof (*hujja*) of perfect knowledge.[42]

Bihbihani states that absolute certainty in "agreement between the early believers is stronger than what is closer to the present time."[43] Therefore, Bihbihani's interpretation of consensus might be construed as fundamentalist because he argues in favor of rejecting more current interpretations of the texts in favor of interpretations of the "original" community. However, he differs from some fundamentalist thinkers in that he does not believe that the past (i.e. the early community) holds all the answers for novel cases or cases that have not yet reached consensus. He does not suggest that the original community should somehow be recreated in the present. However, he does argue that present and future communities must adopt practices on cases in which the early community had already established consensus. Bihbihani favors the idea that Shi'ism must be purified from innovations of Shi'i law and practice that have been changed after the time of the original community. Cases which the early community had either not confronted or those upon which there was disagreement must be resolved through the process of *ijtihad*. Once *ijtihad* is carried out, a *mujtahid's* decision has the power to become truth if it is universally agreed upon by the scholars – which is another form of consensus. Therefore, in Bihbihani's terms, scholarly consensus (*ijma'*) provides evidence for absolute Reality (*haqiqa*).[44] For Bihbihani, scholarly consensus only includes Usuli scholars. Therefore, Akhbaris, Sunnis, Sufis, etc., need not be included in scholarly consensus.

In practice, Bihbihani is open to reinterpretations of the texts. He relies on the consensus of the past or interpretations of previous scholars when he thinks they represent established norms. However, he argues that it is the prerogative of *mujtahids* to establish new rulings on cases that are not yet settled. Therefore, Bihbihani does not take a fully fundamentalist position on this issue. However, he believes that certain norms that are universally agreed upon, such as fasting and the prohibition of alcohol, should never change.

4. Reason (*'aql*)

Bihbihani argues for the permissibility of jurists to make rulings on the basis of sources other than the texts. This fact is more significant than it may appear because many rationalists argue that reason and other sources can only be employed as exegetical tools. According to Bihbihani, reason is an independent source of knowledge and authority. Therefore, *mujtahids* can produce rulings based on reason alone – but only on cases that are not explicit in the texts and have not achieved the status of consensus (*ijma'*). Bihbihani suggests that there are many sound Hadith reports which indicate the validity of reason (*'aql*) as a proof (*hujja*). Additionally, Bihbihani claims that the continuous use of reason is necessary for liberation (*itlaq*) and explains that reason is equivalent to the Truth and therefore "the source of happiness."[45] Bihbihani argues that reason is a proof because of its necessity, without which it would be impossible for Islamic law to operate. Therefore, in addition to his Hadith-based evidence, he employs a utilitarian argument to suggest that reason is fundamental to Islamic law.

Like the possibility of false interpretations of the textual sources, Bihbihani suggests that the law is vulnerable to faulty reasoning. He argues that it is imperative to remove what has wrongly entered into the Shari'a as a result of such false reason.[46] Therefore, he opens up the possibility of reinterpreting Islamic law through a process of purifying it from what has wrongly become part of the tradition.

As did his Usuli predecessors, Bihbihani generally accepts Imami-Mu'tazili theology and therefore believes that God is the ultimate rational being. Thus, God's revelation and reason are in complete agreement (*mulazama*). Bihbihani's explanation of reason (*'aql*) largely focuses on the question of good and evil, addressed by early Mu'tazali scholars. He argues that reason makes it possible to distinguish between good and evil (*al-tahsin wa al-taqbih*) just as ears can differentiate between noise and singing.[47] In other words, the rational faculty naturally senses something evil because it will lead to a disgusting feeling, while something good will produce a positive feeling.

Bihbihani responds to the argument put forward by scholars of the Sunni legal school of Ash'arism, who argued that one might neglect one's prayers because their benefit is not rationally perceivable. Bihbihani agreed that the rational mind does *not* perceive that prayers or other acts of worship are inherently beneficial, but the rational mind also knows that obedience is good and disobedience is bad.[48] Therefore, observing whatever the Lawgiver has enjoined and being obedient to Him equates to good. In other words, Bihbihani says that neglecting prayer is not evil on its own, but it becomes evil once the Lawgiver designates it as a duty.[49]

For this reason, only a rational person (*mukallaf*) can be expected to abide by God's law, whereas insane people, who are irrational, are not bound by the law.[50]

Bihbihani also provides a caveat for committing actions that are inherently evil if they serve a good purpose and vice versa. He says that any rational person can sense that killing and lying are evil, but these acts can be forgiven if they are committed to prevent a greater evil from happening.[51] For example, if someone lies to protect the Prophet, he has committed a sin. However, because this sinner protected the Prophet, God will forgive his transgression. Bihbihani claims that his argument is not the "combining of opposites" and likens his position to "someone sitting (still) in a boat and moving at the same time."[52] In other words, it is possible for someone to be in a state of apparent contradiction. Just as it is possible to say that a person in a boat is moving and still at the same time, it is permissible to commit a crime and a praiseworthy act at the same time. Such reasoning is also employed by scholars explaining just war or *jihad*, which justifies killing someone even though murder is normally forbidden. Bihbihani categorizes this type of moral knowledge as secondary (*idafiyya*), which, he explains, is not inherently moral from a rational point of view, but becomes so through revelation. Bihbihani explains that primary knowledge is produced from reason (*'aql*) and is apparent without the aid of revelation. In this way, Bihbihani argues that reason has the power to produce knowledge independent of revelation, which is rejected by Akhbaris.[53]

However, Bihbihani argues that there are cases in which reason cannot establish new rulings, such as those that concern acts of worship (*'ibadat*). As noted above, the necessity of laws regarding worship are not apparent to the rational mind. Therefore, acts of worship must first be established in the texts, but reason as well as language (*lugha*) and custom (*'urf*) can assist in determining the specifics of how the acts of worship should be performed. For example, prayer is obligatory because it is found in revelatory sources and reason helps to determine that prayer requires prostration.[54] Bihbihani further explains that miracles are not part of God's rational framework.[55]

Finally, Bihbihani argues that the texts contain rational indicators (sing. *dalil 'aqli*), which provide an explanation for legal rulings. In fact, he suggests that there is an indicator from the Lawgiver (*dalil shar'i*) for every rational indicator (*dalil 'aqli*). However, the reverse is not true because some textual references are not necessarily rational.[56] Bihbihani argues that a ruling (*hukm*) that has both a rational and textual indicator has a higher level of epistemological provenance than a ruling that only has a textual indicator.[57]

5. Transference (ta'diyya) vs. Analogy (qiyas)

Any dynamic legal system must include a method of ruling on cases that have no precedent. For this, Sunnis adopted analogy (*qiyas*) as the primary method of using the texts to formulate new rulings. Shi'is, however, rejected the Sunni conception of analogy, partly in order to maintain a distinct legal system.[58] Initially, Shi'is also rejected *ijtihad* in order to differentiate Shi'i law from Sunni law. Bihbihani continues the tradition of rejecting the Sunni conception of analogy because it does not require the determination of a veracious effect cause (*'illa*), which explains the reasoning behind God's laws.[59] For example, the effect cause for the prohibition of wine is presumed to be that it is intoxicating. By analogy, therefore, scholars rule that all intoxicating substances (such as beer or opium) are forbidden. Sunni law generally accepts that the *'illa* is conjectural (*zanni*), whereas Bihbihani, and other Shi'i scholars (including Akhbaris), argue that the *'illa* must be certain (*qat'i*). Although Bihbihani accepts conjecture (*zann*) in other circumstances, he rejects it here and argues that the Sunni form of *qiyas* is not permitted.[60]

In Bihbihani's legal theory, transference (*ta'diyya*) is the closest element in Shi'i jurisprudence to the Sunni conception of analogy. *Ta'diyya* is the broad term used to explain a number of different situations in which a novel case can be determined on the basis of revelatory texts. Bihbihani outlines ten methods for transference that can be divided into three general categories: those that are derived from reason, language, and consensus.[61] Each of these methods is a way for the jurist to produce general legal principles from specific cases and vice versa. The first five are derived from reason:

1. Reason (*'aql*): discussed above.
2. Analogy in which the *'illa* is certain and is identified by reference to two revelatory texts that allow the jurist to determine the *'illa* (*tanqih al-manat*).[62]

3. From general to specific, bigger to smaller, from the whole to the part, etc. (*al-qiyas bi-tariq al-ula*). Similar to *e maiore ad minus*.
4. From specific to general – opposite of 3.
5. Transference of general rules to replacement rules.

The following three are derived from linguistic analysis (*lugha*):

6. A single text that provides the ruling and the reason for the ruling (*al-qiyas al-mansus al-'illa*). In other words, the text itself provides the *'illa*.
7. A general ruling found in the text that can be transferred from a general norm to a specific case.
8. Two cases in the texts can be joined to form a general ruling (*ittihad tariq al-mas'alatayn*).

The final two conditions of transference can be derived from consensus (*ijma'*):

9. Consensus (*ijma'*) that coincides with a similar textual indication of the general rule.
10. A general rule agreed on by all legal scholars, but not found in the texts.[63]

LANGUAGE (*LUGHA*) AND CUSTOM ('*URF*)

Much of Bihbihani's discussion on transferring a textual ruling to another case deals with language (*lugha*) and custom ('*urf*). In fact, Bihbihani argues that it is impossible to comprehend the Qur'an, Hadith, and consensus (*ijma'*) without a clear understanding of the language (*lugha*) and custom ('*urf*) of these sources. He concludes that the context provided by language and custom are necessary keys to understanding what the Lawgiver has laid down in the texts.[64] In service of his argument he cites two Hadith reports: "We did not receive anything from the Prophet of God except through his speech,"[65] and "God, the Almighty, the Most Exalted, addresses [the people] through speech and does not want from them other than [what is known] by their language and what they understand."[66] Therefore, it is imperative that jurists analyze the texts in their proper context, instead of reading them literally, which he suspects is the Akhbari method. Thus Bihbihani concludes that it is imperative for *mujtahids* to be proficient in linguistic sciences and suggests that linguistic training is a basic qualification for a scholar to become a *mujtahid*.

Bihbihani also provides a rational argument in favor of language and custom by suggesting that prophets and Imams are useless unless their message is understandable to the people. He points out that the role of prophets is to establish religious rules and thereby make life better for people in this world and the hereafter. Because God has chosen the medium of speech to disseminate laws and establish norms, the Prophet and Imams must conform to the rules of common language. Therefore, Muhammad and the Imams used terminology, idioms, and grammatical constructions that would maximize understanding of God's intention.[67] Bihbihani seems to agree here with scholars such as Abu Zayd Karami, who argues that God takes the level of comprehension of the people into account.[68] Karami further explains that texts are readily understood by the rational mind. Significantly, he says that scholars must consider the socio-cultural context in which something was written. In other words, the Lawgiver not only provides people with laws suited to their time and place, He packages them in the language (*lugha*) and custom (*'urf*) that are familiar to them.

Since the meaning of words change over time, Bihbihani emphasizes the importance of interpreting words and phrases based on their original context.[69] Therefore, he suggests that it is imperative to interpret the terminology found in the texts the same way as did "the people of the language" (*ahl al-lugha*) (i.e., seventh-century Arabs) and the Imams.[70] Such a change in language over time can prevent a clear understanding of the text and lead to opposing interpretations.

In Bihbihani's approach, language and custom are related to the consensus (*ijma'*) of early Muslims. As noted above, Bihbihani argues that consensus is key to understanding God's laws because it represents how the majority of Muslims understood the laws when they were handed down from God. Consensus, therefore, is the collective interpretation of the Qur'an and Hadith according to Muhammad's community. And since God's speech was directed toward their customs and language, they must have understood the divine commands correctly and properly applied them to their lives. Bihbihani warns that "departing from linguistic and customary meaning is never permissible and its violation is absolute."[71] He, therefore, argues for the preservation of the tradition based on the original linguistic meaning of the texts.

Although Bihbihani argues for the necessity of interpreting texts within the context of the time and place of their issuance, he claims that God's commands are general because God's laws are universal.[72] The laws brought by Muhammad were not simply meant for the community he established in Arabia – although the laws were initially directed toward them. Bihbihani offers the example of prayer: "Since there is no dispute on the necessity of prayer, all are subject to its necessity ... until the day of judgment."[73] Therefore, anything that has achieved consensus can never be changed. Even when the Mahdi returns, he will not have the authority to alter what has been established by Muhammad's companions. In this way, Bihbihani views the tradition as rigid, unchanging, and applicable until the end of days. Change, then, is relegated to issues that are not universally accepted by Muslims or that have not yet been encountered. It should be pointed out, though, that there are few universally accepted laws or obligations, such as prayer and fasting.

Bihbihani specifically explains how the universality of divine decrees can be applied in transference (*ta'diyya*) cases. He argues that specific rulings given to individuals must be applied to everyone. To support this idea, Bihbihani cites the prophetic Hadith which says: "my ruling for one is my ruling for all."[74] He even suggests that rulings address-ing men can also be applied to women and vice versa, unless the text specifically restricts such transference.[75] Therefore, since God's laws (as presented in the Qur'an and Hadith) are meant for all people for all eternity, they are to be applied universally – even when they appear to be addressing specific circumstances. As noted above, a ruling must become accepted by consensus (*ijma'*) prior to achieving the status of a universal command.[76]

Bihbihani acknowledges that even if God's commands are lucid, scholars often disagree on the meaning of the texts. He points out that some scholars argue that any disagreement on the interpretation of a Qur'anic verse or Hadith report is an indicator that the text is ambiguous. Rejecting this analysis, Bihbihani claims that disagreement on a verse simply indicates that some scholars have failed to interpret it correctly because of their misunderstanding of custom and language.[77] In fact, he says that the application, the meaning, and the whole argument of a ruling are tied to language. Therefore, it is necessary for jurists to rely on linguists and the commentary (*tafsir*) of other scholars.[78]

Bihbihani further explains why linguistic misunderstandings occur. Two people at a meeting who hear the same speech may well process the information differently according to their level of intelligence.[79] Thus, according to Bihbihani, there are disagreements regarding the interpretation of the texts, especially Hadith reports which are subject to the understanding of the Hadith reporter and to reinterpretation by later scholars.[80] Therefore, he suggests that in order to understand the Hadiths properly, it is necessary to interpret them as did the narrators.

Bihbihani admits that the texts are not always readily understood to the (untrained) rational mind. Although the Qur'an and Hadith generally follow the rules of speech, they also contain specialized terms that are explained in the text.[81] According to Bihbihani, specialized terms are particularly found in commands related to worship (*'ibadat*). He points out that understanding terminology, such as "prayer" (*salat*), "call to prayer" (*nada'*), and "remembrance of God" (*dhikrullah*), is not possible through recourse to customary, linguistic, or rational methods. These terms are defined in the texts. Because the Lawgiver did not want to simply decree that any type of prayer is lawful, he defined these terms in a specific way.

Therefore, textual sources are composed of both general and specific terminology. The only way for a jurist to know whether a term is general or specific is to determine whether it has been given a special definition in the texts. Bihbihani points out that *mujtahids* should always interpret a specialized term in accordance with its textual definition, unless it is clearly understood through its customary definition (discussed below). Terms defined in the text must be given precedence to what is known according to consensus or custom.[82] Although Bihbihani spills a considerable amount of ink on his conception of general and specific terminology, there seems to be little disagreement between Usuli scholars on the topic.[83]

Bihbihani explains that one of the "irritants" of interpreting Hadith reports is that they contain contradictions between custom and language which divide Shi'i jurists. Nonetheless, a jurist must make a decision. But should custom or language be favored if the two differ? Major figures in the Usuli school disagree on this issue. Bihbihani explicitly states that custom should be preferred over language. In Bihbihani's words, "the fixed term of the Lawgiver is desirable *unless* the text is clearly understood by custom (*'urf*)."[84] He explains that some scholars prefer language because it is documentary proof, while others (like himself) prefer custom because it allows inductive reasoning. The author of

Jawahir al-kalam, Muhammad Hasan al-Najafi, takes a similar position as Bihbihani, whereas 'Allama al-Hilli prefers language.[85]

Bihbihani identifies another problem with textual exegesis – namely that the texts contain both figurative and literal meanings.[86] Although Bihbihani does not provide a framework for jurists to know which terms should be interpreted figuratively, he suggests that many of the pronouncements of the Lawgiver are not to be taken literally, especially when considering ordinances of worship (*'ibadat*) whose commands often *do not* accord with literal meanings.[87]

According to Bihbihani, scholars must deduce rulings from cases of both ritual duties (*'ibadat*) as well as social duties (*mu'amalat*). If they are divided, he argues, Islamic law (*fiqh*) is ruined.[88] Some Muslim scholars argue that since *mu'amalat* are of concern to the public and can be understood by the rational mind, they must receive the attention of scholars. However, *'ibadat* only concern the individual and require an explanation from the texts, which makes ignorance of these duties more acceptable. Bihbihani favors a system in which *mujtahids* are consulted for cases that concern *'ibadat* as well as *mu'amalat*.[89]

To illustrate this point, Bihbihani gives the example of ablutions (*wudhu'*) that are to be carried out before prayer, which is a case of worship (*'ibadat*). He argues that what can be clearly understood from the command "*al-ghasal lil-janaba*" is the expression "to wash" (*al-ghasal*), but "purifying oneself" (*lil-janaba*) is not clear. Therefore, the command is linguistically and rationally incomprehensible. However, the correct understanding of ablutions was issued by an early judge, who clarified the linguistic meaning of the command. In this way, Bihbihani explains that an unclear command in worship (*'ibadat*) becomes similar to a non-worship (*mu'amalat*) command.[90] This is a particularly significant ruling because all sources of law contribute to the final ruling. The original law is given in the text, but is unclear linguistically and rationally. Therefore, consensus (*ijma'*) of the original community is considered, which provides customary clarification that can be used at present to determine the proper practice of ablutions.

CONJECTURE OF *MUJTAHIDS*

Bihbihani's discussion on the authority of *mujtahids* in *Fawa'id al-ha'iriyya* centers on the permissibility of jurists to issue legal opinions on the basis of their scholarly conjecture (*zann*) – which is among the most important issues dividing Akhbaris and Usulis. Bihbihani addresses the Akhbari argument that *mujtahids* claim that conjecture (*zann*) is sure knowledge (*'ilm*) by arguing that what Akhbaris call knowledge is in fact conjecture although it has no basis in reason.[91] In other words, Bihbihani argues that although Akhbaris claim to base their rulings wholly on textual evidence, they actually make inferences, albeit with flawed methodology. And since Akhbaris do not use exegetical methods to interpret the texts properly, their conjecture is less likely to coincide with the Lawgiver's truth than the conjecture of Usulis.

After the textual sources and consensus (*ijma'*), Bihbihani bases the authority of Shi'ism on the conjecture (*zann*) of mujtahids. He argues that the conjecture of a *mujtahid* is always a proof (*hujja*), which is essential for determining divine truth.[92] Although he understands that the conjecture of a *mujtahid* might not result in absolute divine truth, he claims that it is necessary for Islamic law to function.[93] As with his argument in favor of reason (*'aql*), therefore, he employs the argument of necessity to support his acceptance of conjecture.

Bihbihani likens the conjecture of a *mujtahid* to the proof of two witnesses, which the Qur'an allows as evidence in court cases. Like the witness of two people, he argues, it is possible that the conjecture of a *mujtahid* will not lead to absolute truth. Therefore, as it is possible for two witnesses to contribute to the execution of an innocent person, *mujtahids* can produce laws that are contrary to God's law. For practical purposes and as far as lay Shi'is are concerned, therefore, the law is determined by the conjecture of *mujtahids*. Since there is no way to be absolutely sure of what is in the mind of the Lawgiver (other than the texts), the *mujtahid* is the final arbiter on most matters of the law. Bihbihani even argues that once the *mujtahid* takes every piece of evidence into account and makes every effort, God's ruling appears in his decision.[94] However, it does not reach the stage of certainty until it reaches consensus (*ijma'*). As with a Hadith report, the more widely accepted the conjecture of a *mujtahid* is, the more certain it becomes.

CONCLUSION

Bihbihani clings to tradition as embodied in the foundational Shi'i texts and the consensus of Shi'i scholars, and he argues in favor of interpreting the texts on the basis of the language and custom of the early Islamic community. However, he understands the necessity of establishing new cases if Islamic law is to be relevant. In his mind, any ruling that achieves consensus is part of the Shi'i tradition and cannot be changed. Establishing new judgments is in the hands of *mujtahids*, who must master linguistic and rational sciences in order to interpret the texts and establish new rulings. In this way, Bihbihani attempts to strike a balance between tradition and change, text and reason.

In a broad sense, Bihbihani's theoretical approach to the Shi'i tradition is analogous to the dynamic manner in which rationalists working within the framework of any given tradition might operate. Similarly, many Americans approach the Constitution as the "sacred" text upon which their tradition is founded and which may not be changed, while others see the Constitution as a living document which evolves over time. Bihbihani assumed that any aspect of law that is not clearly outlined in the text is open to interpretation and reinterpretation over time until it gains universal credence.

While it may seem convenient to label Akhbaris as fundamentalist conservatives and Usulis as liberal rationalists, Bihbihani's understanding of Shi'i law shows that the application of overarching divisions to the Usuli-Akhbari divide may lead to oversimplification. Bihbihani criticized Akhbaris for viewing Islamic law in black and white terms and accepting a literal reading of the texts. His Usuli system accepted that uncertainties must be overcome through reason and textual criticism and that there are shades of the truth, which may suggest that Usulis accepted a pluralistic view of knowledge. However, this division falls short when considering that it was Usulis, not Akhbaris, who issued death warrants on their enemies because of their "false" interpretations of the texts.

We have now considered the emergence of modern Shi'ism as it developed in the contexts of Iran and southern Iraq as well as the establishment of neo-Usulism, both in practice and theory, by Bihbihani and his successors. As a conclusion to the book, the following chapter considers the extent to which the Usuli movement is comparable to contemporaneous trends in Sufism and Sunnism.

Chapter 7

Founding Fathers of Modern Islam

INTRODUCTION

U suli Shi'ism became part of the fabric of a broader Islamic reformation that occurred in the eighteenth and nineteenth centuries. Sunni, Sufi, and Shi'i Muslim scholars revived and reformed their traditions as politics decentralized in the eighteenth century. As indicated already, I suggest that three movements set the tone for many of the modern Islamic trends that came after them. These movements are: (1) Wahhabism, founded by Muhammad Ibn 'Abd al-Wahhab (1703–92), (2) neo-Sufism (or *tariqa Muhammadiyya*), associated with Ahmad Ibn Idris al-Fasi (1750 or 1760–1837), and (3) neo-Usulism, established by Wahid Bihbihani (1706–92).

Wahhabism has received considerable attention from Western scholars, especially in the wake of 9/11. Since scholars often suggest that Wahhabism helps explain Islamic extremist trends of the past few decades, it has been the subject of several monographs and articles and has received countless citations in studies related to contemporary Islam.[1] In contrast, relatively little has been published on Ahmad Ibn Idris, although he has received more scholarly attention than Bihbihani.[2]

First, let us consider the extent to which reform movements can be considered under a common rubric, a question that has sparked considerable debate in Islamic studies over the past several decades. John Voll attempted to show that reformers were connected in what he calls an "intellectual family tree."[3] Ahmad Dallal, however, rejected any continuity between the Islamic "fundamentalist" movements,[4] an idea that had been supported by Fazlur Rahman,[5] John Esposito,[6] and John Voll.[7] Dallal argued that "the intellectual models produced by these scholars [i.e. eighteenth-century reformers] are quite distinct and cannot be grouped under one rubric."[8] Although Dallal's position is overly deconstructionist, it is a welcome counterweight to over-generalizations. Indeed, the eighteenth-century Islamic revival was not a unified movement. After all, the reformers were reviving distinct traditions within Islam and diversity of thought was prevalent within each tradition. Therefore, Voll suggests that "the difference among fundamentalist movements is primarily a difference in leadership styles or in local contexts."[9]

Even more than local contexts, it is the distinct tradition of the reformers that accounts for the primary difference between each movement. In other words, the critical differences between the movements of Bihbihani, Ibn 'Abd al-Wahhab, and Ibn Idris are the result of Bihbihani's Usuli Shi'i context, Ibn 'Abd al-Wahhab's Hanbali Sunni context, and Ibn Idris's Shadhiliyya Sufi context. As Bihbihani's movement has been referred to as neo-Usulism and Ibn Idris's as neo-Sufism, Ibn 'Abd al-Wahhab's movement might be thought of as neo-Hanbalism. Therefore, I argue that each reformer's school of thought informed their outlook more than their contemporaries. In other words, influence on the reformers was more vertical (historically within a school of thought) than it was horizontal (contemporaries outside a school of thought). This does not mean, however, that contemporary reformers working in distinct traditions had no influence on each other. Certainly, there are broad commonalities that link each of the movements together.

What follows, therefore, is a comparison of the three movements in light of their distinct contexts. First, in the realm of politics, the comparison of Usulism and Wahhabism is apt since the legacies of contemporary Iran and Saudi Arabia are intimately connected with the Usuli and Wahhabi movements, respectively. Although Idrisi Sufism is not currently the state ideology of any country, its legacy was instrumental in the emergence of independent countries in Libya and Sudan. Second, each of the movements can be considered under the rubric of renewal (*tajdid*), since the followers of each reformer considered them as the *mujaddid* of the eighteenth/nineteenth century, even if Ahmad Ibn Idris himself rejected the notion of *tajdid*. Third, each of the reform movements significantly narrowed the field of orthodoxy and they were especially critical of popular Sufism. Bihbihani and Ibn 'Abd al-Wahhab declared infidelity (*takfir*) on their enemies, whereas Ibn Idris did not. In order to delve into these comparisons further, let us become better acquainted with Ibn 'Abd al-Wahhab and Ibn Idris.

IBN ʿABD AL-WAHHAB AND THE WAHHABI MOVEMENT

Muhammad Ibn ʿAbd al-Wahhab was raised in the Arabian Peninsula where he was trained in the Hanbali school (*madhhab*) of Sunni Islam. As already noted, his thought was rooted in the Hanbali tradition and is especially related to the controversial figure of Ibn Taymiyya (1263–1358). Although Hanbalism is widely recognized as one of the four orthodox Sunni legal schools (*maddhabs*), George Makdisi argues that the Hanbali school and Ibn Taymiyya stand "outside the mainstream of Muslim thought."[10] The famous Muslim traveler, Ibn Battuta, who was a contemporary of Ibn Taymiyya, was convinced that Ibn Taymiyya "had a screw loose" even though he "enjoyed great prestige and could discourse on the scholarly disciplines."[11]

Like Bihbihani and Ibn Idris, Ibn ʿAbd al-Wahhab grew up in a family of Muslim scholars. His grandfather (Sulayman ibn ʿAli) was the most prominent scholar in the Najd region of Arabia and his father (ʿAbd al-Wahhab Ibn Sulayman) was the judge (*qadi*) and leading Hanbali scholar in Uyayna (thirty kilometers northwest of the Saudi capital of Riyadh), where Ibn ʿAbd al-Wahhab was born.[12] As a young man, Ibn ʿAbd al-Wahhab traveled to Basra to pursue his studies, where he came into contact with Shiʿis. He later wrote about his debates with "the idolatrous people of Basra," whom he attempted to convince that: "The whole of worship belongs to no one but God," which, he suggests, overwhelmed and silenced them.[13] Ibn ʿAbd al-Wahhab's biographer explains that he was eventually chased out of Basra by leading members of the community and almost died after escaping the city alone and on foot.[14] According to Ibn ʿAbd al-Wahhab's grandson, God revealed the secrets of divine unity to Ibn ʿAbd al-Wahhab while he was in Basra, which were eventually written down in his famous Wahhabi manifesto, *The Book of Divine Unity (Kitab al-tawhid).*[15]

Like Bihbihani and Ibn Idris, Ibn ʿAbd al-Wahhab was remembered by his successors as a charismatic figure, even a savior, inspired by God to revive Islam. The chronicler of the Wahhabi movement, Ibn Bishr, says: "God Almighty expanded his breast for him, enabling him to understand those incongruous matters that led men astray from His path."[16] Ibn ʿAbd al-Wahhab's successors also describe him as the renewer (*mujaddid*) of Islam for the eighteenth century, a title attributed to Ibn Idris and Bihbihani. Ibn Idris, however, argued that Ibn ʿAbd al-Wahhab was not a renewer and in fact rejected the whole tradition of a recurring *mujaddid*. Ibn Idris suggests that the concept of a renewer detracts from the uniqueness of the Prophet Muhammad and contributes to disunity among Muslims.[17]

Ibn 'Abd al-Wahhab is often cited as the eighteenth-century reformer par excellence. He has become emblematic of the eighteenth-century Islamic reformation as a whole and is often cited in Western scholarship as the father of current-day fundamentalist and terrorist movements. As Khalid Abu El Fadl puts it, "every single Islamic group that has achieved a degree of international infamy, such as the Taliban and al-Qaeda, has been heavily influenced by Wahhabi thought."[18] On the opposite end of the spectrum, Natana Delong-Bas presents an apologetic view of Ibn 'Abd al-Wahhab's ideology and movement.[19] She suggests that Wahhabism has wrongly been associated with "xenophobia, militantism, misogyny, extremism, and literalism."[20] Instead, she constructs Ibn 'Abd al-Wahhab as a scholar interested in "the maximum preservation of human life even in the midst of jihad as holy war, tolerance for other religions, and support for a balance of rights between men and women."[21] Delong-Bas further argues that contemporary militant extremists, such as Osama bin Laden, hardly represent Ibn 'Abd al-Wahhab's "moderate, sophisticated, and nuanced interpretation of Islam that emphasizes limitations on violence, killing, and destruction and calls for dialogue and debate as the appropriate means of proselytization and statecraft."[22] Ibn 'Abd al-Wahhab is clearly a controversial figure.

IBN IDRIS AND NEO-SUFISM

Ahmad Ibn Idris was from Morocco and his thought was largely influenced by the Shadhiliyya Sufi tradition as were his disciples. Rex O'Fahey rightly argues that the overall significance of Ibn Idris is not the originality of his teachings, but in the large number of students that he trained, which resulted in "traces of Ibn Idris over a large geographical range."[23] In this regard he was similar to Bihbihani. Ibn Idris's brand of Sufism spread throughout North and East Africa and to Singapore and other parts of Asia. That Ibn Idris's students overshadowed him is indicated by the fact that scholarly references to Ibn Idris are often only found in prefaces to studies of his disciples.[24] Perhaps, Ibn Idris would have become better known had his movement not splintered. After his death, Ibn Idris's most famous pupils established new brotherhoods, including the Sanusiyya, Rashidiyya, and Khatmiyya, which were among the most significant nineteenth-century Sufi networks.[25] The fact that a Sufi order was not directly associated with Ibn Idris was largely the result of his teaching that Muslims should not follow Sufi orders dedicated to individual shaykhs. He also did not establish an organized movement. Instead, he insisted that there was only one true *tariqa*, which is the order of Muhammad guided by the Qu'ran and Hadith. Therefore, Ibn Idris avoided standard Sufi terminology. Instead of referring to his Sufi brotherhood as an order (*tariqa*), he preferred way (*tariq*); instead of shaykh (Sufi master), he preferred professor (*ustad*); and instead of referring to his followers as *murids* (shaykh's followers), he called them students (*talibs*). Additionally, Ibn Idris gave licenses (*ijazas*) to teach his *tariq* to whole groups of people, including children, instead of limiting *ijazas* to his top disciples.[26]

Ibn Idris, like his most prominent student, Muhammad b. 'Ali al-Sanusi (1787–1859), who founded the Sanusiyya brotherhood, followed the Shadhiliyya tradition.[27] Ibn Idris gives a detailed description of his own Shadhiliyya pedigree, which includes each of his Sufi masters.[28] Save for his collections of prayers and litanies, Ibn Idris left few writings, which is a common trait of Shadhiliyya masters.[29] Ibn Idris's modern biographer, Hasan Makki, describes his thought as a continuation of the ideas of Hasan al-Shadhili, the thirteenth-century founder of the Shadhiliyya brotherhood.[30] Makki specifically explains that Ibn Idris promoted the unification of rationalism with Illuminationist philosophy in line with Abu Hamid al-Ghazali (1058–1111).[31]

Although Ibn Idris clearly operated within the Shadhiliyya tradition, he was not completely bound to it. Between the mid-eleventh and the mid-eighteenth centuries most Sufis (including Shadhiliyya scholars) believed their mystical union with the divine freed them from Islamic law, a notion known as antinomianism. Ibn Idris, however, called for complete submission to the letter and spirit of Islamic law and generally gave little attention to miraculous phenomena (*karamat*). In fact, acceptance of Islamic law became a definitive element of Ibn Idris's *tariqa Muhammadiyya*.

The salient features of Ibn Idris's hagiographic biographies, written by his successors who describe him as the "axis of the age" (*qutb al-zaman*), are similar to those of Bihbihani and Ibn 'Abd al-Wahhab. Although Ibn Idris rejected the notion that a Muslim renewer (*mujaddid*) appears once every century, his successors in Sudan describe him as such.[32] Like Bihbihani, Ibn Idris moved from his hometown to a religious center of learning. Ibn Idris was initially educated as a jurist in Fez, after which he traveled to Egypt, where he is reported to have taught at al-Azhar in Cairo before making his way to Mecca and Medina.

Like Bihbihani and Ibn 'Abd al-Wahhab, Ibn Idris was often at odds with the clerical establishment, indicating that as reformers they often came to blows with their colleagues. Unlike Bihbihani who success-fully overthrew the Akhbari establishment, Ibn Idris was expelled from Mecca by the city's religious scholars.[33] His uneasy relationship with the Meccan clerical and political establishment led to his exile in 1827. He spent the last years of his life in the Wahhabi outpost of Sabya (in southern Arabia).[34]

Although Ibn Idris sought protection from Wahhabis, he managed to provoke opposition from them, no doubt as a result of doctrinal dif-ferences. Therefore, it would be a mistake to suggest that Ibn Idris was closely linked to the Wahhabi movement, even if his brand of Sufism was partially inspired by Wahhabism. Although Ibn Idris and Ibn 'Abd al-Wahhab knew each other, their approach to Islam was vastly different. Ibn Idris argues that the intentions of Ibn 'Abd al-Wahhab were genuine, but his approach was wrong. After a falling-out with Wahhabis, Ibn Idris denounced them as "miserable wretches who are bound inflexibly to the externality of the Law. They know the details of knowledge and use them to accuse of heresy those who oppose them."[35] Therefore, Ibn 'Abd al-Wahhab's accusations of heresy (*takfir*) drove a wedge between his movement and that of Ibn Idris, even if both movements had some beliefs in common, such as the rejection of Islamic legal schools (sing. *maddhab*).[36]

The nineteenth-century scholar, Le Chatelier, suggests that Ibn Idris and his successors make up the most powerful school in modern Islam.[37] However, it is more accurate to say that Ibn Idris was the key figure at the head of modern Sufi revival and reform, which has been defined in terms of its orthodoxy, activism, orientation toward Muhammad, commitment to the Qur'an and Sunna, and organization into broth-erhoods. Fazlur Rahman, who coined the term neo-Sufism, defines it as "Sufism reformed on orthodox lines and interpreted in an activist sense."[38] Rahman associates the rise of neo-Sufism with Ibn Idris, point-ing out that the Idrisi movement referred to itself as the "Brotherhood of Muhammad" (*tariqa Muhammadiyya*). Valerie Hoffman explains that the concept of *tariqa Muhammadiyya*, associated with mystic annihilation (*fana'*) in the Prophet, had been in development prior to the eighteenth century.[39]

Additional scholars describe neo-Sufism and *tariqa Muhammadiyya* in the following terms. John Voll elaborates on Rahman's explanation of neo-Sufism as the rejection of Ibn al-'Arabi's (1164–1240) pantheistic conception of God in favor of emphasizing God's transcendence. The goal of the neo-Sufi, therefore, was no longer to be absorbed into God, but rather to be in harmony with the Prophet Muhammad. Voll further suggests that Sufi brotherhoods provided a framework for movements that emphasized purification and adherence to rigorous, literal interpretations of the Qur'an and Sunna.[40] O'Fahey also defines neo-Sufism in terms of the brotherhood, arguing that it is "a new organizational phenomenon that appeared in certain areas of the Muslim world in the eighteenth and nineteenth century."[41] Having dispensed with the term neo-Sufism altogether, Sedgwick argues that

> the *tariqa Muhammadiyya* movement ... was characterized by a new emphasis on a spiritual method for reaching God through a waking vision of the Prophet Muhammad, by a campaign against established Islamic authority as represented by the *madhhabs* (schools of law), and by a rejection of certain aspects of Sufism as then practiced.[42]

POLITICAL INFLUENCE OF THE REFORMERS

Like Usulism, Wahhabism and Idrisi Sufism have been politically influential in the Islamic world. Wahhabis were an integral part of the establishment of the kingdom of Saudi Arabia. Although Idrisi Sufism does not currently have the same political impact as Usulis and Wahhabis, Ibn Idris's successors did become politically active, especially in Libya and Sudan. As already discussed, Usulis played a critical role in establishing Iran's Qajar dynasty in the early nineteenth century. After the Usuli-Qajar honeymoon ended, some Usulis maintained a policy of pious aloofness from politics, while others challenged the political establishment, which eventually culminated in the 1979 Iranian revolution in which Usulis took control of the state.

Prior to allying himself with the Saudi clan, Ibn 'Abd al-Wahhab entered an alliance with Uthman ibn Hamid ibn Mu'ammar, who controlled Ibn 'Abd al-Wahhab's hometown of Uyayna. Ibn 'Abd al-Wahhab returned to Uyayna after escaping an assassination attempt in nearby Huraymila, where he apparently angered some townspeople for insisting that they must abstain from sexual immorality.[43] As part of the alliance, Ibn Mu'ammar became an adherent of Ibn 'Abd al-Wahhab's teachings and offered his aunt to Ibn 'Abd al-Wahhab, who indeed married her. This alliance is strikingly similar to Bihbihani's experience in his hometown of Bihbihan, where he allied himself with the city's most powerful political leader. Like Ibn 'Abd al-Wahhab, Bihbihani married the politician's daughter. These two cases highlight the prevalence of marriage alliances between political and religious officials in the Islamic world.[44] Ibn Mu'ammar eventually withdrew his protection from Ibn 'Abd al-Wahhab because the ruler of nearby Ahsa (Sulayman Ibn Muhammad) threatened to cut economic ties with Uyayna if Ibn 'Abd al-Wahhab was not expelled from the city or executed.[45]

Whereas Bihbihani's political alliances were confined to local officials, Ibn 'Abd al-Wahhab entered an alliance with Muhammad Ibn Saud (d. 1765) whose political ambitions eventually led to the establishment of the first Saudi state. Although Delong-Bas and others argue that an agreement was made in which Ibn Saud would assume political and military responsibilities, while Ibn 'Abd al-Wahhab would be responsible for religious teachings, Abd Allah Salih al-Uthaymin suggests that this arrangement emerged later.[46] Ibn 'Abd al-Wahhab's biographers suggest that it was Ibn 'Abd al-Wahhab, not Muhammad Ibn Saud, who acted as head of state. In addition to receiving the revenue from war booty and alms, Ibn 'Abd al-Wahhab made the final decisions regarding the emerging state, appointed judges (*qadis*), and met with tribal delegations.[47] Furthermore, Ibn 'Abd al-Wahhab seems to have initiated the Wahhabi onslaught in 1746, which lasted nearly three decades. By the mid-eighteenth century, Ibn 'Abd al-Wahhab had amassed a large following whom he had convinced that "opponents of the Wahhabi cause were the enemies of Islam, who could be fought against and whose properties were lawful spoil."[48] According to David Commins, Wahhabis justified the conquest as *jihad*, which could be waged after idolaters were called to change their ways, but instead rejected the Wahhabi interpretation of divine unity (*tawhid*).[49] Therefore, Wahhabis particularly attacked tribal chiefs who had not joined the movement and who had persecuted Wahhabis. Saudi-Wahhabi forces captured the city of Riyadh in 1773, which seems to have prompted Ibn 'Abd al-Wahhab to transfer the political and economic affairs to the Saudi family so he could focus his attention on teaching. Saudi-Wahhabi forces continued to gain territory, including Mecca and Medina, until the Ottomans brought down the first Saudi state in 1818. However, Saudi–Wahhabi forces subsequently re-emerged shortly thereafter to establish a second state.

Ibn Idris seems to have been less interested in influencing politics than Ibn 'Abd al-Wahhab and Bihbihani. There is no evidence that Ibn Idris sustained any long-term or systematic political alliances. This seems to have been a result of his primary interest in spreading Islam through missionary activity (*da'wa*). The Sufi networks established by Ibn Idris and his successors, however, were eventually exploited by politicians. European colonizers, Ottomans, and Wahhabis often courted Ibn Idris's successors in attempts to utilize their network of followers for political gain. Although O'Fahey argues that Ibn Idris's descendants rarely used their high social status for political ends, some of them did.[50] One of Ibn Idris's successors, Muhammad al-Idrisi (1876–1923), established a local dynasty in southern Arabia. He led a revolt in 'Asir, which led to the establishment of a short-lived state that survived from 1906 to 1934, when it was incorporated into Saudi Arabia.[51]

The most successful political enterprise to result from the foundations laid by Ibn Idris developed in Libya from the missionary work of his primary successor, Muhammad b. 'Ali al-Sanusi. His Sanusiyya Sufi order became prominent in the Jabal Akhdar region of eastern Libya which paved the way for a line of successors to gain political power in North Africa, starting with Muhammad al-Mahdi al-Sanusi (d. 1902). In fact, the Sanusiyya has been referred to as a proto-nationalist movement, and Knut Vikor argues that even though the founder of the Sanusiyya was not a political thinker or leader, "the entity called 'Libya' may in many ways be said to have grown out of the activities of the Sanusi order."[52] Supported by the Ottomans, the Sanusiyya order mounted a resistance to the 1911 Italian invasion of Libya under the command of Muhammad al-Mahdi's nephew, Ahmad al-Sharif (d. 1933). During World War One the Sanusiyya continued to support Ottoman forces in Egypt, where they were defeated by the British, which also contributed to the downfall of the Sanusiyya brotherhood.[53] However, Muhammad Idris al-Sanusi (1890–1983), a scion of the Sanusiyya order, was crowned king in 1951 when Libya gained independence from Italy during post-World War Two decolonization. King Idris I, as he came to be known, ruled until the 1969 coup that brought Muammar Gaddafi to power.

A second brotherhood that grew out of Ibn Idris's movement, the Khatmiyya, became a political force in Sudan, where it had become the largest Sufi order in the early nineteenth century. The Khatmiyya remained loyal to Turkish-Egyptian forces and became the fiercest opponents of the Mahdist movement in the late nineteenth century. The Khatmiyya became closely associated with British colonizers who controlled Sudan in the first half of the twentieth century. After Sudan's independence, the Khatmiyya provided the basis for one of two political parties in Sudan – the Democratic Union Party.[54]

KNOWLEDGE AND AUTHORITY

Although Bihbihani, Ibn Idris, and Ibn 'Abd al-Wahhab established their movements under similar circumstances and influenced the political landscape of the Middle East and North Africa, each scholar differed widely in their interpretation of Islam. The only major common denominator in their theoretical approach to knowledge and authority was that they challenged the religious establishments of their day. By rejecting the prevailing schools of thought, they carved out a larger role for their clerical networks. Indeed, the different theoretical approaches of Ibn Idris, Ibn 'Abd al-Wahhab, and Bihbihani to knowledge and authority illustrate the diversity of eighteenth- and nineteenth-century Islamic reform movements and indeed multiple modernities.

Ibn 'Abd al-Wahhab generally followed Hanbali methodology in his approach to Islamic law. Therefore, the only infallible sources of knowledge are the Qur'an and Sunna of the Prophet. Ibn 'Abd al-Wahhab supports taking public interest (*maslaha*) into account when issuing judgments because he views the Qur'an as a source of guidance for the benefit of mankind. He generally does not accept the idea that one Qur'anic verse can be superseded by another verse (*naskh*) because he rejects the idea that the Qur'an contains contradictory verses.[55] Additionally, most Hanbali jurists, including Ibn 'Abd al-Wahhab, accept the consensus of the Prophet's companions as long as they do not contradict the first two sources. Like most Hanbalis, Ibn 'Abd al-Wahhab accepted analogy (*qiyas*) as an interpretive tool, only to be used in rare cases. The same applied for his usage of consensus (*ijma'*), which, he explains, can only be used as an exegetical tool and must result in the general agreement with the Qur'an and Sunna.[56] In practice, he almost never appealed to the consensus of legal scholars. In his absolutist mind, "real" consensus requires all legal scholars to agree, not just scholars of a single school of thought.

It is a bit ironic, therefore, that Ibn 'Abd al-Wahhab used consensus in his rejection of the notion that the Qur'an contains hidden knowledge (*batin*), which indicates that the opinions of Shi'is and Sufis are clearly unnecessary for establishing consensus.[57] Although Shi'is and Sufis generally accept the notion of *batin*, Ibn 'Abd al-Wahhab suggests that any division of knowledge in the Qur'an runs counter to its very purpose, which is to call people equally to believe in absolute monotheism (*tawhid*). According to Ibn 'Abd al-Wahhab, the Qur'an is understandable to every Muslim and, therefore, it is the duty of every Muslim to read it for themselves.

Ibn 'Abd al-Wahhab argues that one jurist cannot emulate (*taqlid*) the judgments of another, but must carry out his own independent judgments (*ijtihad*). He even argues that *taqlid* is a form of idolatry (*shirk*) because it gives jurists the God-like power of infallibility.[58] It is on *ijtihad*, then, that post-prophetic knowledge and authority rest for Ibn 'Abd al-Wahhab. In this sense, he is similar to Bihbihani. He even upholds the theological necessity of the continuous practice of *ijtihad* because it is the only way that absolute truth can be established. However, he specifies that only those who master the Qur'an and Sunna are qualified to carry out *ijtihad*.[59] In addition to his narrow view of who is a "real" Muslim (i.e. one who conforms to his strict interpretation of the oneness of God (*tawhid*)), he restricts the number of people who are fit to carry out *ijtihad* to a small number of jurists. In other words, he defines Muslims as Wahhabis, rejecting any sense of pluralism. Indeed, he accused many contemporary *mujtahids* of supporting immorality, causing divisions among Muslims, supporting unjust practices, etc.[60] Additionally, he singled out Shi'i *mujtahids*, claiming that their *ijtihad* is faulty because it is based on the inner knowledge (*batin*) of the Imams.[61] Sufis, then, would also be restricted from *ijtihad* – because of their reliance on *batin*. Even for the limited few who can engage in *ijtihad*, Ibn 'Abd al-Wahhab suggests that they should only use it on controversial cases.

For Ibn 'Abd al-Wahhab, theology was even more important than Islamic law. In fact, his most famous work, *Kitab al-tawhid*, which became the manifesto of Wahhabism, was a work in theology. This book employs a simple but unique method in which each short chapter starts with a verse from the Qur'an or a Hadith report followed by a short explanation of how the text is to be interpreted. Topics in the book range from prohibitions on magic and intercession from saints, to the obligation of belief in predestination.[62] Indeed, much of the book is dedicated to enumerating actions that violate the belief in God's unity.

For Ibn Idris, post-Prophetic authority rests with Sufi scholars, who are capable of receiving divine revelations. Ibn Idris believed that Sufi shaykhs who possess piety and fear of God (*taqwa*) have the power to attain inner knowledge (*batin*) by mystically communicating with God or the Prophet Muhammad. According to Fazlur Rahman, *taqwa* is a central concept of the Qur'an because of its "positive protective function," which is the "most comprehensive concept for avoiding errors and pursuing the right."[63] Ibn Idris explains that *taqwa* endows a person with intuitive knowledge that allows them to extract absolute knowledge from the Qur'an and Sunna.[64] Conversely, scholars devoid of *taqwa* are like "a donkey carrying books."[65] Those who have achieved the proper fear of God, therefore, have no need for the rational sciences or Islamic legal theory because the texts contain inner knowledge (*batin*) that is only accessible to them. Ibn Idris, then, rejects the legalistic authority assumed by scholars associated with Islamic legal schools (sing. *madhhab*).

No different than the overwhelming majority of Muslims, Ibn Idris's system of knowledge is based primarily on the Qur'an and Sunna of the Prophet. He argues that the Qur'an and Hadith are rarely silent on any question. However, if the texts are silent, it is part of God's mercy. For this reason, any attempt to answer questions that are not found in the texts amounts to polytheism (*shirk*).[66] He also accepts the reports of the Prophet's companions as a source of knowledge.[67] In his *Risalat al-radd*, Ibn Idris explains that all of God's ordinances for mankind are provided through revelation.[68] He further suggests that Muhammad is the only source of authority, explaining that he took his "way (*tariqa*) from the Messenger of God … without any intermediary; thus my way is the Muhammadiyya Ahmadiyya; its beginning and end is from the Muhammadan light."[69] Ibn Idris indicates that religious scholars are often unable to derive correct judgments from the foundational texts.[70] This is not because they are uneducated in the methodology of Islamic law or lack exegetical skills. Rather, it is because they lack the proper fear of God (*taqwa*). According to Ibn Idris, therefore, *taqwa* is the key ingredient needed to derive knowledge, not *ra'y*, *qiyas*, *ijtihad*, or other principles of Islamic law. Ibn Idris even concludes that an individual judgment (*ra'y*) from a legal scholar is equal to a legal ruling from Satan.

Ibn Idris recognized three types of knowledge: legalistic knowledge (*'ilm al-shari'a*), specialized knowledge (*'ilm al-khawass*), and specialized special knowledge (*'ilm khawass al- khawass*). Similarly, Mohammad Ali Amir-Moezzi argues that the Shi'i faithful "are divided into three categories: the masses (*al-'amma*), the elite (*al-khassa*) and the elite of the elite (*khassa al-khassa* or *akhass al-khassa*)."[71] According to Ibn Idris, only legalistic knowledge is accessible to everyone. The second and third categories of knowledge are secret (*batin*) and not accessible to lay Muslims. Only adept Sufis, such as Ibn Idris himself, have access to inner, specialized knowledge and the authority to dispense it.

Although greater acceptance of independent legal judgments seems to be a feature of the eighteenth-century Islamic reformation, Ibn Idris's approach to *ijtihad* is a bit ambiguous. O'Fahey argues that Ibn Idris defined *ijtihad* narrowly, claiming that it is "not a matter within the capacity of everyone."[72] In all, *ijtihad* was not central to Ibn Idris's approach to attaining knowledge and he forcefully rejects the use of rational methods for deriving legal judgments. He even says that one should only engage in the rational sciences when absolutely necessary.[73] Ibn Idris not only rejects the use of personal judgments (sing. *ra'y*), he is hostile to those who accept *ra'y* and praises those who reject it. He says that Muslims should not converse with anyone who makes use of personal judgments.[74] Although Ibn Idris does not declare infidelity on those who disagree with him, this is an example of the tendency of eighteenth-century reformers to draw distinct lines between Muslims on the basis of scholarly methodology.

Ibn Idris's reliance on attaining knowledge through intuition and the fear of God sets him apart from both Ibn 'Abd al-Wahhab and Bihbihani. Neither reformer advocated use of divine inspiration in their methodology of knowledge production. However, divine inspiration does factor into the authority of Bihbihani and Ibn 'Abd al-Wahhab. Bihbihani's successors claimed that his writings were the result of divine inspiration and that dreams of the Imams assisted him to overcome the Akhbaris. Similarly, Wahhabis claim that God revealed special aspects of His unity and attributes to Ibn 'Abd al-Wahhab. In Commins's words: "Wahhabi sources concur that gifted inspiration is the wellspring for his monotheist manifesto."[75]

Bihbihani, Ibn Idris, and Ibn 'Abd al-Wahhab all cast themselves as revivers of tradition while insisting on the necessity of reinterpreting or reapplying the principles of Islam anew for the modern period. Their disagreements are primarily a result of their adherence to their particular school of thought. Ibn 'Abd al-Wahhab's Hanbali Sunni school emphasizes a literal, traditionist reading of the foundational texts. Ibn Idris's Shadhiliyya Sufism focuses on inner knowledge (*batin*). Bihbihani's Usuli Shi'i school promotes a rationalist approach to the texts. The three scholars also advocated change by reinterpreting their tradition for the eighteenth century. Openness to change allowed the successors of these reformers a degree of interpretive latitude that bolstered their authority. In an effort to consolidate their positions of authority, they challenged contemporary scholars representing alternative schools of thought. In sum, then, these scholars were revivers and reformers – entrenched in the traditions that they sought to revive, yet advocates of reform in the new age of political decentralization.

Opponents of the Reformers

Sectarian divisions are a hallmark of the modern reform movements, even if sectarianism did not begin in the modern period. In other words, the fault-lines between Sunnis, Sufis, and Shi'is are nearly as old as Islam, but during the transitional period of the eighteenth century, these divisions became more acute. This is partly because alternative movements and ideologies vied for power in an Islamic world that was decreasing in central authority. Additionally, Shi'is, Sunnis, and Sufis competed among themselves for supremacy and vied to define orthodoxy anew for the modern age. Therefore, the period witnessed increased intra-Shi'i, -Sunni, and -Sufi divisions. Sectarianism notwithstanding, Wahhabis, Idrisis, and Usulis did have a common enemy in popular Sufism and each movement sought to suppress popular rituals that were thought to be un-Islamic.

Many elements of Sufism, such as saint worship, were unacceptable to Ibn 'Abd al-Wahhab because he equated such acts with polytheism (*shirk*). This line of argument has led to many well-known Wahhabi raids on Sufi shrines and the Wahhabi policy of destroying anything deemed an idol. Additionally, Wahhabis attacked the social structure of Sufism, including the brotherhood and the relationship between shaykhs and their followers.[76]

As a scholar who combined mysticism with strict adherence to the revelatory texts, Ibn Idris's approach was also incongruent with popular Sufi practices. In fact, he blamed popular Sufism for the decline of Islamic society. However, unlike Wahhabis and Usulis, there are no records indicating that Ibn Idris violently persecuted Sufis. That Ibn Idris was against the practice of declaring infidelity (*takfir*) on other Muslims reinforces the idea that he refrained from harming anyone who practiced rituals associated with popular Sufism.

As noted already, Bihbihani claimed that Imam Husayn told him in a dream that Sufis are destroyers of Islam and he viewed the authority of Sufi masters in direct conflict with Shi'i *mujtahids*.[77] Additionally Bihbihani's son, Muhammad 'Ali Bihbihani, was infamous for his anti-Sufi activity, exemplified by his nickname, "the Sufi killer" (*Sufi-kush*). Muhammad 'Ali particularly targeted the Ni'matullahi order and infamously killed one of its leaders, Sayyid Ma'sum 'Ali Shah.[78] Additionally, Muhammad 'Ali convinced Fath 'Ali Shah to banish all Sufi dervishes from the Qajar capital of Tehran.[79]

Unlike Ibn Idris, both Bihbihani and Ibn 'Abd al-Wahhab revived the practice of declaring infidelity (*takfir*) on other Muslims. Bihbihani reserved the declaration of infidelity primarily for Akhbari Shi'is. His successors claimed that Sufis, Shaykhis, Akhbaris, Babis, Baha'is and Wahhabis were infidels. Ibn 'Abd al-Wahhab declared infidelity on anyone who did not adhere to his narrow view of monotheism (*tawhid*), including all Sufis, Shi'is, and many non-Wahhabi Sunnis. Ibn Idris condemns Wahhabis for their willingness to declare unbelief (*takfir*) on Muslims with whom they disagreed. Ibn Idris says Ibn 'Abd al-Wahhab "declared those Muslims who had belief in anything other than God ... to be unbelievers and ... allowed them to be killed and their property to be seized without justification."[80] According to Ibn Idris, it is not the prerogative of jurists to declare anyone an unbeliever since the declaration of infidelity can only be issued by infallible prophets.[81] However, this did not stop his successors from declaring infidelity on their opponents and indeed on each other. In 1857, for example, leaders of the Khatmiyya declared that the founder of the Ahmadiyya order and prominent successor of Ibn Idris (Ibrahim al-Rashid, d. 1874) was a heretic.[82]

PRIMARY CONCERNS OF THE REFORMERS

The overarching concerns that spurred the activities of the three reformers were vastly different. Ibn 'Abd al-Wahhab had two major concerns that informed his ideology and activism. First and foremost, he thought it was necessary for Muslims to return to a strict adherence to monotheism (*tawhid*). In fact, his followers were known among themselves not as Wahhabis, but as Monotheists (*Muwahiddun*). Second, Ibn 'Abd al-Wahhab was convinced that the Muslim community was in need of socio-moral reconstruction. Ibn 'Abd al-Wahhab lamented that many Muslims during his day did not observe the most basic moral teachings of the Qur'an, such as abstaining from extramarital sex and drinking wine. In fact, he thought that Arabs had sunk into the state of ignorance (*jahiliyya*), which had plagued them before the advent of Islam.[83] Therefore, he emphasized the necessity of promoting the moral teachings of the Qur'an by launching a public campaign against licentiousness. He was especially concerned about the moral degradation of those in power and even chastised the Saudi royal family for their opulent lifestyle.[84] Further, Ibn 'Abd al-Wahhab declared that Muslim clerics had abandoned morality and thus forfeited their religious authority, which pitted him against the Sunni clerical establishment, including that of Mecca.[85]

Three controversial events illustrate Ibn 'Abd al-Wahhab's methods of countering polytheism and immorality. First, he sent his followers to cut down trees that some of the inhabitants of Uyayna believed had special powers. He destroyed the most venerated tree himself. Second, accompanied by Ibn Mu'ammar's men, Ibn 'Abd al-Wahhab destroyed the shrine built over the remains of one of the Prophet Muhammad's companions, Zayd b. al-Khattab.[86] Because this was a pilgrimage site, many Muslims considered this act of destruction as especially heinous. Ibn 'Abd al-Wahhab justified his actions by recalling Muhammad's example of destroying idols in Mecca. Third, Ibn 'Abd al-Wahhab sentenced a woman to be stoned to death after committing adultery. According to reports of the trial, he ordered her to be stoned after she repeatedly admitted her guilt, even though Ibn 'Abd al-Wahhab urged her to claim that she had been raped. After determining that she was sane, she was stoned to death.[87] News of each of these actions spread far and wide, which propagated the Wahhabi message of anti-idolatry and anti-immorality. Muslims in the region became polarized over the Wahhabi movement. On one hand, Ibn 'Abd al-Wahhab gained prestige as someone who would enforce Islamic law. On the other, the Sharifs of Mecca declared infidelity (*takfir*) on Wahhabis and the ruler of Ahsa ordered Ibn Mu'ammar to execute or exile Ibn 'Abd al-Wahhab, as noted already.[88]

Ibn Idris was firmly committed to spreading his message of salvation in Muhammad. His scant record of writings indicates that preaching was far more important to him than scholarship. His successors continued his missionary activities and established religious schools, which were active in spreading the *tariqa Muhammadiyya* across much of the Islamic world, especially in Africa. As indicated above, Ibn Idris focused much of his activity on training the next generation of Sufi scholars, who became influential in the nineteenth century similar to the disciples of Bihbihani.

Bihbihani's primary concerns were quite different from those of Ibn 'Abd al-Wahhab and Ibn Idris. Idolatry and immorality were not issues on which Bihbihani or Ibn Idris focused much attention. Bihbihani's overarching goal was to overthrow the Akhbari clerical establishment in southern Iraq and establish his rationalist Usuli school of thought in its place. From his scholarship, it is clear that he thought this battle would be won by debating the philosophy of Islamic law, and training the next generation of scholars in Usuli methodology. Bihbihani also regularly debated with his colleagues, especially his Akhbari nemesis, Yusuf al-Bahrani (d. 1772). His activity as a teacher-scholar, therefore, far outweighs his role as a preacher.

CONCLUSION

Ibn 'Abd al-Wahhab, Ibn Idris, and Bihbihani founded the most influential modern Islamic movements that began in the critical period of the late eighteenth century. Ibn 'Abd al-Wahhab's movement contributed to the spread of a puritanical, militant interpretation of Islam throughout much of the Islamic world. Bihbihani's movement has become known for political activism and Iranian Usulis have since set a new standard for political Islam. Ahmad Ibn Idris promoted an orthodox Sufism that was oriented toward Muhammad, and the brotherhoods that emerged out of his scholarly circle were especially influential in defining Libya and Sudan as independent countries.

It would be anachronistic to suggest that Ibn 'Abd al-Wahhab, Bihbihani, and Ibn Idris promoted political Islam. However, these figures planted a seed that evolved over time. Ibn 'Abd al-Wahhab may not have condoned the wanton acts of terror that are associated with contemporary jihadi networks. However, in hindsight, his puritanical movement was a critical step in the development of the Islamic extremism that took a darker turn in the twentieth century. Ibn 'Abd al-Wahhab's acts of destruction and puritanical interpretations de-emphasized the peaceful, pluralistic dynamic of Islam that was widespread between the eleventh and the eighteenth centuries. He advocated a fundamentalist path that was taken to a new extreme by his successors. Bihbihani and Ibn Idris could not have dreamed that their movements would eventually gain political power. However, they set processes in motion that made political gains possible. Bihbihani carved out a more independent, prominent, and authoritative social role for Shi'i clerics, which made them politically and economically influential. Likewise, Sufi brotherhoods of Ibn Idris's successors became useful for social, political, and economic ends. These outcomes were not inevitable. They are the current results of processes that evolved over time.

The Islamic revival and reformation that began in the eighteenth century was a response to a perceived crisis in Islamic civilization accompanied by the decentralization and collapse of the Islamic "gunpowder" empires. Scholars from each major Islamic tradition (i.e. Sufism, Sunnism, and Shi'ism) grappled with the challenge of reconstructing Islamic society for the new age. Idrisi Sufism, Wahhabism, and neo-Usulism are distinct movements that coincided at a critical stage in world history. Taken together, they can be referred to as an Islamic revival and reformation. Because these movements advocated change, they defied established Muslim scholars who did not support their reformist ideology. Each of the three movements agreed that the Qur'an and Hadith were the primary sources of sure knowledge and authority. However, they disagreed on how to produce new knowledge on the basis of these texts. Even more, they disagreed on the authority that such knowledge might carry. Islam in the contemporary world has remained decentralized, yet organized around semi-independent movements. Wahhabism in Saudi Arabia and Usulism in Iran have been particularly decisive on the regional and global stage – both towering examples of the prevalence of political Islam and bitter rivals, partially because they compete for the very soul of the Islamic world.

GLOSSARY

ahl al-bayt	lit. people of the house, family of the Prophet Muhammad. A term Shi'is use to refer to the Shi'i community
Akhbari	traditionist, scripturalist, Twelver Shi'i school of thought that stresses the importance of the Qur'an and Hadith as sources of knowledge and authority
'aql	reason, intellect
'Atabat	lit. thresholds, Shi'i shrine cities in Iraq, including Najaf, Karbala', Hilla, and Samara, which are pilgrimage sites and contain tombs for six Imams
bab al-ijtihad	lit. the gate of *ijtihad*. An important debate among Muslim scholars was whether the gate of *ijtihad* was opened or closed. See also *ijtihad*
bab al-'ilm	gate of knowledge
batin	inner, hidden, or esoteric, often associated with knowledge derived through inspiration, as opposed to exoteric knowledge (*zahir*)
dalil	(pl. *'adilla*) lit. indicator or indication, argument, evidence, or proof on which a ruling is derived
dalil 'aqli	rational indicator
dalil shar'i	indicator from the Lawgiver (God)
da'wa	missionary activity
dhikrullah	remembrance of God
fana'	ceasing to exist, annihilation in God, highest state of Islamic mysticism

fatwa	response, the legal opinion of a jurist in response to a question
fiqh	Islamic law, human understanding of divine law (*shari'a*)
furu' al-fiqh	lit. branches of jurisprudence, positive law
Hadith	tradition, collection of reports of the sayings and actions of Muhammad (and the Imams for Shi'is), which have been transmitted from one generation to the next and provide knowledge of the sunna
haqiqa	absolute reality, the ultimate non-relative truth, truth according to God, also literal meaning of a text
hawza	Shi'i seminary or educational system
hikma	(or *hikmat*) mystical philosophy, wisdom
hikmat al-ilahi	see *Ishraqiyya*
hujja	(or *hujjat*) proof, evidence
hujjiyya	probative force, authoritativeness, evidential
hukm	(pl. *ahkam*) legal ruling related to what is enjoined by God, the Lawgiver
'ibadat	(or *'ibada*) commands related to worship or ritual duty
Idrisi	Sufi movement established by Ahmad Ibn Idris al-Fasi (1760–1837)
ihtiyat	caution, a procedural principle to ensure that one is in compliance with divine injunctions
ijaza	lit. permission, license, similar to a diploma, issued from cleric to student indicating the permissibility for the student to exercise the rights of a jurist
ijma'	legal consensus, agreement of Muslims or scholars of a legal school

ijma' zanni	conjectural consensus
ijtihad	juristic reasoning, derivation of a ruling exercised by a jurist (*mujtahid*) based on the principles of Islamic law (*usul al-fiqh*)
ikhtilaf	disagreement, difference of opinion, opposite of consensus (*ijma'*)
'illa	ratio legis, rationale, effect cause
'ilm	knowledge
'ilm al-khawass	special knowledge
Imam	According to Shi'is, Imams are successors of Muhammad, believed to be endowed with infallibility (*'isma*)
imam jum'a	Friday prayer leader
Ishraqiyya	(or *hikmat al-ilahi*) theosophy or Illuminationist philosophy that originated with Shihab al-Din Yahya Suhrawardi (d. 1191), who promoted the idea that true knowledge is the result of both rational and intuitive emanations from the mind
'isma	sinless, infallible, see *ma'sum*
isnad	chain of transmission of a Hadith report
istihsan	juristic preference, discretionary opinion
istishab al-hal	presumption of continuance
istislah	public welfare or interest
jahiliyya	ignorance
jihad	holy war, struggle
jizya	head tax paid to Muslim rulers by non-Muslims
kadkhoda	village leader
kafir	(pl. *kuffar*) infidel, unbeliever
kalam	theology

karamat	miraculous phenomena
kashf	divine inspiration, intuitive revelation
Kashfiyya	see Shaykhi
khabar	(pl. *akhbar*) Hadith report
khabar al-wahid	(pl. *akhbar al-ahad*) Hadith report that only has one chain of transmitters
khawass	elite, special
khums	(lit. one-fifth) Islamic tax paid on specific items
lisan	language
lugha	language, linguistic
al-lugha al-'urfiyya	customary language
luti	thug, gang, homosexual
madhhab	school of Islamic legal thought
madrasa	school, often denoting religious school
mafhum	(pl. *mafahim*) linguistic implication
Mahdi	Hidden Imam. According to Twelver Shi'is, the Mahdi (Muhammad al-Mahdi) is the twelfth Imam, who has been in a state of spiritual occultation since 873 CE. In other words, the Mahdi (or *qa'im*, lit. the one who will arise) did not die, but is also not physically present in the world – although he allegedly may periodically manifest himself on the physical plane
marja' al-taqlid	(lit. source of emulation) Shi'i jurist (*mujtahid*) whose legal judgments are emulated by lay Shi'is (*muqallid*)
maslaha	public interest, common benefit
ma'sum	infallible, sinless, attributed to the Shi'i Imams

matn	text of a Hadith report
millet	confessional community
mirghadab	executioner
mu'amalat	non-ritual legal duties
mu'assis	founder
mufti	legal expert
mujaddid	renewer, reformer, or reviver of Islam thought to appear every century. Based on the prophetic Hadith: "At the beginning of every hundred years, God will send a person who will revive the religion (i.e. Islam) for the community (*ummah*)"
mujtahid	jurisconsult, jurist, legal scholar who carries out *ijtihad*
mukallaf	legal agent, sane person who is subject to the law
mulazama	belief that revelation and reason are in complete agreement
mullabashi	head jurist, religious scholar and administrator. The office of the *mullabashi* began in the late Safavid period
muqallid	emulator, follower of a *mujtahid*, lay Shi'i
murawwij	reviver
mutashabih	unclear, ambiguous Qur'an verse
mutawatir	widespread, Hadith report transmitted through multiple chains of Hadith transmitters
Muwahiddun	(lit. Monotheists, Unitarians) title by which Wahhabis initially referred to themselves
na'ib	deputy, see *niyaba 'amma*
najis	ritual impurity

naql	scripture, foundational Islamic texts (i.e. Qur'an and Hadith)
niyaba 'amma	general deputyship or vicegerency of the Hidden Imam
qadi	legal judge
qat'	legal certainty, assurance
qiyas	analogy, Sunni source of law (*usul al-fiqh*), rejected by Shi'i scholars
qizilbash	(lit. red head) supporters of Shah Isma'il who assisted him in establishing the Safavid dynasty
qutb al-zaman	axis of the age
ra'y	personal opinion
rijal	Hadith transmitters
riwayat	companions of Muhammad
sadr	Safavid religious official, administrator of charitable endowments (sing. *waqf*)
sahib al-zaman	Lord of the age, one of the titles of the Mahdi
salat	prayer
shakk	legal doubt, opposite of certainty (*qat'*)
sharh	(pl. *shuruh*) textual commentary
shari'a	God's law or divine law, see also *fiqh*, which is often used interchangeably with *shari'a*
shaykh	(or *pir*) Sufi master or tribal head
Shaykhi	Shi'i school of thought established by Shaykh Ahmad al-Ahsa'i, also known as Kashfiyya
shirk	idolatry, polytheism
silsila	chain

sunna	what is known about Muhammad and the Imams, which provides the basis for Islamic legal custom and practice
ta'arud	contradiction found within revelatory texts
tabaqat	biographical dictionaries of clerics
ta'diyya	transference, method of transferring a ruling from an original case to a novel case
tafsir	commentary
takfir	declaration of unbelief or infidelity
takhyir	legal choice
taklif	legal obligation, injunction
tanqih al-manat	discovering the rationale of a law with certainty
taqiyya	dissimulation
taqlid	emulation of a Muslim scholar's legal judgment(s), precedent
taqwa	fear of God
tariqa Muhammadiyya	Sufi order or brotherhood focused on the example of the Prophet Muhammad
ta'wil	interpretation of a text, exegesis
tawqifi (or *tawaqquf*)	suspension of a legal decision
tawhid	monotheism, oneness of God
'ulama'	religious scholars
'urf	customary, common usage, often related to language
usul al-din	theological principles
usul al-fiqh	lit. "sources or principles of Islamic law," jurisprudence
usul	sources, principles, roots

Usuli	rationalist Twelver Shi'i school of thought that accepts the use of *ijtihad* and other extra-textual methods of deriving knowledge and authority. Usulis are often referred to as *ijtihadis*
Wahhabi	puritanical Sunni movement established by Muhammad Ibn 'Abd al-Wahhab (1703–92), also known as Muwahiddun
wahy	prophetic revelation, the manner in which Muhammad received the Qur'an from God
waqf	religious endowment
wilayat al-faqih	guardianship of the jurist
zahir	outer or exoteric knowledge, as opposed to esoteric knowledge (*batin*)
zann	conjecture, probability, supposition. Arguments based on conjecture generally do not have probative force

NOTES

INTRODUCTION

1 Imams are Shi'i successors of Muhammad, who should not be confused with prayer leaders (*imams*).

2 Muhammad Baqir Khwansari, *Rawdat al-jannat fi ahwal al-'ulama' wa as-sadat*, Vol. 2 (Beirut, 1991), 95; Hamid Algar, *Religion and State in Iran 1785–1906: The Role of the Ulama in the Qajar Period* (Berkeley: University of California Press, 1969), 35.

3 Wahid Bihbihani, *al-Risala al-akhbar wa al-ijtihad* (Tab'-i Mahalli, 1895), 9. See also Devin J. Stewart, *Islamic Legal Orthodoxy: Twelver Shiite Responses to the Sunni Legal System* (Salt Lake City: University of Utah Press, 1998), 216.

4 For more on Muharram rituals, see Babak Rahimi, *Theater State and the Formation of Early Modern Public Sphere in Iran: Studies on Safavid Muharram Rituals, 1590–1641 CE* (Leiden: Brill, 2012).

5 The Iraqi shrine cities, often referred to as the 'Atabat (lit. thresholds), include Najaf, Karbala', Samarra, and Kazimayn. See H. Algar, "'Atabat," *Encyclopaedia Iranica*, Vol. II: 902–4.

6 For the "rivalry" between Najaf and Qum, see Devin J. Stewart, "The Portrayal of an Academic Rivalry: Najaf and Qum in the Writings and Speeches of Khomeini, 1964–78," in Linda S. Walbridge, ed., *The Most Learned of the Shi'i: The Institution of the Marja' Taqlid* (New York: Oxford University Press, 2001).

7 For more on Shi'ism and politics, see Said Amir Arjomand, *The Shadow of God and the Hidden Imam: Religion, Political Order, and Societal Change in Shi'ite Iran from the Beginning to 1890* (Chicago: The University of Chicago Press, 1984); Algar, *Religion and State*; Said Amir Arjomand, ed., *Authority and Political Culture in Shi'ism* (Albany: SUNY Press, 1988); Nikki R. Keddie, ed., *Religion and Politics in Iran: Shi'ism from Quietism to Revolution* (New Haven: Yale University Press, 1983).

8 Things or people related to Shi'ism are rendered in English as Shi'i, Shi'a, Shi'ite, Shii, Shia, etc. For the sake of uniformity and simplicity, I use the terms Shi'i, Shi'is, and Shi'ism.

9 Arjomand, *Shadow of God*, 34.

10   Algar, *Religion and State*, 4.

11   Henry Corbin, "Pour une Morphologie de la Spiritualite Shi'ite," *Eranos-Jahrbuch*, XXXIX (Zurich, 1960), 69. See also Algar, *Religion and State*, 5.

12   Arjomand, *Shadow of God*, 122, 159.

13   Quoted in Ann K. S. Lambton, "A Nineteenth Century View of Jihad," *Studia Islamica*, 32 (1970), 189.

14   Jean Chardin, *Les Voyages du Chevalier Chardin en Perse*, L. Langles, ed., Vol. 5 (Paris: Le Normant, 1811), 215. See also Arjomand, *Shadow of God*, 185, and Kathryn Babayan, *Mystics, Monarchs, and Messiahs: Cultural Landscapes of Early Modern Iran* (Cambridge: Harvard University Press, 2002), 404–5.

15   Said Amir Arjomand, "History, Structure, and Revolution in the Shi'ite Tradition in Contemporary Iran," *International Political Science Review / Revue internationale de science politique*, Vol. 10, No. 2, The Historical Framework of Revolutions/Le contexte historique des révolutions (April, 1989): 112.

16   On the Saudi exportation of Wahhabism, see Khalid Abou El Fadl, *The Great Theft: Wrestling Islam from the Extremists* (New York: HarperCollins, 2007); David Commins, *The Wahhabi Mission and Saudi Arabia* (London: I.B. Tauris, 2009).

17   Mark Sedgwick, *Saints and Sons: The Making of the Rashidi Ahmadi Sufi Order, 1799–2000* (Leiden: Brill, 2005), xi, 27–8; Rex Sean O'Fahey and Bernd Radtke, "Neo-Sufism Reconsidered," *Der Islam*, 70 (1993): 52–87.

18   E. J. Hobsbawm, *The Age of Revolution: 1789–1848* (New York: Mentor, 1962).

19   See Jonathan Israel, *A Revolution of the Mind: Radical Enlightenment and the Intellectual Origins of Modern Democracy* (Princeton: Princeton University Press, 2010).

20   Marshall G. S. Hodgson, *The Venture of Islam*, Vol. 2 (Chicago: University of Chicago Press, 1974), 3, 18. Stephen Dale prefers to use the term "patrimonial-bureaucratic" to refer to the empires, instead of "gunpowder" or "early modern," and he emphasizes Islam as the common denominator between the three empires. Stephen F. Dale, *The Muslim Empires of the Ottomans, Safavids, and Mughals* (Cambridge: Cambridge University Press, 2010), 5. In reference to the Safavids, Matthee argues that "despite their documented eagerness to acquire firearms, there are few signs that the Safavids seriously attempted, let alone succeeded, in integrating the new technology into their army." Rudi Matthee, "Unwalled Cities and Restless Nomads: Firearms and Artillery in Safavid Iran," in Charles

Melville, ed., *Safavid Persia* (London: I.B.Tauris, 1996), 408. See also Douglas E. Streusand, *Islamic Gunpowder Empires: Ottomans, Safavids, and Mughals* (Boulder: Westview Press, 2011).

21 Others, especially Philip Hitti, argue that the "decline" occurred much earlier. Revealing his association of the greatness of Islamic civilization with Arab culture, he argues the following: "The fall of the Moslem caliphate in the mid-thirteenth century, the successive Mongol invasions, and the rise of the successor states – mostly Persian and Turkish – left the Arab world in a state of blackout that lasted for no less than six centuries." Hitti goes on to say that the cause of "political and spiritual stagnation" was "internal rather than external." Further, he suggests that Ottoman Turks accelerated the "downward drift of Arab culture." Philip K. Hitti, *Islam: A Way of Life* (Minneapolis: University of Minnesota Press, 1970), 176.

22 See, for example, Dana Sajdi, ed., *Ottoman Tulips, Ottoman Coffee: Leisure and Lifestyle in the Eighteenth Century* (London: I.B.Tauris, 2007).

23 Cemal Kafadar, "The Question of Ottoman Decline," *Harvard Middle Eastern and Islamic Review*, 4 (1997–8): 32. See also Rudi Matthee, *Persia in Crisis: Safavid Decline and the Fall of Isfahan* (London: I.B.Tauris, 2012), xxii.

24 See Reinhard Schulze, "Was ist Die Islamische Aufklärung?" *Die Welt des Islams*, New Series, Vol. 36, Issue 3 (November, 1996): 276–325. Bernd Radtke, "Erleuchtung und Aufklärung: Islamische Mystik und europaischer Rationalismus," *Die Welt des Islams*, New Series, Vol. 34, Issue 1 (April, 1994): 48–66.

25 Ira M. Lapidus, "Islamic Revival and Modernity: The Contemporary Movements and the Historical Paradigms," *Journal of the Economic and Social History of the Orient*, Vol. 40, No. 4 (1997): 457.

26 Ibid., 453.

27 Ibid., 448.

28 Rula Jurdi Abisaab, *Converting Persia: Religion and Power in the Safavid Empire* (London: I.B.Tauris, 2004); Yitzhak Nakash, *The Shi'is of Iraq* (Princeton: Princeton University Press, 2003), 27.

29 Ibid., 13.

30 For Shi'ism in Iraq, see Joyce N. Wiley, *The Islamic Movement of Iraqi Shi'as* (Boulder: Lynee Rienner Publishers, 1992); Chibli Mallat, *Renewal of Islamic Law, Muhammad Baqer as-Sadr, Najaf and the Shi'i International* (Cambridge: Cambridge University Press, 1993); Nakash, *Shi'is of Iraq*; Meir Litvak, *Shi'i Scholars of Nineteenth Century Iraq: The 'Ulama' of Najaf and Karbala'* (Cambridge: Cambridge University Press, 1997); Graham E. Fuller and Rend Rahim Francke, *The Arab Shia:*

The Forgotten Muslims (New York: St. Martin's Press, 1999). For Shi'ism in Lebanon, see Fouad Ajami, *The Vanished Imam: Musa al-Sadr and the Shia of Lebanon* (Ithaca: Cornell University Press, 1986); Rodger Shanahan, *The Shi'a of Lebanon: Clans, Parties and Clerics* (London: I.B.Tauris, 2005); Tamara Chalabi, *The Shi'is of Jabal 'Amil and the New Lebanon: Community and Nation State, 1918–1943* (New York: Palgrave Macmillan, 2006); Max Weiss, *In the Shadow of Sectarianism: Law, Shi'ism, and the Making of Modern Lebanon* (Cambridge: Harvard University Press, 2010); Stefan Winter, *The Shiites of Lebanon Under Ottoman Rule, 1516–1788* (Cambridge: Cambridge University Press, 2010). For Shi'ism in Saudi Arabia and the Gulf, see Fouad N. Ibrahim, *The Shi'is of Saudi Arabia* (London: Saqi, 2006); Laurence Louer, *Transnational Shia Politics: Religious and Political Networks in the Gulf* (New York: Columbia University Press, 2008); Toby Matthiesen, *The Other Saudis: Shiism, Dissent and Sectarianism* (Cambridge: Cambridge University Press, 2015). For Shi'ism in South Asia, see J. R. I. Cole, *Roots of North Indian Shi'ism in Iran and Iraq: Religion and State in Awadh, 1722–1859* (Berkeley: University of California Press, 1988); David Pinault, *The Shiites: Ritual and Popular Piety in a Muslim Community* (New York: St. Martin's Press, 1992). For Shi'ism in North America, see Linda S. Walbridge, *Without Forgetting the Imam: Lebanese Shi'ism in an American Community* (Detroit: Wayne State University Press, 1997); Liyakat Nathani Takim, *Shi'ism in America* (New York: New York University Press, 2009). For a general overview on Shi'i communities in these countries, see chapter 14 of Moojan Momen, *An Introduction to Shi'i Islam* (New Haven: Yale University Press, 1985).

31 Baqer Moin, *Khomeini: Life of the Ayatollah* (New York: I.B.Tauris, 1999); Said Amir Arjomand, *The Turban for the Crown: The Islamic Revolution in Iran* (Oxford: Oxford University Press, 1988).

32 On the twentieth century revival of Shi'ism, see Vali Nasr, *The Shia Revival: How Conflicts within Islam Will Shape the Future* (New York: W. W. Norton & Co., 2006).

33 Peter Mandaville, *Global Political Islam* (New York: Routledge, 2007), 57.

34 For more on the Muslim Brotherhood, see Richard P. Mitchell, *The Society of the Muslim Brothers* (Oxford: Oxford University Press, 1993); Carrie Rosefsky Wickham, *The Muslim Brotherhood: Evolution of an Islamist Movement* (Princeton: Princeton University Press, 2013).

35 Quoted in Mandaville, *Global*, 60.

36 For more on Hezbollah, see Augustus Richard Norton, *Hezbollah: A Short History* (Princeton: Princeton University Press, 2007).

37 For more on the Iran-Iraq war, see Dilip Hiro, *The Longest War: The Iran-Iraq Military Conflict* (New York: Routledge, 1991).

38 Hodgson, *Venture*, Vol. 2, 36.

39 See, for example, Hossein Modarressi Tabatabai, "Rationalism and Traditionalism in Shi'i Jurisprudence: A Preliminary Survey," *Studia Islamica*, No. 59 (1984): 141–58.

40 For messianism and occultation, see Abdulaziz Sachedina, *Islamic Messianism: Idea of Mahdi in Twelver Shi'ism* (Albany: SUNY Press, 1981); Jassim Hussain, *Occultation of the Twelfth Imam: A Historical Background* (London: Muhammadi Trust, 1982); Omid Ghaemmaghami, "Seeing the Proof: The Question of Contacting the Hidden Imam in Early Twelver Shi'i Islam" (PhD Dissertation, University of Toronto, 2013).

41 Reported by Ibn Babuya (d. 991). Quoted in Said Amir Arjomand, "Introduction: Shi'ism, Authority, and Political Culture," in Arjomand, ed., *Authority and Political*, 5.

42 For more on Shi'i authority, see Liyakat N. Takim, *The Heirs of the Prophet: Charisma and Religious Authority in Shi'ite Islam* (Albany: SUNY Press, 2006); Ahmad Kazemi Moussavi, *Religious Authority in Shi'ite Islam: From the Office of Mufti to the Institution of Marja* (Kuala Lumpur: International Institute of Islamic Thought and Civilization (ISTAC), 1996).

43 Roy Parviz Mottahedeh, "Introduction," in Muhammad Baqir as-Sadr, *Lessons in Islamic Jurisprudence* (Oxford: Oneworld Publications, 2003), 2.

44 For more on Shi'i law, see Hossein Modarressi Tabatabai, *An Introduction to Shi'i Islam: A Bibliographical Study* (London: Ithaca Press, 1984); Robert Gleave, *Inevitable Doubt: Two Theories of Shi'i Jurisprudence* (Leiden: Brill, 2000); Stewart, *Islamic Legal Orthodoxy*; Sadr, *Lessons*.

45 Sadr, *Lessons*, 51. See also Sadr's discussion on the history of the term *ijtihad* on pp. 46–51.

46 Wael Hallaq, *A History of Islamic Legal Theories: An introduction to Sunni usul al-fiqh* (Cambridge: Cambridge University Press, 2002), vii.

47 Modarressi, "Rationalism," 143.

48 See Martin McDermott, *The Theology of al-Shaikh al-Mufid* (Beirut: Dar el-Machreq, 1986).

49 Andrew Newman, "The Development and Political Significance of the Rationalist (Usuli) and Traditionist (Akhbari) Schools in Imami Shi'i History from the Third/Ninth to the Tenth/Sixteenth Century" (PhD Thesis, UCLA, 1986), 195.

50 Quoted in ibid., 511.

51 Robert Gleave, *Scripturalist Islam: The History and Doctrines of the Akhbari Shi'i School* (Leiden: Brill, 2007), 6, chapter 1.

52   Ibid., xx, chapter 3.

53   Ibid., 99.

54   See Mehdi Amin Razavi, *Suhrawardi and the School of Illumination* (London: Curzon Press, 1997).

55   Muhammad ibn Ibrahim Sadra al-Din Shirazi, *Sharh Usul al-Kafi* (Tehran: Mu'assasa Mutal'at wa Tahqiqat Farhangi, 1987), 25; quoted in Kazemi, *Religious Authority*, 119–20.

56   Most of the teaching licences (*ijazas*) that Shaykh Ahmad received were from students of Wahid Bihbihani (Bahr al-'Ulum, Mirza Muhammad Mahdi Shahristani, Sayyid 'Ali Tabataba'i, and Muhammad Ibrahim Kalbasi), indicating that his formal training was firmly in the Usuli school.

57   Vahid Rafati, "The Development of Shaykhi Thought in Shi'i Islam" (PhD Thesis, UCLA, 1979), 42; see also Todd Lawson, "Orthodoxy and Heterodoxy in Twelver Shiism: Ahmad al-Ahsai on Fayd Kashani (The *Risala al-'ilmiyya*)," in Robert Gleave, ed., *Religion and Society in Qajar Iran* (London: Routledge, 2005).

58   Algar, *Religion and State*, 7–8.

1.   THE TIMES AND PLACES OF REFORM IN THE MODERN WORLD

1   Jonathan D. Spence, *The Search for Modern China* (New York: Norton, 1990), 102–6.

2   See, for example, Shmuel N. Eisenstadt, ed., *Multiple Modernities* (New Jersey: Transaction Publishers, 2002).

3   Andre Gunder Frank, *ReOrient: Global Economy in the Asian Age* (Berkeley: University of California Press, 1998), 27. For a discussion on "diffusionism," see J. M. Blaut, *The Colonizer's Model of the World: Geographical Diffusionism and Eurocentric History* (New York: The Guilford Press, 1993), 11–17.

4   Samuel Huntington, *The Clash of Civilizations and the Remaking of World Order* (London: Free Press, 2004); Francis Fukuyama, *The End of History and the Last Man* (Harmondsworth: Penguin, 1992).

5   For Enlightenment views on progress, see Israel, *Revolution of the Mind*, chapter 1.

6   See Arjun Appadurai, *Modernity at Large: Cultural Dimensions of Globalization* (Minneapolis: University of Minnesota Press, 1996), 3.

7   Marshall G. S. Hodgson, *Rethinking World History: Essays on Europe, Islam, and World History* (Cambridge: Cambridge University Press, 1993), 58.

8   See, for example, Appadurai, *Modernity*, 1.

9   Frank, *ReOrient*, 37, 2.

10   Eisenstadt, ed., *Multiple Modernities*.

11   Appadurai, *Modernity*, 9.

12   Samir Amin, *Eurocentrism* (New York: Monthly Review Press, 1989), 7.

13   Ibid., 53, 67–8.

14   Appadurai, *Modernity*, 6–7.

15   Timothy Mitchell, "The Stage of Modernity," in Timothy Mitchell, ed., *Questions of Modernity* (Minneapolis: University of Minnesota, 2000), 3–4.

16   Ibid., 15.

17   Ibid., 15–16.

18   Ibid.

19   Blaut, *Colonizer's Model*, 3–8; Hodgson, *Rethinking*, 6.

20   Edward W. Said, *Orientalism* (New York: Vintage Books, 1979).

21   Martin Bernal, *Black Athena: The Afroasiatic Roots of Classical Civilization*, 2 vols (New Brunswick: Rutgers University Press, 1987).

22   For an exception, see James L. Gelvin, *The Modern Middle East: A History* (New York: Oxford University Press, 2005).

23   Karl Marx, *Capital: A Critique of Critical Economy*, Vol. 1 (Chicago: Charles H. Kerr and Company, 1915), 823.

24   Immanuel Wallerstein, *World-Systems Analysis: An Introduction* (Durham: Duke University Press, 2004), 17.

25   Ibid., 23.

26   Ibid., 2.

27   Ibid., 1–3.

28   Ibid., 21.

29   Frank, *ReOrient*, xxv, 5.

30   Ibid., 328.

31   Ibid., 5.

32   Ibid., 37.

33   Janet L. Abu-Lughod, *Before European Hegemony: The World System A. D. 1250–1350* (Oxford: Oxford University Press, 1989), x.

34   Ibid., 12–14.

35   Terence K. Hopkins and Immanuel Wallerstein, eds., *Processes of the World-System* (London: Sage, 1980), 174.

36   Ibid.

37   Masoud Kamali, *Multiple Modernities, Civil Society and Islam: The Case of Iran and Turkey* (Liverpool: Liverpool University Press, 2006), 16.

38   S. N. Eisenstadt, *Comparative Civilizations and Multiple Modernities*, Vol. 2 (Leiden: Brill, 2003), 536.

39   Ibid.

40   Timothy Mitchell, ed., *Questions of Modernity* (Minneapolis: University of Minnesota Press, 2000), xii.

41   Ann K. S. Lambton, "Some New Trends in Islamic Political Thought in Late 18th and Early 19th Century Persia," *Studia Islamica*, No. 39 (1974), 96.

42   Abdul-Hadi Hairi, "Why Did the 'Ulama Participate in the Persian Constitutional Revolution of 1905–1909?" *Die Welt des Islams*, New Series, Vol. 17, Issue 1/4 (1976–1977): 127–54.

43   See Kamali, *Multiple Modernities*, 49.

44   Peter N. Stearns, *The Industrial Revolution in World History* (Boulder: Westview Press, 1993), 11–12.

45   Ibid., 5; Bonnie Smith, et al., *Crossroads and Cultures: A History of the World's Peoples*, Vol. 2 (Boston: Bedford/St. Martin's, 2012), 794.

46   Stearns, *Industrial Revolution*, 11.

47   For more on defensive developmentalism in the Middle East, see Gelvin, *Modern Middle East*, chapter 5.

48   Edmund Burke, "Introduction," in Hodgson, *Rethinking*, xx.

49   Hodgson, *Rethinking*, 56.

50   Ibid., 60–1.

51   Abu-Lughod, *Before European*, 144.

52   Ibid., 363.

53   Ibid., 361.

54   Hodgson, *Venture*, Vol. 3, 11–15.

55   Sajdi, *Ottoman Tulips*, 2.

56   Reinhard Schulze, "Das Islamische Achtzehntes Jahrhundert: Versuch einer Historiographischen Kritik," *Die Welt des Islams*, New Series, Bd. 30, Nr. ¼ (1990): 140–59. Schulze, "Islamische Aufklarung?"

57   Radtke, "Erleuchtung und Aufklarung."

58   Rudolph Peters, "Reinhard Schulze's Quest for an Islamic Enlightenment," *Die Welt des Islams*, New Series, Bd. 30, Nr. ¼ (1990): 160–2.

59   Ali A. Allawi, *The Crisis of Islamic Civilization* (New Haven: Yale University Press, 2009), 249.

60   Ibid., 23.

61   Ibid., 250.

62   John Obert Voll, *Islam: Continuity and Change in the Modern World*, (Syracuse: Syracuse University Press, 1994), 29.

63   O'Fahey argues the same for Ibn Idris. R. S. O'Fahey, *Enigmatic Saint, Ahmad Ibn Idris and the Idrisi Tradition* (Evanston: Northwestern University Press, 1990), 5.

64   John L. Esposito, *Islam and Politics* (New York: Syracuse University Press, 1984), 32.

2. Shi'ism and the Emergence of Modern Iran

1   See Cole, *Indian Shi'ism*.

2   Babayan, *Mystics*, xxiv.

3   Rudi Matthee, "Safavid Dynasty," *Encyclopaedia Iranica*, online edition, www.iranicaonline.org/articles/safavids (accessed 27 September 2014).

4   Andrew J. Newman, *Safavid Iran: Rebirth of a Persian Empire* (London: I.B.Tauris, 2009), 13–14.

5   Babayan, *Mystics*, xxviii-xxix.

6   Quoted in Babayan, *Mystics*, 312.

7   Babayan, *Mystics*, 296.

8   Michael J. McCaffrey, "Battle of Chaldiran," *Encyclopaedia Iranica*, Vol. IV, 656–8. See also Homa Katouzian, *The Persians: Ancient, Mediaeval, and Modern Iran* (New Haven: Yale University Press, 2009), 115.

9   Adel Allouche, *The Origins and Development of the Ottoman-Safavid Conflict (906–962/1500–1555)* (Berlin: Klaus Schwarz Verlag, 1983).

10 Katouzian, *The Persians*, 118. See also Babayan, *Mystics*, 301.

11 Newman, *Safavid Iran*, 28.

12 Abisaab, *Converting*, 20.

13 Babayan, *Mystics*, 312.

14 Ibid., 295–348.

15 Ibid., 311–17.

16 Newman, *Safavid Iran*, 32.

17 Abisaab, *Converting*; Albert Hourani, "From Jabal 'Amil to Persia," *Bulletin of the School of Oriental and African Studies*, University of London, Vol. 49, No. 1 (1986): 133–40. See also Devin J. Stewart, "An Episode in the 'Amili Migration to Safavid Iran: Husayn b. 'Abd al-Samad al-'Amili's Travel Account," *Iranian Studies*, Vol. 39, No. 4 (December 2006): 481–508.

18 Abisaab, *Converting*, 10–13.

19 Andrew Newman, "The Myth of Clerical Migration to Safawid Iran: Shiite Opposition to 'Ali al-Karaki and Safawid Shiism," *Die Welt des Islams*, 33 (1993): 66–112.

20 Newman, *Safavid Iran*, 36.

21 Babayan, *Mystics*, 403.

22 Andrew Newman argues that Karaki was the only "Arab Twelver Shi'i cleric … to have journeyed East specifically to associate himself with Safavid Shi'ism." See *Safavid Iran*, 24.

23 Abisaab, *Converting*, 22; Newman, *Safavid Iran*, 37.

24 Babayan, *Mystics*, 306–7.

25   Newman, *Safavid Iran*, 38.

26   Abisaab, *Converting*, 21. See also Roger M. Savory, *Iran under the Safavids* (Cambridge: Cambridge University Press, 1980), 28–9.

27   Abisaab, *Converting*, 24, 27.

28   Katouzian, *The Persians*, 126.

29   For more on Safavid economics, see Rudi Matthee, *Politics of Trade in Safavid Iran: Silk for Silver 1600–1730* (Cambridge: Cambridge University Press, 1999); Rudi Matthee, Willem Floor, Patrick Clawson, *The Monetary History of Iran: From the Safavids to the Qajars* (London: I.B. Tauris, 2013).

30   Babayan, *Mystics*, 350–1.

31   Ibid., 359.

32   Ibid., 360.

33   Ibid., 352.

34   Edward G. Browne, *Literary History of Persia*, Vol. 4 (New Delhi: Goodword Books), 408.

35   Sajjad Rizvi, *Mulla Sadra Shirazi: His Life and Works and the Sources of Safavid Philosophy* (Oxford: Oxford University Press, 2007), 1.

36   See Gleave, *Scripturalist Islam*.

37   Abisaab, *Converting*, 111.

38   Denis MacEoin, *The Messiah of Shiraz: Studies in Early and Middle Babism* (Leiden: Brill, 2009), 42, 48.

39   Modarressi, "Rationalism," 155.

40   Newman, *Safavid Iran*, 7.

41   Matthee, *Persia in Crisis,* xxvii-xxxiv.

42   Ibid., xxxiv.

43   Ibid., xxix–xxx.

44   Babayan, *Mystics*, 471.

45   Algar, *Religion and State*, 29.

46   Majlisi I clearly states, "most of what Mulla Muhammad Amin [Astarabadi] has said is true." Quoted in Khwansari, *Rawdat*, 38.

47   Quoted in Khwansari, *Rawdat*, 38.

48   For further discussion on Muhammad Baqir al-Majlisi's position in the Akhbari-Usuli dispute, see Gleave, *Scripturalist Islam*.

49   A. K. S. Lambton, "Tribal Resurgence and the Decline of the Bureaucracy in Eighteenth Century Persia," in Thomas Naff and Roger Owen, eds., *Studies in Eighteenth Century Islamic History* (Carbondale: Southern Illinois University Press, 1977).

50   For more on Nadir Shah, see Michael Axworthy, *The Sword of Persia: Nader Shah, from Tribal Warrior to Conquering Tyrant* (London: I.B. Tauris, 2009); Ernest S. Tucker, *Nadir Shah's Quest for Legitimacy in Post-Safavid*

Iran (Gainesville: University Press of Florida, 2006); Laurence Lockhart, *Nadir Shah: A Critical Study Based Mainly upon Contemporary Sources* (London: Luzac, 1938).

51 Axworthy, *Sword of Persia*, xv, 11.

52 Ibid., 8.

53 Lockhart, *Nadir Shah*, 213–15.

54 Tucker, *Nadir Shah's Quest*, 1.

55 'Abdullah b. Husayn al-Suwaydi, *al-Hujaj al-qat'iya li-ittifaq al-firaq al-Islamiya* (Cairo: al-Matba'a al-Halabiya, 1905), 11. Quoted in Ernest Tucker, "Nadir Shah and the Ja'fari Madhhab Reconsidered," *Iranian Studies*, Vol. 27, No. 1/4, Religion and Society in Islamic Iran during the Pre-Modern Era (1994): 171.

56 Tucker, "Ja'fari Madhhab," 163–79.

57 Lockhart, *Nadir Shah*, 197.

58 Tucker, "Ja'fari Madhhab," 164

59 Arjomand, *Shadow of God*, 217.

60 Hamid Algar, "Shi'ism and Iran in the Eighteenth Century," in Naff and Owen, eds., *Islamic History*, 294.

61 Arjomand, *Shadow of God*, 215.

62 Algar, "Shi'ism and Iran," 292, 298.

63 John R. Perry, "Karim Khan Zand," *Encyclopaedia Iranica*, Vol. XV, 561–4.

64 John R. Perry, *Karim Khan Zand: A History of Iran, 1747–1779* (Chicago: University of Chicago Press, 1979), 221.

65 Arnold T. Wilson, *The Persian Gulf: An Historical Sketch from the Earliest Times to the Beginning of the Twentieth Century* (Oxford: Oxford University Press, 1928), 178–87.

66 Gelvin, *Modern Middle East*, 82.

67 John R. Perry, "Aga Mohammad Khan Qajar," *Encyclopaedia Iranica*, Vol. I, 602–5.

68 Nikki R. Keddie, *Modern Iran: Roots and Results of Revolution* (New Haven: Yale, 2006), 37; see also, Perry, "Aga Mohammad."

69 Katouzian, *The Persians*, 139.

70 Ibid., 140.

71 Elton L. Daniel, *The History of Iran* (Westport: Greenwood Press, 2001), 103.

72 Abbas Amanat, "Fath Ali Shah Qajar," *Encyclopaedia Iranica*, Vol. IX, 407–21.

73 Meir Litvak, "A Failed Manipulation: The British, the Oudh Bequest and the Shi'i 'ulama' of Najaf and Karbala'," *British Journal of Middle Eastern Studies*, Vol. 27, No. 1 (May 2000): 69–89.

74 See, for example, Katouzian, *The Persians*, 141.

75   John Foran, "The Concept of Dependent Development as a Key to the Political Economy of Qajar Iran (1800–1925)," *Iranian Studies*, Vol. 22, No. 2/3 (1989): 9.

76   Gelvin, *Modern Middle East*, 83.

77   See Elton L. Daniel, "The Golestan Treaty," *Encyclopaedia Iranica*, Vol. XI, 86–90.

78   Firuz Kazemzadeh, *Russia and Britain in Persia: Imperial Ambitions in Qajar Iran* (London: I.B.Tauris, 2013), 236–9. See also Charles Issawi, ed., *The Economic History of Iran: 1800–1914* (Chicago: University of Chicago Press, 1971), 184.

79   J. Calmard, "Anglo Persian War," *Encyclopaedia Iranica*, Vol. II, 65–8.

80   Foran, "Dependent Development," 11.

81   For imperialism in Iran during this period, see Kazemzadeh, *Russia and Britain*.

82   George N. Curzon, *Persia and the Persian Question*, Vol. 2 (London: Longman, Green and Co., 1892), 480.

83   For more on Nasir al-Din Shah, see Abbas Amanat, *Pivot of the Universe: Nasir al-Din Shah Qajar and the Iranian Monarchy, 1831–1896* (Berkeley: University of California Press, 1997).

84   Quoted in Nikki R. Keddie, *Roots of Revolution: An Interpretive History of Modern Iran* (New Haven: Yale University Press, 1981), 95–6.

85   Foran, "Dependent Development," 11. See also Chris Pain, "Iranian Nationalism and the Great Powers: 1872–1954," *MERIP Reports*, No. 37 (1975): 3–28, and R. W. Ferrier, *The History of the British Petroleum Company*, Vol. 1 (Cambridge: Cambridge University Press, 1982).

3. Shi'ism and the Emergence of Modern Iraq

1   Mohammad Salman Hasan, "The Growth and Structure of Iraq's Population, 1867–1947," *Bulletin of the Oxford University Institute of Economics and Stastistics* (1958): 344. See also Nakash, *Shi'is of Iraq*, 25.

2   According to a British census conducted in 1919, Shi'is were fifty-three percent of Iraq and by 1932 that number rose to fifty-six percent. Iranians accounted for five percent of the Shi'i population. See Yitzhak Nakash, "The Conversion of Iraq's Tribes to Shi'ism," *International Journal of Middle East Studies*, Vol. 26, No. 3 (August 1994): 443.

3   Hala Fattah, *The Politics of Regional Trade in Iraq, Arabia, and the Gulf: 1745–1900* (Albany: SUNY Press, 1997); Thabit A. J. Abdullah, *Merchants, Mamluks, and Murder: The Political Economy of Trade in Eighteenth Century Basra* (Albany: SUNY Press, 2001).

4   Fattah, *Politics of Regional Trade*, 1, 13. Compare this definition of frontier to the work of William H. McNeill, *Europe's Steppe Frontier, 1500–1800* (Chicago: University of Chicago Press, 1964), *The Great Frontier: Freedom and Hierarchy in Modern Times* (Princeton: Princeton University Press, 1983).

5   Hanna Batatu, *The Old Social Classes and the Revolutionary Movements in Iraq: A Study of Iraq's Old Landed and Commercial Classes and of its Communists, Ba'thists, and Free Officers* (Princeton: Princeton University Press, 1989), 8–9.

6   Thabit A. J. Abdullah, *A Short History of Iraq: From 636 to the Present* (Harlow: Pearson Education, 2003), 67.

7   Ibid., 74.

8   See, for example, Abdullah, *Short History*, 74; Ebubekir Ceylan, *The Ottoman Origins of Modern Iraq: Political Reform, Modernization and Development in the Nineteenth-Century Middle East* (London: I.B.Tauris, 2011), 26–9; Tom Nieuwenhuis, *Politics and Society in Early Modern Iraq: Mamluk Pashas, Tribal Shaykhs and Local Rule Between 1802 and 1831* (The Hague: Martinus Nijhoff Publishers, 1982), 75–6.

9   Ceylan, *Ottoman Origins*, 27.

10 Ibid., 29.

11 Nieuwenhuis, *Politics and Society*, 76.

12 Abdullah, *Short History*, 79.

13 For more on Basra, see Abdullah, *Merchants*; Willem Floor, *The Persian Gulf: A Political and Economic History of Five Port Cities, 1500–1730* (Washington, DC: Mage Publishers, 2006); Reidar Visser, *Basra, the Failed Gulf State: Separatism and Nationalism in Southern Iraq* (Munster: Lit Verlag, 2005).

14 Rudi Matthee, "Between Arabs, Turks and Iranians: The Town of Basra, 1600–1700," *Bulletin of the School of Oriental and African Studies*, Vol. 69, No. 1 (2006): 55.

15 Ibid., 53–78.

16 Ceylan, *Ottoman Origins*, 157. See also Abdullah, *Short History*, 78.

17 Nieuwenhuis, *Politics and Society*, 4.

18 Ibid., 5.

19 Ceylan, *Ottoman Origins*, 57.

20 For more on the Land Code, see Marion Farouk-Sluglett and Peter Sluglett, "The Transformation of Land Tenure and Rural Social Structure in Central and Southern Iraq, c. 1870–1958," *International Journal of Middle East Studies*, Vol. 15, No. 4 (Nov., 1983): 491–505.

21 See also Ehud Toledano, "The Emergence of Ottoman-Local Elites (1700–

1900): A framework for Research," in Ilan Pape and Moshe Ma'oz, eds., *Middle Eastern Politics and Ideas: A History from Within* (London: I.B.Tauris, 1997).

22   See Litvak, *Shiʻi Scholars*, 120–1.

23   Ceylan, *Ottoman Origins*, 38.

24   Ibid., 38–9.

25   Nieuwenhuis, *Politics and Society*, 25.

26   Ibid., 26.

27   Abdullah, *Merchants*, 25.

28   For more on the plague, see John T. Alexander, *Bubonic Plague in Early Modern Russia: Public Health and Urban Disaster* (Oxford: Oxford University Press, 2003); Michael W. Dols, "The Second Plague Pandemic and its Recurrences in the Middle East: 1347–1894," *Journal of the Economic and Social History of the Orient*, Vol. 22, No. 2 (May 1979): 162–89.

29   For a description of the siege, see Perry, *Karim Khan Zand*.

30   Ibid., 174.

31   Ibid., 192.

32   Ibid., 194.

33   A branch of the Muntafiq tribe, the Al Mughamis dynasty, had ruled Basra in the fifteenth century, prior to the first attempt of Ottomans to take the city. For more on the Muntafiq, see Peter Sluglett, "al-Muntafiq," *Encyclopaedia of Islam*, 2nd edn., P. Bearman et al., eds. Brill Online.

34   Perry, *Karim Khan Zand*, 194.

35   Abdullah, *Short History*, 87.

36   Litvak, *Shiʻi Scholars*, 120.

37   Abdullah, *Short History*, 90.

38   Stephen Hemsley Longrigg, *Four Centuries of Modern Iraq* (Oxford: Oxford University Press, 1925), 260. See also Ceylan, *Ottoman Origins*, 56.

39   For a primary source description, see Charles Issawi, ed., *The Fertile Crescent, 1800–1914: A Documentary History* (Oxford: Oxford University Press, 1988), 102.

40   Abdullah, *Short History*, 92.

41   Ibid., 91.

42   For more on *Tanzimat* in Iraq, see Ceylan, *Ottoman Origins*, chapter 4. See also Moshe Mo'az, *Ottoman Reform in Syria and Palestine, 1840–1861* (London: Oxford University Press, 1968).

43   Ceylan, *Ottoman Origins*, 19.

44   Farouk-Sluglett, "Transformation of Land Tenure," 493.

45 Muhammad Salman Hasan, "The Role of Foreign Trade in the Economic Development of Iraq, 1864–1964: A Study in the Growth of a Dependent Economy," in Michael Cook, ed., *Studies in the Economic History of Middle East: From the Rise of Islam to the Present Day* (London: Oxford University Press, 1970), 346–72.

46 Robert Fernea, *Shaykh and Effendi: Changing Patterns of Authority Among the El Shabana of Southern Iraq* (Cambridge: Harvard University Press, 1970), 1.

47 Farouk-Sluglett, "Transformation of Land Tenure," 493.

48 Hasan, "Iraq's Population," 339–52. See also Farouk-Sluglett, "Transformation of Land Tenure."

49 Farouk-Sluglett, "Transformation of Land Tenure," 495.

50 Ceylan, *Ottoman Origins*, 142.

51 Gokhan Cetinsaya, *Ottoman Administration of Iraq, 1890–1908* (New York: Routledge, 2006), 73. See also Charles Tripp, *A History of Iraq* (Cambridge: Cambridge University Press, 2007), 18.

52 Nieuwenhuis, *Politics and Society*, 31.

53 Ismail Safa Ustan, "The Ottoman Dilemma in Handling the Shi'i Challenge in Nineteenth Century Iraq," in Ofra Bengio and Meir Litvak, eds., *The Sunna and Shi'a in History: Division and Ecumenism in the Muslim Middle East* (New York: Palgrave Macmillan, 2011), 89; Litvak, *Shi'i Scholars*, 122.

54 Nieuwenhuis, *Politics and Society*, 31; Ceylan, *Ottoman Origins*, 54 and 243, fn. 55.

55 Ceylan, *Ottoman Origins*, 53–4.

56 Fattah, *Politics of Regional Trade*, 41.

57 Nakash, *Shi'is of Iraq*, 34.

58 Ibid., 27. For a list of converted tribes, see Ibrahim Fasih al-Haydari, *Unwan al-majd fi bayan ahwal Baghdad wa al-Basra wa al-Najd* (Baghdad, 1962), 110–15, 118.

59 Uwaidah M. al-Juhany, *Najd before the Salafi Movement: Social, Political, and Religious Conditions during the Three Centuries Preceding the Rise of the Saudi State* (London: Ithaca Press, 2002).

60 Longrigg, *Modern Iraq*, 217; Litvak, *Shi'i Scholars*, 121.

61 Nakash, *Shi'is of Iraq*, 28.

62 Litvak, *Shi'i Scholars*, 131.

63 Batatu, *The Old Social Classes*, 42.

64 Carsten Niebuhr, *Voyage en Arabie et en d'autres pays circonvoisins* (Amsterdam, 1780), 180, 220.

65 Tripp, *History of Iraq*, 12; Litvak, *Shi'i Scholars*, 130; Nakash, *Shi'is of Iraq*, 45; Jean-Pierre Luizard, *La Formation de l'Irak Contemporain: Le*

Role Politique des Ulema Chiites a la Fin de la Domination Ottomane et au Moment de la Construction de l'Etat Irakien (Paris: CNRS, 1991), 112.

66   Nakash, *Shi'is of Iraq*, 28.

67   Ibid., 46.

68   Nakash, "Conversion," 447.

69   Juan R. I. Cole, "'Indian Money' and the Shi'i Shrine Cities of Iraq, 1786–1850," *Middle Eastern Studies*, Vol. 22, No. 4 (October 1986): 463; See also Nakash, *Shi'is of Iraq*, 31.

70   Nieuwenhuis, *Politics and Society*, 130; Nakash, *Shi'is of Iraq*, 31.

71   Nakash, "Conversion," 448.

72   Batatu, *Old Social Classes*, 41–2; Litvak, *Shi'i Scholars*, 131.

73   Litvak, *Shi'i Scholars*, 152. An additional example is Muhammad Ibrahim from the prominent Usuli family of Bahr al-'Ulum, who married the daughter of Shaykh Satter of the Bani Hasan tribe. See Nakash, *Shi'is of Iraq*, 40.

74   Litvak, *Shi'i Scholars*, 132.

75   Nakash, *Shi'is of Iraq*, 46–7; Litvak, *Shi'i Scholars*, 133.

76   Litvak, *Shi'i Scholars*, 131–2.

77   Nakash, *Shi'is of Iraq*, 29; Litvak, *Shi'i Scholars*, 131.

78   Gokhan Cetinsaya, "Caliph and Mujtahids: Ottoman Policy towards the Shiite Community of Iraq in the Nineteenth Century," *Middle Eastern Studies*, Vol. 41, No. 4 (July 2005): 562. See also John Robert Barnes, *An Introduction to Religious Foundations in the Ottoman Empire* (Leiden: Brill, 1986), 67–153.

79   Quoted in Selim Deringil, "The Struggle against Shiism in Hamidian Iraq: A Study in Ottoman Counter-Propaganda," *Die Welt des Islams*, New Series, Bd. 30, Nr. ¼ (1990): 49.

80   Quoted in Cetinsaya, "Caliph and Mujtahids," 566.

81   Ibid., 564.

82   Ibid., 564–5.

4. Wahid Bihbihani: Shi'i Reviver and Reformer

1   MacEoin, *Messiah*, 47.

2   Zackery M. Heern, "Thou Shalt Emulate the Most Knowledgeable Living Cleric: Redefinition of Islamic Law and Authority in Usuli Shi'ism," *Journal of Shi'a Islamic Studies*, Vol. VII, No. 3 (Summer 2014): 321–44.

3   Arjomand, *Shadow of God*, 218, 246.

4   The work of Robert Gleave is an exception.

5   Some Shi'i sources, including the major biographical dictionaries of the

nineteenth century, claim that Bihbihani was the renewer of the thirteenth Islamic century since he lived until 1206 AH.

6   'Abdallah Mamaqani, *Nukhbat al-maqal*, unpublished. See Ahmad Bihbihani, *Mir'at al-ahwal jahan-nama* (Tehran: Amir Kabir, 1370), 146, and 'Ali Davani, *Aqa Muhammad Baqir Bin Muhammad Akmal Isfahani ma'ruf bih Vahid Bihbihani* (Tehran: Amir Kabir, 1983), 130.

7   Sayyid 'Ali Tabataba'i. Quoted in MacEoin, *Messiah*, 47.

8   Khwansari, *Rawdat*, 93.

9   Muhammad b. Sulayman Tunikabuni, *Qisas al-'ulama'* (Shiraz, 1964), 251.

10 Quoted in Wael Hallaq, "Was the Gate of Ijtihad Closed?" *International Journal of Middle East Studies*, 16 (1984), 27–8. For more on the Sunni tradition of *tajdid*, see Ella Landau-Tasseron, "The 'Cyclical Reform': A Study of the mujaddid Tradition," *Studia Islamica*, No. 70 (1989): 79–117.

11 Muhammad Khan Kirmani, *al-Kitab al-mubin* (Kirman: Chapkhana-yi Sa'adat, 1975), Vol. 1, 435. Quoted in MacEoin, *Messiah*, 20.

12 Muhammad b. 'Umar Kashhi, *Ikhtiyar ma'rifa al-rijal* (Mashhad: Danishgah-e Mashhad, 1969), 155. Quoted in Takim, *Heirs of the Prophet*, 81.

13 Bihbihani, *al-Akhbar wa al-ijtihad*, quoted in Davani, *Aqa Muhammad*, 129.

14 Landau-Tasseron, "Cylical Reform," 85–6.

15 Bihbihani's father, Muhammad Akmal Bihbihani, was Majlisi's student and married into the Majlisi family. Therefore, Wahid Bihbihani is a direct descendant of the Majlisi family through his mother. For a family tree that includes the Bihbihani, Majlisi families, and others, see Momen, *Shi'i Islam*, 132–3. See also Davani, *Aqa Muhammad*, 107.

16 Arjomand, *Shadow of God*, 217.

17 Khwansari, *Rawdat*, 331.

18 See Davani, *Aqa Muhammad*, 129.

19 Ibid., 95. Davani bases his claim that Bihbihani is a descendant of Shaykh al-Mufid on a notation from Sayyid Ja'far A'raji Kazimayni Baghdadi, *al-Asas fi insab al-nas*.

20 See McDermott, *Theology*.

21 Sayyid Muhammad Hasan Zunuzi, *Riyad al-jinna*, unpublished. Cited in Davani, *Aqa Muhammad*, 135.

22 MacEoin, *Messiah*, 43.

23 Ibid.

24 Muhammad 'Ali Mu'allim Habibabadi, *Makaraim al-athar*, Vol. 1 (Isfahan: Kamal, 1978), 231. Quoted in MacEoin, *Messiah*, 43.

25 Bihbihani, *Mir'at al-ahwal*, 147.

26 Ibid.

27 Litvak, *Shi'i Scholars*, 14.

28 Ibid., 148.

29 Zunuzi, *Riyad al-jinna*. Cited in Davani, *Aqa Muhammad*, 135.

30 Bihbihani, *Mir'at al-ahwal*, 148.

31 Quoted in Davani, *Aqa Muhammad*, 128.

32 Lockhart, *Nadir Shah*, 77–8.

33 Davani, *Aqa Muhammad*, 112.

34 Juan Cole, "Shi'i Clerics in Iran and Iraq, 1722–1780: The Akhbari-Usuli Controversy Reconsidered," *Iranian Studies*, 18:1 (1985): 16.

35 Davani, *Aqa Muhammad*, 120.

36 Bihbihani, *Mir'at al-ahwal*, 147.

37 Davani, *Aqa Muhammad*, 120.

38 Bihbihani, *Mir'at al-ahwal*, 147.

39 Davani, *Aqa Muhammad*, 121.

40 Ibid.

41 Litvak, *Shi'i Scholars*, 14.

42 Muhammad ibn Isma'il Abu 'Ali, *Muntaha al-maqal fi ahwal al-rijal* (Beirut: al-Mu'assasa, 1998). Quoted in Davani, *Aqa Muhammad*, 122.

43 Ibid.

44 Muhammad 'Ali Kashmiri, *Nujum al-sama'* (Lucknow: Lithograph, 1885), 204.

45 Khwansari, *Rawdat*, Vol. 2, 93. Quoted in Robert Gleave, "The Akhbari-Usuli Dispute in *Tabaqat* Literature: An Analysis of the Biographies of Yusuf al-Bahrani and Muhammad Baqir al-Bihbihani," *Jusur*, 10 (1994): 97.

46 Kashmiri, *Nujum*, 305. Abu 'Ali, *Muntaha*, 29. Khwansari, *Rawdat*, Vol. 2, 95. Quoted in Gleave, "Akhbari-Usuli Dispute," 97.

47 Davani, *Aqa Muhammad*, 122.

48 Ibid., 138.

49 'Ali Akbar Nahavardi, *Khazinat al-jawahir fi zinat al-manabir* (Tehran: Kitabfurushi-ye Islamiyeh, 1962–3). Quoted in Davani, *Aqa Muhammad*, 138.

50 Bihbihani, *Mir'at al-ahwal*, 151.

51 Ibid., 147.

52 Tunikabuni, *Qisas*, 251; Khwansari, *Rawdat*, Vol. 2, 95; Algar, *Religion and State*, 35.

53 Cole, "Shi'i Clerics," 19.

54 Juan R. I. Cole and Moojan Momen, "Mafia, Mob and Shi'ism in Iraq:

The Rebellion of Ottoman Karbala 1824–1843," *Past and Present*, No. 112 (August 1986): 112–43.

55 Algar, *Religion and State*, 19.

56 Juan Cole has already pointed out that after the fall of the Safavid dynasty many of the descendants of the Majlisi clerical dynasty adopted merchant professions and those that became clerics were closely allied with merchants. See Cole, "Shi'i Clerics."

57 Cole, "Shi'i Clerics," 11.

58 'Abdullah Mamaqani, *Tanqih al-maqal fi ahwal al-rijal* (Qum: Mu'assasat Al al-Bayt li-Ihya al-Turath, 2002). Quoted in Davani, *Aqa Muhammad*, 123.

59 Ibid.

60 Davani, *Aqa Muhammad*, 124.

61 Ibid.

62 Tunikabuni, *Qisas*, 264.

63 Ibid., 201. Quoted in Gleave, "Akhbari-Usuli Dispute," 100.

64 Muhaddath Qummi, *Fawa'id al-radhwiyya*, unpublished. Quoted in Davani, *Aqa Muhammad*, 124.

65 See Gleave, "Akhbari-Usuli Dispute."

66 Ibid., 99–100.

67 See Gleave, *Inevitable Doubt*.

68 Bahrani states that Astarabadi was "the first to open the door of reviling against the *mujtahids* [Usulis]," Yusuf ibn Ahmad al-Bahrani, *Lu'lu'at al-Bahrayn* (Najaf, 1966), 122. See also MacEoin, *Messiah*, 37; Etan Kohlberg, "Aspects of Akhbari Thought in Seventeenth and Eighteenth Centuries," in Nehemia Levtzion and John Olbert Voll, eds., *Eighteenth-Century Renewal and Reform in Islam* (New York: Syracuse University Press, 1987), 149.

69 For more on Samahiji, see Andrew J. Newman, "The Nature of the Akhbari/Usuli Dispute in Late Safawid Iran. Part 1: 'Abdallah al-Samahiji's "*Munyat al-Mumarisin*," *Bulletin of the School of Oriental and African Studies*, Vol. 55, No. 1 (1992): 22–51.

70 Kohlberg, "Aspects of Akhbari Thought."

71 Bihbihani, *Mir'at al-ahwal*, 152.

72 Cole, "Shi'i Clerics," 21–2.

73 Ibid., 22.

74 Cited in Algar, *Religion and State*, 35–6.

75 Tunikabuni, *Qisas*, 251.

76 Ibid., 252.

77 Ibid., 253.

78   Ibid., 251.

79   Ibid.

80   Ibid., 252.

81   Kashmiri, *Nujum*, 303.

82   For references to dreams attributed to Bihbihani, see Zunuzi, *Riyad al-jinna*, and Davani, *Aqa Muhammad*, 136–8.

83   Zunuzi, *Riyad al-jinna*. Quoted in Davani, *Aqa Muhammad*, 137.

84   Ibid.

85   Ibid.

86   Ibid.

87   Ibid.

88   Davani, *Aqa Muhammad*, 144.

89   Gleave, *Inevitable Doubt*, 14.

90   See Davani, *Aqa Muhammad*, 136.

91   See also Gleave, *Scripturalist Islam*, 303–4.

5. Bihbihani's Usuli Network In Iraq And Iran

1   Arjomand, *Shadow of God*, 242.

2   Juan R. Cole, "Imami Jurisprudence and the Role of the Ulama: Mortaza Ansari on Emulating the Supreme Exemplar," in Nikki R. Keddie, ed., *Religion and Politics in Iran: Shi'ism from Quietism to Revolution* (New Haven: Yale University Press, 1983), 46.

3   Arjomand, *Shadow of God*, 229–30.

4   According to Algar, the shah spent more than 100,000 tomans on shrines in Iraq and Iran. *Religion and State*, 46.

5   Andre Godard, *The Art of Iran* (New York: Praeger, 1965), 168. See also Algar, *Religion and State*, 47.

6   Rida Quli Khan Hidayat, *Ta'rikh-i rawdat al-safa-i nasiri dar dhikr padshahan-i dawra-i safaviyya afshariyya zandiyya qajariyya* (Qum, 1399). Quoted in Algar, *Religion and State*, 56.

7   Tunikabuni, *Qisas*, 93. See also Algar, *Religion and State*, 57.

8   According to Tunikabuni, Kashif al-Ghita's permission to allow the shah to rule was conditioned on the appointment of a prayer leader for each battalion of the Qajar army. He also required the troops to listen to a weekly sermon. *Qisas*, 141.

9   Algar, *Religion and State*, 57.

10   Bihbihani's grandson, for example, addresses Fath 'Ali Shah as "the august king, protector of the world, Shadow of God." See Arjomand, *Shadow of God*, 224.

11   Lambton, "Political Thought," 114.

12   Quoted in Lambton, "Jihad," 188.

13   Mulla Ahmad Naraqi, *'Awa'id al-ayyam* (Qum: Maktaba Basirati, 1903) 185, 188. Quoted in Ahmad Kazemi Moussavi, "The Establishment of the Position of Marja'yyat-i Taqlid in the Twelver-Shi'i Community," *Iranian Studies*, Vol. 18, No. 1 (Winter 1985): 41, 43.

14   Moussavi, *Religious Authority*, 155.

15   Algar, *Religion and State*, 12–13; Arjomand, *Shadow of God*, 220.

16   Arjomand, *Shadow of God*, 218.

17   D. M. MacEoin, "Changes in Charismatic Authority in Qajar Shi'ism," in Edmund Bosworth and Carole Hillenbrand, eds., *Qajar Iran: Political, Social and Cultural Change, 1800–1925* (Edinburgh: Edinburgh University Press, 1983), 164.

18   The declarations and treatises on *jihad* were compiled in a volume titled *Kitab al-jihadiyya*.

19   Lambton, "Jihad," 192. Arjomand relies on Lambton's assessment. See Arjomand, *Shadow of God*, 224.

20   Arjomand, *Shadow of God*, 225–6.

21   Robert Gleave, "Jihad and Religious Legitimacy of the Early Qajar State," in Robert Gleave, ed., *Religion and Society in Qajar Iran* (New York: Routledge, 2005): 42.

22   Ibid., 65.

23   Gleave, "Jihad," 47–8. See also Robert Gleave, "Two Classical Shi'i Theories of qada'," in G. Hawting, et al., eds., *Studies in Islamic and Middle Eastern Texts and Traditions in Memory of Norman Calder* (Oxford: Oxford University Press, 2000).

24   Litvak, *Shi'i Scholars*, 46.

25   For more on the relationship between Bahrani and Bahr al-'Ulum, see Robert Gleave, "The Ijaza from Yusuf al-Bahrani (d. 1186/1772) to Sayyid Muhammad Mahdi Bahr al-'Ulum (d. 1212/1797-8)," *Iran*, Vol. 32 (1994): 115–23.

26   Tunikabuni, *Qisas*, 213.

27   Vera B. Moreen, "A Shi'i-Jewish 'Debate' (Munazara) in the Eighteenth Century," *Journal of the American Oriental Society*, Vol. 119, No. 4 (October – December 1999): 570–89.

28   Muhsin al-Amin 'Amili, *al-Shi'a fi masarihim al-tarikhi: muqaddimat A'yan al-Shi'a* (Beirut: Markaz al-Ghadir li al-darasat al-Islamiyya, 2000), Vol. 58, 165. Quoted in Litvak, *Shi'i Scholars*, 47.

29   Quoted in Litvak, *Shi'i Scholars*, 47.

30   The following are among Bahr al-'Ulum's students: Kashif al-Ghita',

Mulla Ahmad Naraqi, Muhammad Ibrahim Kalbasi, and Shaykh Ahmad al-Ahsa'i.

31 Litvak, *Shi'i Scholars*, 47.

32 Ibid., 48.

33 Kashmiri, *Nujum*, 316–17.

34 Quoted in Davani, *Aqa Muhammad*, 195.

35 His list of students includes some of Bihbihani's younger students as well as some of the most prominent scholars that carried on Bihbihani's school of thought into the next generation. Among Kashif al-Ghita's students were Muhammad Baqir Shafti, Muhammad Ibrahim Kalbasi, Shaykh Muhammad Hasan Najafi, Sayyid Sadr al-Din Musavi 'Amili, and Shaykh Muhammad Taqi Isfahani.

36 Davani, *Aqa Muhammad*, 257–64.

37 Moussavi, *Religious Authority*, 37. See also Litvak, *Shi'i Scholars*, 49.

38 Abdulaziz A. Sachedina, *The Just Ruler in Shi'ite Islam: The Comprehensive Authority of the Jurist in Imamite Jurisprudence* (New York: Oxford University Press, 1988), 22.

39 Tunikabuni, *Qisas*, 141.

40 Abdul-Hadi Hairi, "The Legitimacy of the Early Qajar Rule as Viewed by the Shi'i Religious Leaders," *Middle Eastern Studies*, Vol. 24, No. 3 (July 1988): 277.

41 Davani, *Aqa Muhammad*, 195. See also Bihbihani, *Mir'at al-ahwal*.

42 *Manhaj al-rashad li-man arada al-sadad* (Najaf: 1925).

43 Meir Litvak, "Encounters between Shi'i and Sunni 'Ulama' in Ottoman Iraq," in Ofra Bengio and Meir Litvak, eds., *The Sunna and Shi'a in History: Division and Ecumenism in the Muslim Middle East* (New York: Palgrave Macmillan, 2011).

44 Ann K. S. Lambton, *State and Government in Medieval Islam: An Introduction to the Study of Islamic Political Theory* (Oxford: Oxford University Press, 1981), 247–8; Arjomand, *Shadow of God*, 231.

45 Litvak, *Shi'i Scholars*, 124.

46 Davani, *Aqa Muhammad*, 196.

47 Ibid., 200.

48 Algar, *Religion and State*, 65–6.

49 Zunuzi, *Riyad al-jinna*. Cited in Davani, *Aqa Muhammad*, 187.

50 Meir Litvak, "The Finances of the 'ulama' Communities of Najaf and Karbala', 1796–1904," *Die Welt des Islams*, new series Vol. 40, Issue 1 (March 2000): 47.

51 Juan Cole, "Indian Money," 465.

52 Litvak, "Finances," 47.

53 Litvak, *Shi'i Scholars*, 50.

54 Ibid.

55 Ibid.

56 Khwansari, *Rawdat*. Cited in Davani, *Aqa Muhammad*, 191.

57 Tunikabuni, *Qisas*. Quoted in Davani, *Aqa Muhammad*, 202.

58 See Momen, *Shi'i Islam*, 194; Arjomand, *Shadow of God*, 225–9.

59 Lambton, "Political Thought." See also Arjomand, *Shadow of God*, 223.

60 Quoted in Hairi, "Legitimacy," 273.

61 Ibid., 272–5.

62 Ibid., 275.

63 Davani, *Aqa Muhammad*, 204.

64 Mirza Abu al-Qasim Qummi, *Qawanin al-usul* (Tehran, 1958), 239–412.

65 Quoted in Moussavi, *Religious Authority*, 195.

66 Qummi, *Qawanin*, 384.

67 Moussavi, *Religious Authority*, 190–1.

68 Qummi, *Qawanin*, 356, 373. See also Moussavi, *Religious Authority*, 191.

69 Mulla Ahmad Naraqi, *Mi'raj al-Sa'ada* (Tehran, 1864), 358–60. See also Hairi, "Legitimacy," 278.

70 Ibid.

71 Hairi, "Legitimacy," 278.

72 Naraqi, *'Awa'id*, 185. Quoted in Hairi, "Legitimacy," 279.

73 Quoted in Hairi, "Legitimacy," 279.

74 Hairi, "Legitimacy," 279.

75 Naraqi, *'Awa'id*, 151.

76 Naraqi, *'Awa'id*, 189. Quoted in Moussavi, *Religious Authority*, 154.

77 For more on Naraqi's influence on Khomeini, see Vanessa Martin, *Creating an Islamic State: Khomeini and the Making of a New Iran* (London: I.B.Tauris, 2000), 117.

78 Moussavi, *Religious Authority*, 272–3.

79 Quoted in Algar, *Religion and State*, 62.

80 Algar, *Religion and State*, 89.

81 Tunikabuni, *Qisas*. Cited in Davani, *Aqa Muhammad*, 227.

82 Arjomand and Moussavi suggest that Shafti was the first to take the title of *Hujjat al-Islam*. *Shadow of God*, 238; *Religious Authority*, 210–1.

83 Tunikabuni, *Qisas*, 103.

84 Walbridge, *Most Learned*, 60–1.

85 Tunikabuni, *Qisas*, 104–9. See also Roy Mottahedeh, *The Mantle of the Prophet: Religion and Politics in Iran* (Oxford: Oneworld Publications, 2002), 207; Algar, *Religion and State*, 60–1.

86 Moussavi, *Religious Authority*, 239.

87 See Walbridge, *Most Learned*, 61.

88 Quoted in Deringil, "Struggle against Shiism," 49–50.

89 Algar, *Religion and State*, 61.

90 Mottahedeh, *Mantle*, 207–10.

91 Khwansari, *Rawdat*, Vol. 2, 294. See also Moussavi, *Religious Authority*, 129.

92 Arjomand, *Shadow of God*, 223.

93 See Litvak, *Shi'i Scholars*, 52–3.

94 Tunikabuni, *Qisas*, 104–5.

95 Arjomand, *Shadow of God*, 239.

96 Hasan Fasa'i, *History of Persia under Qajar Rule*, trans. Heribert Busse (New York: Columbia University Press, 1972), 233.

97 Tunikabuni, *Qisas*, 110; Arjomand, *Shadow of God*, 243; Moussavi, *Religious Authority*, 128, 257.

98 See Algar, *Religion and State*, 109–12; Arjomand, *Shadow of God*, 243.

99 Tunikabuni, *Qisas*, 106; Arjomand, *Shadow of God*, 239.

100 Habibabadi, *Makarim al-athar*, Vol. 1, 231–3.

101 Davani, *Aqa Muhammad*, 169–252.

102 For more on these scholars, see also Khwansari, *Rawdat*; Tunikabuni, *Qisas*; Kashmiri, *Nujum*.

6. Bihbihani's Conception of Islamic Law

1 Wahid Bihbihani, *al-Fawa'id al-ha'iriyya* (Qum: Maja' al-Fikr al-Islami, 1995), 130.

2 Ibid.

3 For more on the closing of the gate of *ijtihad*, see Wael Hallaq who argues from a historical perspective that "the gate of ijtihad was not closed in theory nor in practice." "Gate of Ijtihad," 4.

4 Bihbihani, *Fawa'id*, 142.

5 Ibid., 91.

6 Ibid.

7 Ibid., 93.

8 See Bihbihani, *Fawa'id*, 207–29. See also Gleave, *Inevitable Doubt*, 137–44.

9 Bihbihani, *Fawa'id*, 93.

10 Ibid., 94.

11 Bernard G. Weiss, *The Spirit of Islamic Law* (Athens: University of Georgia Press, 1998), 120.

12 *Qur'an*, 5:47, trans., Arberry.

13 Bihbihani, *Fawa'id*, 93.

14 Ibid., 284.

15 *Qur'an*, 17:32, Bihbihani, *Fawa'id*, 285.

16 Bihbihani, *Fawa'id*, 284.

17 This is the primary subject of section (*fa'ida*) 28 of *Fawa'id*, 283–7.

18 Ibid., 283.

19 Ibid., 284.

20 Ibid., 286. Robert Gleave translates Bihbihani's position on the Qur'an as follows: "It is clear from the many *akhbar* that [corruption] occurred … Our position is that it is permitted to act upon one of the famous seven variants [of the Qur'an]. The indicator for this position is the statement, or rather the order, of the Imams that 'You must recite as the people recite until the day of the return of the *qa'im*'." *Inevitable Doubt*, 64–5.

21 Bihbihani, *Fawa'id*, 286.

22 Gleave, *Inevitable Doubt*, 65.

23 Bihbihani, *Fawa'id*, 284.

24 Ibid., 284, 316.

25 Ibid., 317.

26 Ibid., 118.

27 Ibid.

28 Ibid.

29 Ibid., 119.

30 Gleave, *Inevitable Doubt*, 69.

31 Bihbihani, *Fawa'id*, 284.

32 Ibid.

33 Ibid., 285.

34 Gleave, *Inevitable Doubt*, 163.

35 Bihbihani, *Fawa'id*, 119.

36 Ibid., 140.

37 Ibid., 296.

38 Ibid., 298.

39 Ibid., 297–8.

40 Ibid., 299.

41 Ibid.

42 Ibid., 302.

43 Ibid., 314.

44 Gleave, *Inevitable Doubt*, 81–2.

45 Bihbihani, *Fawa'id*, 109.

46 Ibid., 96.

47 Gleave, *Inevitable Doubt*, 205.

48   Ibid., 206.

49   Ibid., 207.

50   Ibid., 208.

51   Ibid., 211.

52   Ibid., 212.

53   Ibid., 215.

54   Ibid., 216.

55   Ibid., 209.

56   Ibid., 214.

57   Ibid., 215.

58   Norman Calder, "Doubt and Prerogative: The Emergence of an Imami Shi'i Theory of Ijtihad," *Studia Islamica*, 70 (1989): 57–78.

59   Gleave points out that Yusuf al-Bahrani and Bihbihani agree on this issue. See *Inevitable Doubt*, 130.

60   Gleave, *Inevitable Doubt*, 130.

61   These principles have already been listed by Gleave, but he does not divide them into categories as they are here. See *Inevitable Doubt*, 131–2.

62   Bihbihani, *Fawa'id*, 147.

63   Ibid., 149.

64   Ibid., 97.

65   Ibid., 105.

66   Ibid.

67   Bihbihani makes this argument in several places: *al-Rasa'il al-usuliyya* (Qum, 1416). Qum, 1416. 29; *Hashiyya majma' al-fa'ida wa al-burhan* (Qum. al-Mu'assasa. 1996), 24; *Hashiyyat al-Wafi* (Qum: al-Mu'assasa, 2005), 205; *Fawa'id*, 106.

68   Abu Zayd Tusit Muhammad Taqi Karami, *Majal-i nuqd wa nazar*, 412. Karami explains that texts can easily be understood through textual and cultural context and the rational faculty.

69   Bihbihani, *Usuliyya*, 474.

70   Ibid., 21.

71   Bihbihani, *Fawa'id*, 145.

72   Ibid., 109.

73   Ibid., 154.

74   Ibid., 155.

75   Ibid., 146, 154.

76   Ibid., 201.

77   Ibid., 113.

78   Ibid., 109.

79   Bihbihani, *Usuliyya*, 29.

80 Bihbihani, *al-Risa'il al-fiqhiyya*, unpublished, 90.

81 Bihbihani, *Fawa'id*, 95–7.

82 Bihbihani, *Fiqhiyya*, 104.

83 See similar explanations in Ruhullah Khomeini, *al-Bi'* (Iran: Wizarat al-Thaqafah wa-al-Irshad, 1987), 381; Said Muhammad Taqi, *al-Usul al-'amma lil-fiq al-maqarin*, 422; Shahid al-Thani, *al-Rawdha al-bahiyya fi sharh al-lam'a al-damashqiyya*, 64.

84 Bihbihani, *Fawa'id*, 106. Italics mine.

85 Shaykh Muhammad Hasan Najafi, *Jawahir al-kalam fi Sharh Shara'i' al-Islam*, Abbas al-Quchani, ed. 23 vols (Tehran: Dar al-Kutub al-Islamiyya, 1972), Vol. 1, 189, 323.

86 Bihbihani, *Fawa'id*, 107, 114.

87 Gleave, *Inevitable Doubt*, 164, and Bihbihani, *Fawa'id*, 168.

88 Bihbihani, *Fawa'id*, 100.

89 Gleave, *Inevitable Doubt*, 26, and Bihbihani, *Fawa'id*, 98.

90 Bihbihani, *Fawa'id*, 98. See also Gleave, *Inevitable Doubt*, 217.

91 Ibid., 127–8.

92 Ibid., 276.

93 Ibid., 136.

94 Ibid., 138.

7. Founding Fathers of Modern Islam

1 Commins, *Wahhabi Mission*; Natana J. Delong-Bas, *Wahhabi Islam: From Revival and Reform to Global Jihad* (New York: Oxford University Press, 2004); George S. Rentz, *The Birth of the Islamic Reform Movement in Saudi Arabia* (London: Arabian Publishing, 2004); Abd Allah Salih al-'Uthaymin, *Muhammad Ibn 'Abd al-Wahhab: The Man and his Works* (London: I.B.Tauris, 2009); Hamid Algar, *Wahhabism: A Critical Essay* (Oneonta: Islamic Publication International, 2002).

2 O'Fahey, *Enigmatic Saint*; Einar Thomassen and Bernd Radtke, eds., *The Letters of Ahmad Ibn Idris* (Evanston: NorthWestern University Press, 1993); Rex S. O'Fahey and Ali Salih Karrar, "The Enigmatic Imam: The Influence of Ahmad Ibn Idris," *International Journal of Middle East Studies*, Vol. 19, No. 2 (May 1987): 205–19.

3 See John Voll, "Muhammad Hayya al-Sindi and Muhammad ibn 'Abd al-Wahhab: An Analysis of an Intellectual Group in Eighteenth-Century Madina," *Bulletin of the School of Oriental and African Studies*, University of London, Vol. 38, No. 1 (1975): 32–9.

4 Ahmad Dallal, "The Origins and Objectives of Islamic Revivalist Thought,

1750–1850," *Journal of the American Oriental Society*, Vol. 113, No. 3 (1993): 341.

5   Fazlur Rahman, *Islam* (Chicago: University of Chicago Press, 1979).

6   Esposito, *Islam and Politics.*

7   John O. Voll, "Linking Groups in the Networks of Eighteenth-Century Revivalist Scholars: The Mizjaji Family in Yemen," in Levtzion and Voll, *Eighteenth-Century Renewal*; Voll, *Islam.*

8   Dallal, "The Origins," 341.

9   John Voll, "The Sudanese Mahdi: Frontier Fundamentalist," *International Journal of Middle East Studies*, Vol. 10, No. 2 (May 1979): 159.

10   George Makdisi, "Ibn Taymiyya: A Sufi of the Qadiriya Order," *American Journal of Arabic Studies*, I (1973): 119.

11   See Donald P. Little, "Did Ibn Taymiyya Have a Screw Loose?" *Studia Islamica*, No. 41 (1975): 93–111.

12   'Uthaymin, *Ibn 'Abd al-Wahhab*, 28.

13   Quoted in 'Uthaymin, *Ibn 'Abd al-Wahhab*, 35.

14   'Uthaymin, *Ibn 'Abd al-Wahhab*, 36.

15   Michael Cook, "On the Origins of Wahhabism," *Journal of the Royal Asiatic Society*, Third Series, Vol. 2, No. 2 (July 1992): 202; Commins, *Wahhabi Mission*, 12.

16   Quoted in Hamid Algar, *Wahhabism*, 6.

17   O'Fahey, *Enigmatic Saint*, 21, 105.

18   Abou El Fadl, *The Great Theft*, 45.

19   Delong-Bas, *Wahhabi Islam*. That a portion of the funding for this book came from the King Abd al-Aziz Foundation for Research and Archives may indicate why Delong-Bas takes a pro-Wahhabi slant. See the preface of the book for details. For a more even-handed history of Wahhabism, see Commins, *Wahhabi Mission.*

20   Delong-Bas, *Wahhabi Islam*, 5.

21   Ibid.

22   Ibid.

23   O'Fahey, *Enigmatic Saint*, 9.

24   O'Fahey, "The Enigmatic Imam," 205.

25   See, for example, Trimingham's section on "movements deriving from Ahmad Ibn Idris." J. Spencer Trimingham, *The Sufi Orders In Islam* (Oxford: Oxford University Press, 1971), 114–21.

26   Sedgwick, *Saints and Sons*, 12–17.

27   See, for example, Bernd Radtke, "Sufism in the 18th Century: An Attempt at a Provisional Appraisal," *Die Welt des Islams*, New Series, Vol. 36, Issue 3 (November 1996): 326–64.

28 O'Fahey, *Enigmatic Saint*, 38.

29 For additional trends within the Shadhiliyya tradition, see P. Lory, "Shadhiliyya," *Encyclopaedia of Islam*, 2nd edn. online version, P. Bearman, et al., eds. 2010.

30 Hasan Makki, *al-Sayyid Ahmad ibn Idris al-Fasi* (Khartoum: al-Markaz al-Islami al-Ifriqi bi al-Khartoum, 1986).

31 Makki's assessment is similar to the Enlightenment definition of rationality, which equates rationality with nature and Illuminationism with the supernatural. Since Ibn Idris rejected such a division between the natural and supernatural, it seems more correct to suggest that Ibn Idris embraced the notion that rationality includes both the natural universe and the divine.

32 Makki, *Sayyid Ahmad*, 21.

33 Thomassen, *Letters*, 168–9.

34 See discussion in Bernd Radtke, et al., *The Exoteric Ahmad Ibn Idris: A Sufi's Critique of the Madhahib and the Wahhabis* (Leiden: Brill, 2000), 27–8.

35 Quoted in O'Fahey, *Enigmatic Saint*, 74.

36 Radtke, *Exoteric*, 28.

37 A. Le Chatelier, *Les Conferies Musulmanes du Hedjaz* (Paris, 1887), 97.

38 Rahman, *Islam*, 206.

39 Valerie J. Hoffman, "Annihilation in the Messenger of God: The Development of a Sufi Practice," *International Journal of Middle East Studies*, Vol. 31, No. 3 (August 1999): 351–69.

40 Voll, *Islam*, 27–9.

41 O'Fahey, *Enigmatic Saint*, 4.

42 Sedgwick, *Saints and Sons*, xi.

43 'Uthaymin, *Ibn 'Abd al-Wahhab*, 39–41; Delong-Bas, *Wahhabi Islam*, 23.

44 See, for example, Michael H. Fisher, "Political Marriage Alliances at the Shi'i Court of Awadh," *Comparative Studies in Society and History*, Vol. 25, No. 4 (October 1983): 593–616.

45 'Uthaymin, *Ibn 'Abd al-Wahhab*, 49–50.

46 Delong-Bas, *Wahhabi Islam*, 34–5; 'Uthaymin, *Ibn 'Abd al-Wahhab*, 55.

47 Uthman Ibn Bishr, *Unwan al-Majd fi tarikh Najd*, Vol. 1, 'Abd al-Rahman 'Abd al-Latif bin 'Abdullah Al al-Shaykh, ed. (Riyadh: Matbu'at Darat al-Malik 'Abd al-Aziz, 1982), 36. See also 'Uthaymin, *Ibn 'Abd al-Wahhab*, 73–4.

48 'Uthaymin, *Ibn 'Abd al-Wahhab*, 58–66.

49 Commins, *Wahhabi Mission*, 24–5.

50 O'Fahey, *Enigmatic Saint*, 7.

51 Anne K. Bang, *The Idrisi State in 'Asir 1906–1934: Politics, Religion and Prestige in Arabia* (London: Hurst, 1997).

52   Knut S. Vikor, *Sufi and Scholar on the Desert Edge: Muhammad b. 'Ali al-Sanusi and his Brotherhood* (Evanston: Northwestern University Press, 1995), 1; See also E. E. Evans-Pritchard, *The Sanusi of Cyrenaica* (London: Oxford University Press, 1949).

53   Sedgwick, *Saints and Sons*, 61.

54   Ali Salih Karrar, *Sufi Brotherhoods in the Sudan* (London: Hurst, 1992); Sedgwick, *Saints and Sons*, 62–3.

55   See Delong-Bas, *Wahhabi Islam*, 101–5 for a lengthier discussion on *maslaha* and *naskh*.

56   Muhammad Ibn 'Abd al-Wahhab, "Kitab al-Nikah," in *Mu'allafat al-Shaykh al-Imam Muhammad Ibn 'Abd al-Wahhab*, Vol. 2 (Riyadh: Jami'at al-Imam Muhammad bin Saud al-Islamiyya, 1298), 670.

57   Ibn 'Abd al-Wahhab, "Fatwa wa masa'il," in *Mu'allafat*, Vol. 3, 24.

58   Ibid., 23.

59   Delong-Bas, *Wahhabi Islam*, 109.

60   Ibn 'Abd al-Wahhab, "Fatwa wa masa'il," 38.

61   Ibn 'Abd al-Wahhab, "Risala fi al-radd 'ala al-rafidah," in *Mu'allafat*, Vol. 4, 29.

62   Ibn 'Abd al-Wahhab, *Kitab al-tawhid*, trans. Ismail al-Faruqi (Kuwait: al-Faisal Printing, 1986).

63   Fazlur Rahman, "Some Key Ethical Concepts of the Qur'an," *The Journal of Religious Ethics*, Vol. 11, No. 2 (Fall 1983): 178.

64   Ibid., 14.

65   Ahmad Ibn Idris al-Fasi, *Risalat al-radd 'ala ahl al-ra'y*, unpublished, 3.

66   Ibn Idris, *Risalat al-radd*, 6; Sedgwick, *Saints and Sons*, 15.

67   Ibn Idris, *Risalat al-radd 'ala ahl al-ra'y* (unpublished), #3.

68   Ibn Idris, *Risalat al-radd*, #16.

69   Quoted in O'Fahey, "Enigmatic Imam," 209.

70   Ibn Idris, *Risalat al-radd*, #5.

71   Mohammad Ali Amir-Moezzi, *The Spirituality of Shi'i Islam: Beliefs and Practices* (London: I.B.Tauris, 2011), xiii.

72   O'Fahey, *Enigmatic Saint*, 26; Ahmad Ibn Idris, *al-'Iqd al-nafs fi nazm jawahir al-tadris Sayyid Ahmad ibn Idris* (Cairo: Mustafa al-Babi al-Halabi, 1979), 20.

73   See Radtke, "Sufism," 14.

74   Ibn Idris, *Risalat al-radd*, # 26.

75   Commins, *Wahhabi Mission*, 12.

76   See Esther Peskes, "The Wahabiyya and Sufism in the Eighteenth Century," in Frederick De Jong and Bernd Radtke, eds., *Islamic Mysticism Contested: Thirteen Centuries of Controversies and Polemics* (Leiden: Brill, 1999).

77   Davani, *Aqa Muhammad*, 127.

78   Nasrollah Pourjavady and Peter Lamborn Wilson, *Kings of Love: The Poetry and History of the Ni'matullahi Sufi Order* (Tehran: Imperial Iranian Academy of Philosophy, 1978), 128–131. Muhammad 'Ali is also known for his polemics against Judaism and Christianity. See Reza Pourjavady and Sabine Schmidtke, "Muslim Polemics Against Judaism and Christianity in 18th Century Iran: The Literary Sources of Aqa Muhammad Ali Bihbihani's (1144/1732–1216/1801) *Radd-i Shubuhat al-Kuffar*." *Studia Iranica*, 35, (2006): 893–924.

79   See Algar, *Religion and State*, 39.

80   Quoted in O'Fahey, "The Enigmatic Imam," 208.

81   O'Fahey, *Enigmatic Saint*, 69.

82   Sedgwick, *Saints and Sons*, 72; Karrar, *Sufi Brotherhoods*, 107.

83   Commins, *Wahhabi Mission*, 3.

84   Ibn Bishr, *Unwan*, 44–6.

85   Delong-Bas, *Wahhabi Islam*, 30.

86   'Uthaymin, *Ibn 'Abd al-Wahhab*, 42.

87   For different interpretations of these events, see Delong-Bas, *Wahhabi Islam*, 27–8; 'Uthaymin, *Ibn 'Abd al-Wahhab*, 44; Commins, *Wahhabi Mission*, 18.

88   'Uthaymin, *Ibn 'Abd al-Wahhab*, 49, 68.

BIBLIOGRAPHY

Abdullah, Thabit A. J. *Merchants, Mamluks, and Murder: The Political Economy of Trade in Eighteenth Century Basra*. Albany: SUNY Press, 2001.

———. *A Short History of Iraq: From 636 to the Present*. Harlow: Pearson Education, 2003.

Abisaab, Rula Jurdi. *Converting Persia: Religion and Power in the Safavid Empire*. London: I.B.Tauris, 2004.

Abou El Fadl, Khalid. *The Great Theft: Wrestling Islam from the Extremists*. New York: HarperCollins, 2007.

Abrahamian, Ervand. *Iran between Two Revolutions*. Princeton: Princeton University Press, 1981.

Abraham, Marcus. *The Middle East on the Eve of Modernity: Aleppo in the Eighteenth Century*. New York: Columbia University Press, 1989.

Abu 'Ali, Muhammad ibn Isma'il. *Muntaha al-maqal fi ahwal al-rijal*. Beirut: al-Mu'assasa, 1998.

Abu-Lughod, Janet L. *Before European Hegemony: The World System A. D. 1250–1350*. Oxford: Oxford University Press, 1989.

Abu Zahra, Muhammad. *Muhadarat fi usul al-fiqh al-ja'fari*. Cairo: Dirasat al-'Arabiyya, 1956.

Abu Zahra, Nadia. *The Pure and Powerful: Studies in Contemporary Muslim Society*. New York: Ithaca Press, 2001.

Adamiyat, Fereydun. *Andisha-yi Mirza Fath 'Ali Akhundzada*. Tehran: Amir Kabir, 1970.

Aghaie, Kamran Scot. *The Martyrs of Karbala: Shi'i Symbols and Rituals in Modern Iran*. Seattle: University of Washington Press, 2004.

Akhavi, Shahrough. *Religion and Politics in Contemporary Iran: Clergy-State Relations in the Pahlavi Period*. Albany: SUNY Press, 1980.

'Akish, Hasan. *Munazarat Ahmad ibn Idris ma' fuqaha 'Asir*. 'Abd Allah Abu Dahish, ed. Jiddah: Dar al-Madani, 1986.

Alexander, John T. *Bubonic Plague in Early Modern Russia: Public Health and Urban Disaster*. Oxford: Oxford University Press, 2003.

Algar, Hamid. *Mirza Malkum Khan: A Biographical Study in Iranian Modernism*. Berkeley: University of California Press, 1973.

———. *Religion and State in Iran 1785 – 1906: The Role of the Ulama in the Qajar Period*. Berkeley: University of California Press, 1969.

——. "Shi'ism and Iran in the Eighteenth Century." In *Studies in Eighteenth-Century Islamic History*, Thomas Naff and Roger Owen, eds. Carbondale: Southern Illinois University Press, 1977.

——. *Wahhabism: A Critical Essay*. Oneonta: Islamic Publication International, 2002.

'Ali, Nur al-Din. *Bahr al-'Ulum*. Translated by Kamal al-Sayyid. Qum: Sadr, 1995.

Allawi, Ali A. *The Crisis of Islamic Civilization*. New Haven: Yale University Press, 2009.

Allouche, Adel. *The Origins and Development of the Ottoman-Safavid Conflict (906–962/1500–1555)*. Berlin: Klaus Schwarz Verlag, 1983.

Amanat, Abbas. *Apocalyptic Islam and Iranian Shi'ism*. London: I.B.Tauris, 2009.

——. "In Between the Madrasa and the Market Place: The Designation of Clerical Leadership in Modern Shi'ism." In *Authority and Political Culture in Shi'ism*, Said Amir Arjomand, ed. Albany: SUNY Press, 1988.

——. "Fath Ali Shah Qajar." *Encyclopaedia Iranica* Vol. IX, 407–421.

——. *Pivot of the Universe: Nasir al-Din Shah Qajar and the Iranian Monarchy, 1831–1896*. Berkeley: University of California Press, 1997.

——. *Resurrection and Renewal: The Making of the Babi Movement in Iran*. Ithaca: Cornell University Press, 1989.

'Amili, Muhsin al-Amin. *al-Shi'a fi masarihim al-tarikhi: muqaddimat A'yan al-Shi'a*. 60 vols. Beirut: Markaz al-Ghadir li al-Darasat al-Islamiyya, 2000.

Amin, Samir. *Eurocentrism*. New York: Monthly Review Press, 1989.

Amir-Moezzi, Mohammad Ali. *Divine Guide in Early Shi'ism: The Sources of Esotericism in Islam*. Albany: SUNY Press, 1994.

——. *The Spirituality of Shi'i Islam: Beliefs and Practices*. London: I.B.Tauris, 2011.

Amuli, Haydar. *Jami' al-Asrar*. Henry Corbin and Osman Yahya, eds. Tehran: L'Institut Franco-Iranien de Recherche, 1969.

——. *La Philosophie Shi'ite*. Henry Corbin and Osman Yahia, eds. Bibliothèque Iranienne, No. 16. Tehran and Paris: L'Institut Franco-Iranien de Recherche, 1969.

Amr, Yusuf Muhammad. *al-Madkhal ila usul al-fiqh al-ja'fari*. Beirut: Dar al-Zahra, 1981.

Ansari, Murtada b. Muhammad Amin. *al-Makasib*. Tabriz: Math'at Ittila'at, 1955.

——. *Sirat al-najat*. Iran: Hajj 'Ali Akbar, 1883.

——. *Turath al-shaykh al-a'zam: Fara'id al-usul*. 24 vols, Qum: Majma' al-Fikr al-Islami, 1994.

Ansari, Murtada b. Muhammad Ja'far. *Zendagani va shakhsiyyat-e Shaykh Ansari*. Qum: Kungrih-i Shaykh-i A'zam Ansari, 1960.

Appadurai, Arjun. *Modernity at Large: Cultural Dimensions of Globalization*. Minneapolis: University of Minnesota Press, 1996.

Arjomand, Kamran Amir. *Katalog der Bibliothek des Schiitischen Schrifttums im Orientalischen Seminar der Universitat zu Koln*. Munchen: K.G. Saur, 1996.

Arjomand, Said Amir, ed. *Authority and Political Culture in Shi'ism*. Albany: SUNY Press, 1988.

——. "The Clerical Estate and the Emergence of a Shi'ite Hierocracy in Safavid Iran: A Study in Historical Sociology." *Journal of the Economic and Social History of the Orient* Vol. 28, No. 2 (1985): 169–219.

——. "History, Structure, and Revolution in the Shi'ite Tradition in Contemporary Iran." *International Political Science Review/Revue internationale de science politique* Vol. 10, No. 2, The Historical Framework of Revolutions / Le contexte historique des révolutions (April 1989): 111–119.

——. "The Office of the Mulla-Bashi in Shi'ite Iran." *Studia Islamica* 57 (1983): 135–146.

——. "Religious Extremism (Ghuluww), Sufism, and Sunnism in Safavid Iran: 1501–1722." *Journal of Asian History* 15 (1981): 24–8.

——. *The Shadow of God and the Hidden Imam: Religion, Political Order, and Societal Change in Shi'ite Iran from the Beginning to 1890*. Chicago: University of Chicago Press, 1984.

——. "The Shiite Hierocracy and the State in Pre-Modern Iran: 1785–1890." *Archives of European Sociology* 22 (1981): 40–78.

——. *The Turban for the Crown: The Islamic Revolution in Iran*. Oxford: Oxford University Press, 1988.

Asifi, Muhammad Mahdi. *Madrasat al-Najaf wa-tatawwur al-haraka al-'ilmiyya fi-ha*. Najaf, 1964.

al-Astarabadi, Muhammad Amin. *Al-Fawa'id al-madaniyya*. Qum: Mu'assasat al-Nashr al-Islami, 1424.

Avery, Peter. "Nadir Shah and the Afsharid Legacy." In *From Nadir Shah to the Islamic Republic*. Peter Avery, Gavin Hambly, and Charles Melville, eds. Vol. 7 of *The Cambridge History of Iran*. Cambridge: Cambridge University Press, 1991.

'Awaj, 'Abd al-Amir. *Surat Karbala' al-mansiyya: Munjaz lil-'ulama' al-muhaqqiq*. Beirut: Dar al-Mahajja al-Bayda', 2012.

Axworthy, Michael. *The Sword of Persia: Nader Shah, from Tribal Warrior to Conquering Tyrant*. London: I.B.Tauris, 2009.

al-'Azzawi, Abbas. *Ta'rikh al-Iraq bayn ihtilalayn*, 8 vols. Baghdad, 1955.

Babayan, Kathryn. *Mystics, Monarchs, and Messiahs: Cultural Landscapes of Early Modern Iran*. Cambridge: Harvard University Press, 2002.

Bahadili, 'Ali. *al-Hawzah al-'ilmiyya fi al-Najaf: ma'alimuha wa-harakatuha al-islahiyya*. Beirut: Dar al-Zahra', 1993.

———. *al-Najaf: Jami'atuha wa-dawruha al-qiyad*. Beirut: Mu'assasat al-Wafa', 1989.

Bahrani, Yusuf. *al-Hada'iq al-nadira*. Najaf: Dar al-Kutub al-'Ilmiyya, 1957.

———. *Lu'lu'at al-Bahrayn*. Najaf, 1966.

Bakhash, Shaul. *Iran: Monarchy, Bureaucracy and Reform under the Qajars: 1858–1896*. Ithaca: Ithaca Press, 1994.

Bamdad, Mahdi. *Sharh-i hal-i rijal-i Iran dar qarn-i 12, 13, 14 Hijri*. 6 vols. Tehran: Kitabfurushi-i Zuvvar, 1968–74.

Bang, Anne K. *The Idrisi State in 'Asir 1906–1934: Politics, Religion and Prestige in Arabia*. London: Hurst, 1997.

Barnes, John Robert. *An Introduction to Religious Foundations in the Ottoman Empire*. Leiden: Brill, 1986.

Batatu, Hanna. "Iraq's Underground Shi'a Movements; Characteristics, Causes and Prospects." *Middle East Journal* 35 (1981): 578–94.

———. *The Old Social Classes and the Revolutionary Movements of Iraq: A Study of Iraq's Old Landed and Commercial Classes and of its Communists, Ba'thists, and Free Officers*. Princeton: Princeton University Press, 1989.

Bayat, Mangol. "Anti-Sufism in Qajar Iran." In *Islamic Mysticism Contested: Thirteen Centuries of Controversies and Polemics*. F. de Jong and B. Radtke, eds. Leiden: Brill, 1999.

———. *Mysticism and Dissent: Socioreligious Thought in Qajar Iran*. New York: Syracuse University Press, 1982.

Bayhom-Daou, Tamima. *Shaykh Mufid*. Oxford: Oneworld, 2005.

Bengio, Ofra and Meir Litvak, eds. *The Sunna and Shi'a in History: Division and Ecumenism in the Muslim Middle East*. New York: Palgrave Macmillan, 2011.

Benjamin, Samuel G. W. *Persia*. London: T. Fisher Unwin, 1889.

Berkey, Jonathan. *The Formation of Islam: Religion and Society in the Near East, 600–1800*. Cambridge: Cambridge University Press, 2003.

———. *The Transmission of Knowledge in Medieval Cairo: A Social History of Islamic Education*. Princeton: Princeton University Press, 1992.

Bernal, Martin. *Black Athena: The Afroasiatic Roots of Classical Civilization*, 2 vols. New Brunswick: Rutgers University Press, 1987.

Bey, Sulayman Fa'iq. *Ta'rikh Baghdad*. Trans. M. K. Nawras. Baghdad, 1962.

Bihbihani, Aqa Ahmad. *Mir'at al-ahwal jahan-nama*. Tehran: Amir Kabir, 1370.

Bihbihani, Muhammad Baqir "Wahid" ibn Muhammad Akmal. *Adab al-tijara.* Tehran: Dar al-Khilafa, 1898.

——. *al-Fa'ida wa al-burhan.* Qum: al-Mu'assasa, 1996.

——. *al-Fawa'id al-ha'iriyya.* (including *al-Fawa'id al-jadida*) Qum: Majma' al-Fikr al-Islami, 1995.

——. *Hashiyya majma' al-fa'ida wa al-burhan.* Qum: al-Mu'assasa, 1996.

——. *Hashiyyat al-Wafi.* Qum: al-Mu'assasa, 2005.

——. *Ma'alim al-din,* (includes 21 treatises and books), unpublished.

——. *Madarik al-ahkam.* Qum: al-Mu'assasa, 1998–9.

——. *Masabih al-zalam.* Qum: al-Mu'assasa, 2003.

——. *al-Risa'il al-fiqhiyya.* Unpublished.

——. *al-Rasa'il al-usuliyya* (including *al-Risala fi al-ijtihad wa al-akhbar*). Qum, 1416.

——. *al-Risala al-akhbar wa al-ijtihad.* Tab'-i Mahalli, 1895.

——. *Sharh mafatih al-shara'i.* Unpublished.

——. *Tahqiq fi al-qiyas.* Unpublished.

——. *al-Ta'liqat al-Bihbihanniyya.* In Muhammad b. 'Ali al-Astarabadi, *Minhaj al-maqal*, Tehran, n.d.

——. *'Uddat al-usul.* Matba'at Ustad al-Mahir, 1899.

Blaut, J. M. *The Colonizer's Model of the World: Geographical Diffusionism and Eurocentric History.* New York: The Guilford Press, 1993.

Bosworth, Clifford Edmund, ed. *Iran and Islam: In Memory of the Late Vladimir Minorsky.* Edinburgh: Edinburgh University Press, 1971.

Bosworth, Clifford Edmund and Hillenbrand, Carole, eds. *Qajar Iran: Political, Social, and Cultural Change, 1800–1925.* Edinburgh: Edinburgh University Press, 1983.

Browne, Edward G. *A Literary History of Persia.* 4 vols. New Delhi: Goodword Books, 2002.

——. *The Persian Revolution, 1905–1909.* Cambridge: Cambridge University Press, 1910.

——. *A Year among the Persians.* Cambridge: Cambridge University Press, 1926.

Brunner, Rainer and Werner Ende, eds. *The Twelver Shia in Modern Times: Religious Culture & Political History.* Leiden: Brill, 2001.

Calder, Norman. "Doubt and Prerogative: The Emergence of an Imami Shi'i Theory of Ijtihad." *Studia Islamica* 70 (1989): 57–78.

——. "The Structure of Authority in Imami Shi'i Jurisprudence." PhD Thesis, University of London, 1980.

——. "Zakat in Imami Shi'i Jurisprudence, from the Tenth to the Sixteenth Century AD." *Bulletin of the School of Oriental and African Studies* 44:3 (1981): 468–80.

Cetinsaya, Gokhan. "Caliph and Mujtahids: Ottoman Policy towards the Shiite Community of Iraq in the Nineteenth Century." *Middle Eastern Studies* Vol. 41, No. 4 (July 2005): 561–574.

——. *Ottoman Administration of Iraq, 1890–1908*. New York: Routledge, 2006.

Ceylan, Ebubekir. *The Ottoman Origins of Modern Iraq: Political Reform, Modernization and Development in the Nineteenth-Century Middle East.* London: I.B.Tauris, 2011.

Chardin, Jean. *Chardin, Les Voyages du Chevalier Chardin en Perse.* L. Langles, ed., Vol. 5. Paris: Le Normant, 1811.

Chittick, William. "Islamic Mysticism Versus Philosophy in Earlier Islamic History: The Al-Tusi, Al-Qunawi Correspondence." *Religious Studies* Vol. 17, No. 1 (Mar. 1981): 87–104.

Cole, Juan. "Imami Jurisprudence and the Role of the Ulama: Mortaza Ansari on Emulating the Supreme Exemplar." In *Religion and Politics in Iran: Shi'ism from Quietism to Revolution*, Nikki R. Keddie, ed. New Haven: Yale University Press, 1983.

——. "'Indian Money' and the Shi'i Shrine Cities of Iraq, 1786–1850." *Middle Eastern Studies* Vol. 22, No. 4 (Oct. 1986): 461–80.

——. "Iranian Millenarianism and Democratic Thought in the Nineteenth Century." *International Journal of Middle East Studies* 24 (1992): 1–26.

——. "Rival Empires of Trade and Imami Shi'ism in Eastern Arabia, 1300–1800." *International Journal of Middle East Studies* 19 (1987): 196–8.

——. *Roots of North Indian Shi'ism in Iran and Iraq: Religion and State in Awadh, 1722–1859.* Berkeley: University of California Press, 1988.

——. *Sacred Space and Holy War: Politics, Culture and History in Shi'ism.* London: I.B.Tauris, 2001.

——. "Shi'i Clerics in Iran and Iraq, 1722–1780: The Akhbari-Usuli Controversy Reconsidered." *Iranian Studies* 18:1 (1985): 7–34.

Cole, Juan R. I. and Nikki R. Keddie, eds. *Shi'ism, and Social Protest.* New Haven: Yale University Press, 1986.

Cole, Juan R. I. and Moojan Momen. "Mafia, Mob and Shi'ism in Iraq: The Rebellion of Ottoman Karbala, 1824–1843." *Past and Present* 112 (1986): 112–43.

Commins, David. *The Wahhabi Mission and Saudi Arabia.* London: I.B.Tauris, 2009.

Cook, Michael. "On the Origins of Wahhabism." *Journal of the Royal Asiatic Society* Third Series, Vol. 2, No. 2 (July 1992): 191–202.

Corbin, Henry. *History of Islamic Philosophy.* Trans. Liadain Sherrard. London: Kegan Paul Intl, 1993.

——. *En Islam Iranien.* 4 vols. Paris: Gallimard, 1971–2.

———. *L'Ecole Shaykhie en Theologie Shi'ite.* Tehran, 1957.

Crone, Patricia. *God's Rule: Government and Islam.* New York: Columbia University Press, 2004.

Curzon, George N. *Persia and the Persian Question.* 2 vols. London: Longman, Green and Co., 1892.

Dabashi, Hamid. "The Sufi Doctrine of the 'Perfect Man' and the View of the Hierarchical Structure of Islamic Culture." *Islamic Quarterly* 30:2 (1986): 118–30.

Daiber, H. and Ragep, F. J. "al-Tusi, Nasir al- Din, Abu Dja'far Muhammad." *Encyclopaedia of Islam.* Second Edition, online edition, P. Bearman, et al., eds. Brill, 2009.

Dakake, Maria Mass. *The Charismatic Community: Shi'ite Identity in Early Islam.* Albany: SUNY Press, 2007.

Dale, Stephen F. *The Muslim Empires of the Ottomans, Safavids, and Mughals.* Cambridge: Cambridge University Press, 2010.

Dallal, Ahmad. "The Origins and Objectives of Islamic Revivalist Thought, 1750–1850." *Journal of the American Oriental Society* Vol. 113, No. 3 (1993): 341–59.

Daniel, Elton L. "The Golestan Treaty." *Encyclopaedia Iranica* Vol. XI, 86–90.

———. *The History of Iran.* Westport: Greenwood Press, 2001.

Davani, 'Ali. *Aqa Muhammad Baqir bin Muhammad Akmal Isfahani ma'ruf bih Vahid Bihbihani.* Tehran: Amir Kabir, 1983.

Delong-Bas, Natana J. *Wahhabi Islam: From Revival and Reform to Global Jihad.* New York: Oxford University Press, 2004.

Deringil, Selim. "The Struggle against Shiism in Hamidian Iraq: A Study in Ottoman Counter-Propaganda." *Die Welt des Islams* New Series, Bd. 30, Nr. ¼ (1990): 45–62.

Dols, Michael W. "The Second Plague Pandemic and its Recurrences in the Middle East: 1347–1894." *Journal of the Economic and Social History of the Orient* Vol. 22, No. 2 (1979): 162–89.

Donaldson, Dwight M. *The Shi'ite Religion: A History of Islam in Persia and Irak.* London: Luzac, 1933.

Eisenstadt, Shmuel N. *Comparative Civilizations and Multiple Modernities.* 2 vols. Leiden: Brill, 2003.

Eisenstadt, Shmuel N., ed. *Multiple Modernities.* New Jersey: Transaction Publishers, 2002.

Eliash, Joseph. "The Ithna'ashari-Shi'i Juristic Theory of Political and Legal Authority." *Studia Islamica* Vol. 29 (1969): 17–30.

Enayat, Hamid. *Modern Islamic Political Thought: The Response of the Shi'i and Sunni Muslims to the Twentieth Century.* London: Macmillan, 1982.

Esposito, John L. *Islam and Politics*. New York: Syracuse University Press, 1984.

Evans-Pritchard, E. E. *The Sanusi of Cyrenaica*. London: Oxford University Press, 1949.

Ezzati, Abu'l-Fadl. *An Introduction to Shi'i Islamic Law and Jurisprudence*. Lahore: Ashraf Press, 1976.

al-Fadli, 'Abd al-Hadi. *Dalil al-Najaf al-ashraf*. Najaf, 1966.

Farouk-Sluglett, Marion and Peter Sluglett. "The Transformation of Land Tenure and Rural Social Structure in Central and Southern Iraq, c. 1870–1958." *International Journal of Middle East Studies* Vol. 15, No. 4 (Nov. 1983): 491–505.

Fasa'i, Hasan. *History of Persia under Qajar Rule*. Trans. Heribert Busse. New York: Columbia University Press, 1972.

al-Fasi, Ahmad Ibn Idris. *al-'Iqd al-nafs fi nazm jawahir al-tadris Sayyid Ahmad ibn Idris*. Cairo: Mustafa al-Babi al-Halabi, 1979.

———. *Risalat al-radd 'ala ahl al-ra'y*. Unpublished.

Fattah, Hala. *The Politics of Regional Trade in Iraq, Arabia, and the Gulf: 1745–1900*. Albany: SUNY Press, 1997.

Fernea, Robert. *Shaykh and Effendi: Changing Patterns of Authority Among the El Shabana of Southern Iraq*. Cambridge: Harvard University Press, 1970.

Ferrier, R. W. *The History of the British Petroleum Company*. Vol. 1. Cambridge: Cambridge University Press, 1982.

Fischer, Michael, M. J. *Iran: From Religious Dispute to Revolution*. Cambridge: Harvard University Press, 1980.

Fisher, Michael H. "Political Marriage Alliances at the Shi'i Court of Awadh." *Comparative Studies in Society and History* Vol. 25, No. 4 (October 1983): 593–616.

Floor, Willem. ed. and trans. *The Afghan Occupation of Safavid Persia, 1721–1729*. Paris: Association pour l'Avancement des Etudes Iraniennes, 1998.

———. *The Persian Gulf: A Political and Economic History of Five Port Cities, 1500–1730*. Washington, DC: Mage Publishers, 2006.

———. "The Lutis: A Social Phenomenon in Qajar Persia: A Reappraisal." *Die Welt des Islams* New Series, Vol. 13, Issue 1/2 (1971): 103–120.

Frank, Andre Gunder. *ReOrient: Global Economy in the Asian Age*. Berkeley: University of California Press, 1998.

Gelvin, James L. *The Modern Middle East: A History*. New York: Oxford University Press, 2005.

Gharawi, Muhammad. *Ma' 'ulama' al-Najaf al-ashraf*. Beirut: Dar al-Thaqalayn, 1999.

Gleave, Robert. "The Akhbari-Usuli Dispute in *Tabaqat* Literature: An Analysis of the Biographies of Yusuf al-Bahrani and Muhammad Baqir al-Bihbihani." *Jusur* 10 (1994): 79–109.

——. "The Ijaza from Yusuf al Bahrani (d. 1186/1772) to Sayyid Muhammad Mahdi Bahr al-'Ulum (d. 1212/1797–8)." *Iran* Vol. 32 (1994): 115–23.

——. *Inevitable Doubt: Two Theories of Shi'i Jurisprudence*. Leiden: Brill, 2000.

——. "Jihad and Religious Legitimacy of the Early Qajar State." In *Religion and Society in Qajar Iran*. Robert Gleave, ed. New York: Routledge, 2005.

——. "Marrying Fatimid Women: Legal Theory and Substantive Law in Shi'i Jurisprudence." *Islamic Law and Society* Vol. 6, No. 1 (1999): 38–66.

——. ed. *Religion and Society in Qajar Iran*. New York: RoutledgeCurzon, 2005.

——. *Scripturalist Islam: The History and Doctrines of the Akhbari Shi'i School*. Leiden: Brill, 2007.

——. "Two Classical Shi'i Theories of *qada'*." In *Studies in Islamic and Middle Eastern Texts and Traditions in Memory of Norman Calder*. G. Hawting, et al. eds. Oxford: Oxford University Press, 2000.

Gommans, Jos. *The Rise of the Indo-Afghan Empire, c. 1710–1780*. Leiden: Brill, 1995.

Gran, Peter. *Islamic Roots of Capitalism: Egypt, 1760–1840*. New York: Syracuse University Press, 1998.

Habibabadi, Muhammad 'Ali Mu'allim. *Makaraim al-athar*. 5 vols. Isfahan: Kamal, 1978.

Haddad, Fanar. *Sectarianism in Iraq: Antagonistic Views of Unity*. London: C. Hurst & Co., 2011.

Hairi, Abdul-Hadi. "The Legitimacy of the Early Qajar Rule as Viewed by the Shi'i Religious Leaders." *Middle Eastern Studies* Vol. 24, No. 3 (July 1988): 271–286.

——. *Shi'ism and Constitutionalism in Iran: A Study of the Role Played by the Persian Residents of Iraq in Iranian Politics*. Leiden: Brill, 1977.

——. "Why Did the 'Ulama Participate in the Persian Constitutional Revolution of 1905–1909?" *Die Welt des Islams* New Series, Vol. 17, Issue 1/4 (1976–1977): 127–54.

al-Hakim, Muhammad Taqi. *Da'ira al-ma'arif al-Islamiyya al-Shi'a*. Beirut: al-Ta'arif, 1986.

Hallaq, Wael. *A History of Islamic Legal Theories: An Introduction to Sunni usul al-fiqh*. Cambridge: Cambridge University Press, 2002.

——. "On the Origins of the Controversy about the Existence of Mujtahids and the Gate of Ijtihad." *Studia Islamica* No. 63 (1986): 129–141.

——. "Was the Gate of Ijtihad Closed?" *International Journal of Middle East Studies* 16 (1984): 3–41.

Hasan, Mohammad Salman. "The Growth and Structure of Iraq's Population, 1867–1947." *Bulletin of the Oxford University Institute of Economics and Statistics* (1958): 339–352.

——. "The Role of Foreign Trade in the Economic Development of Iraq, 1864–1964: A Study in the Growth of a Dependent Economy." In *Studies in the Economic History of Middle East: From the Rise of Islam to the Present Day*. Michael Cook, ed. Oxford: Oxford University Press, 1970.

al-Haydari, Ibrahim Fasih. *Unwan al-majd fi bayan ahwal Baghdad wa al-Basra wa al-Najd*. Baghdad, 1962.

Heern, Zackery M. "Thou Shalt Emulate the Most Knowledgeable Living Cleric: Redefinition of Islamic Law and Authority in Usuli Shi'ism." *Journal of Shi'a Islamic Studies* Vol. VII, No. 3 (Summer 2014): 321–344.

Hidayat, Rida Quli Khan. *Ta'rikh-i rawdat al-safa-i nasiri dar dhikr padshahan-i dawra-i Safaviyya Afshariyya Zandiyya Qajariyya*. 10 vols. Qum, 1399.

al-Hilli, Ibn Idris. *al-Sara'ir*. Unpublished.

al-Hilli, Ibn al-Mutahhar. *Kashf al-Murad*. Mashhad: Muhammadiyya, n.d.

——. *Tahdhid al-wusul ila 'ilm al-usul*. Tehran: Dar al-Khilafa, 1890.

al-Hilli, Muhaqqiq. *al-Mu'tabar*. Tehran, 1318.

Hiro, Dilip. *The Longest War: The Iran-Iraq Military Conflict*. New York: Routledge, 1991.

Hirz al-Din, Muhammad. *Ma'arif al-rijal fi tarajim al-'ulama' wa al-udaba'*. 3 vols. Najaf, 1964.

Hisri, Ahmad. *al-Ta'rikh al-fiqh al-Islami*. Beirut: Dar al-Jayl, 1991.

Hitti, Philip K. *Islam: A Way of Life*. Minneapolis: University of Minnesota Press, 1970.

Hobsbawm, E. J. *The Age of Revolution: 1789–1848*. New York: Mentor, 1962.

——. *Primitive Rebels: Studies in Archaic Forms of Social Movement in the 19th and 20th Centuries*. New York: W. W. Norton, 1965.

Hodgson, Marshall G. S. *Rethinking World History: Essays on Europe, Islam, and World History*. Cambridge: Cambridge University Press, 1993.

——. *The Venture of Islam*. 3 vols. Chicago: University of Chicago Press, 1974.

Hoffman, Valerie J. "Annihilation in the Messenger of God: The Development of a Sufi Practice." *International Journal of Middle East Studies* Vol. 31, No. 3 (August 1999): 351–369.

Hopkins, Terence K. and Immanuel Wallerstein, eds. *Processes of the World-System*. London: Sage, 1980.

Hourani, Albert. "From Jabal 'Amil to Persia." *Bulletin of the School of Oriental and African Studies* University of London, Vol. 49, No. 1 (1986): 133–40.

al-Hurr al-'Amili, Muhammad b. al-Husayn. *Amal al-amil fi 'ulama' al-Jabal 'Amil*. 2 vols. Baghdad: Maktabat al-Andalus, 1965.

Hussain, Jassim M. *Occultation of the Twelfth Imam: A Historical Background*. London: Muhammadi Trust, 1982.

Ibn 'Abd al-Wahhab, Muhammad. "Fatwa wa masa'il." In *Mu'allafat al-Shaykh al-Imam Muhammad Ibn 'Abd al-Wahhab*. Vol. 3. Riyadh: Jami'at al-Imam Muhammad bin Saud al-Islamiyya, 1298.

——. "Kitab al-nikah." In *Mu'allafat al-Shaykh al-Imam Muhammad Ibn 'Abd al-Wahhab*. Vol. 2. Riyadh: Jami'at al-Imam Muhammad bin Saud al-Islamiyya, 1298.

——. *Kitab al-tawhid*. Trans. Ismail al-Faruqi. Kuwait: al-Faisal Printing, 1986.

——. "Risala fi al-radd 'ala al-rafida." In *Mu'allafat al-Shaykh al-Imam Muhammad Ibn 'Abd al-Wahhab*. Vol. 4. Riyadh: Jami'at al-Imam Muhammad bin Saud al-Islamiyya, 1298.

Ibn Babawayh. *al-I'tiqadat*. Tehran, 1370.

Ibn Babuya, Muhammad ibn 'Ali. *A Shiite Creed*. Trans. A. A. Fyzee. Oxford: Oxford University Press, 1942.

Ibn Bishr, Uthman. *Unwan al-majd fi tarikh Najd*. 'Abd al-Rahman 'Abd al-Latif bin 'Abdullah Al al-Shaykh, ed. Vol. 1. Riyadh: Matbu'at Darat al-Malik 'Abd al-Aziz, 1982.

Ibn Shahrashub, Muhammad b. 'Ali. *Ma'alim al-'ulama'*. 'Abbas Iqbal, ed. Najaf, 1961.

Israel, Jonathan. *A Revolution of the Mind: Radical Enlightenment and the Intellectual Origins of Modern Democracy*. Princeton: Princeton University Press, 2010.

Issawi, Charles, ed. *The Economic History of Iran: 1800–1914*. Chicago: University of Chicago Press, 1971.

——. *The Economic History of the Middle East, 1800–1914: A Book of Readings*. Chicago: University of Chicago Press, 1966.

——. *The Fertile Crescent, 1800–1914: A Documentary Economic History*. Oxford: Oxford University Press, 1988.

Jabar, Faleh, A. *The Shi'ite Movement in Iraq*. London: Saqi, 2003.

Jafri, S. Husain M. *Origins and Early Development of Shi'a Islam*. London: Longman, 1979.

al-Juhany, Uwaidah M. *Najd before the Salafi Movement: Social, Political, and Religious Conditions during the Three Centuries Preceding the Rise of the Saudi State*. London: Ithaca Press, 2002.

Kafadar, Cemal. "The Question of Ottoman Decline." *Harvard Middle Eastern and Islamic Review* 4 (1997–8).

Kalbasi, Muhammad Ibrahim. *Isharat al-usul*. Tehran, 1830.

Kamali, Masoud. *Multiple Modernities, Civil Society and Islam: The Case of Iran and Turkey*. Liverpool: Liverpool University Press, 2006.

Kamali, Mohammad Hashim. *Principles of Islamic Jurisprudence*. Kuala Lumpur: Pelanduk Publishers, 1989.

al-Karaki, 'Ali b. 'Abd al-'Ali "Muhaqqiq". *Rasa'il al-Muhaqqiq al-Karaki*. 2 vols. Muhammad al-Hassun, ed. Qum, 1988.

Karami, Abu Zayd Tusit Muhammad Taqi. *Majal-i nuqd wa nazar*. Unpublished.

Karimi, Nazim al-Islam. *Ta'rikh-i bidari-yi Iranian*. Tehran, 1978–9.

Karrar, Ali Salih. *Sufi Brotherhoods in the Sudan*. London: Hurst, 1992.

Kashmiri, Muhammad 'Ali. *Nujum al-sama'*. Lucknow: Lithograph, 1885.

Kashshi, Muhammad b. 'Umar. *Ikhtiyar ma'rifa al-rijal*. Mashhad: Danishgah-e Mashhad, 1969.

al-Katib, Ahmad. *Tatawwur al-fikr al-siyasi al-Shi'i min al-shuru ila wilayat al-faqih*. Giza: Maktabat al-Nafida, 2007.

Katouzian, Homa. *The Persians: Ancient, Mediaeval, and Modern Iran*. New Haven: Yale University Press, 2009.

Kazemzadeh, Firuz. *Russia and Britain in Persia: Imperial Ambitions in Qajar Iran*. London: I.B.Tauris, 2013.

Keddie, Nikki R. *Modern Iran: Roots and Results of Revolution*. New Haven: Yale, 2006.

Keddie, Nikki R., ed. *Religion and Politics in Iran: Shi'ism from Quietism to Revolution*. New Haven: Yale University Press, 1983.

Kelly, J. B. *Britain and the Persian Gulf: 1795–1880*. Oxford: Clarendon Press, 1968.

Khalili, Ja'far. *Mawsu'at al-atabat al-muqaddasa, Najaf*, 10 vols. Baghdad and Beirut, 1965–70.

Khomeini, Ruhullah. *al-Bi'*. Iran: Wizarat al-Thaqafa wa al-Irshad, 1987.

Khurmuji, Muhammad Ja'far. *Tarikh-i Qajar: Haqa'iq al-akhbar-i Nasiri*. Tehran: Kitabfurushi-yi Zavvar, 1965.

Khwansari, Muhammad Baqir. *Rawdat al-jannat fi ahwal al-'ulama' wa al-sadat*. 8 vols. Beirut, 1991.

———. *Rawdat al-jannat*. Trans. into Persian by Sa'idi Khurasani. Unpublished.

Kilidar, Muhammad Hasan. *Ta'rikh Karbala' wa-ha'ir al-Husayn 'alayhi al-salam*. Najaf, 1967.

Kirmani, Muhammad Khan. *al-Kitab al-mubin*. Kirman: Chapkhana-yi Sa'adat, 1975.

Kohlberg, Etan. "Aspects of Akhbari thought in the Seventeenth and Eighteenth Centuries." in *Eighteenth-Century Renewal and Reform in Islam*. Nehemia Levtzion and John Olbert Voll, eds. Syracuse: Syracuse University Press, 1987.

———. *Belief and Law in Imami Shi'ism*. Brookfield: Variorum, 1991.

Kraemer, Joel L. *Humanism in the Renaissance of Islam: The Cultural Revival During the Buyid Age*. Leiden: Brill, 1993.

Kramer, Martin. *Shi'ism, Resistance and Revolution*. London: Mansell, 1987.

al-Kulayni, Muhammad b. Ya'qub. *al-Kafi*. 8 vols. 'Ali-Akbar al-Ghaffari, ed. Tehran: Dar al-Kutub al-Islamiyya.

——. *al-Usul min al-kafi*. 2 vols. 'Ali-Akbar al-Ghaffari, ed. Tehran: Dar al-Kutub al-Islamiyya, 1984.

Lambton, Ann K. S. "Tribal Resurgence and the Decline of the Bureaucracy in Eighteenth Century Persia." In *Studies in Eighteenth Century Islamic History*. Thomas Naff and Roger Owen, eds. Carbondale: Southern Illinois University Press, 1977.

——. "A Reconstruction of the Position of *Marja' al-Taqlid* and the Religious Institution." *Studia Islamica* 20 (1964): 115–35.

——. "Some New Trends in Islamic Political Thought in Late 18th and Early 19th Century Persia." *Studia Islamica* 39 (1974): 95–128.

——. *State and Government in Medieval Islam: An Introduction to the Study of Islamic Political Theory*. Oxford: Oxford University Press, 1981.

Landau-Tasseron, Ella. "The 'Cyclical Reform': A Study of the *mujaddid* Tradition." *Studia Islamica* No. 70 (1989): 79–117.

Lapidus, Ira M. *A History of Islamic Societies*. Cambridge: Cambridge University Press, 1988.

——. "Islamic Revival and Modernity: The Contemporary Movements and the Historical Paradigms." *Journal of the Economic and Social History of the Orient* Vol. 40, No. 4 (1997): 444–460.

Lawson, Todd. "Akhbari Shi'i Approaches to *tafsir*." In *Approaches to the Qur'an*. G. R. Hawting and Abdul-Kader A. Shareef, eds. New York: Routledge, 1993.

——. "Orthodoxy and Heterodoxy in Twelver Shiism: Ahmad al-Ahsai on Fayd Kashani (The *Risala al-'ilmiyya*)." In *Religion and Society in Qajar Iran*. Robert Gleave, ed. London: Routledge, 2005.

——. ed. *Reason and Inspiration in Islam*. London: I.B.Tauris, 2005.

Le Chatelier, A. *Les Conferies Musulmanes du Hedjaz*. Paris, 1887.

Levtzion, Nehemia and John Olbert Voll, eds. *Eighteenth-Century Renewal and Reform in Islam*. New York: Syracuse University Press, 1987.

Little, Donald P. "Did Ibn Taymiyya Have a Screw Loose?" *Studia Islamica* No. 41 (1975): 93–111.

Litvak, Meir. "Continuity and Change in the Ulama Population of Najaf and Karbala, 1791–1904: A Socio-Demographic Study." *Iranian Studies* Vol. 23, No. 1/4 (1990): 31–60.

——. "Encounters between Shi'i and Sunni 'Ulama' in Ottoman Iraq." In *The Sunna and Shi'a in History: Division and Ecumenism in the Muslim Middle East*. Ofra Bengio and Meir Litvak, eds. New York: Palgrave Macmillan, 2011.

——. "A Failed Manipulation: The British, the Oudh Bequest and the Shi'i 'ulama' of Najaf and Karbala'." *British Journal of Middle Eastern Studies* Vol. 27, No. 1 (May 2000): 69–89.

——. "The Finances of the 'Ulama' Communities of Najaf and Karbala', 1796–1904." *Die Welt des Islams* New Series, Vol. 40, Issue 1 (March 2000): 41–66.

——. *Shi'i Scholars of Nineteenth Century Iraq: The 'ulama' of Najaf and Karbala'.* Cambridge: Cambridge University Press, 1997.

Lockhart, Laurence. *The Fall of the Safavi Dynasty and the Afghan Occupation of Persia.* Cambridge: Cambridge University Press, 1938.

——. *Nadir Shah: A Critical Study Based Mainly upon Contemporary Sources.* London: Luzac, 1938.

Longrigg, Stephen H. *Four Centuries of Modern Iraq.* Oxford: Oxford University Press, 1925.

Lory, P. "Shadhiliyya." *Encyclopaedia of Islam*, Second Edition. Online version, P. Bearman, et al., eds. 2010.

Luizard, Jean-Pierre. *La Formation de l'Irak Contemporain: Le Role Politique des Ulema Chiites a la Fin de la Domination Ottomane et au Moment de la Construction de l'Etat Irakien.* Paris: CNRS, 1991.

MacEoin, Dennis. "Changes in Charismatic Authority in Qajar Shi'ism." In *Qajar Iran: Political, Social and Cultural Change: 1800–1925.* Edmund Bosworth and Carole Hillenbrand, eds. Edinburgh: Edinburgh University Press, 1983.

——. *The Messiah of Shiraz: Studies in Early and Middle Babism.* Leiden: Brill, 2009.

——. "Mulla Sadra Shirazi Sadr al-Din Muhammad b. Ibrahim Kawami Shirazi." *Encyclopaedia of Islam,* Second Edition. Online version, P. Bearman, et al., eds. 2009.

Mahbuba, Ja'far. *Madhi al-Najaf wa hadiruhu.* 3 vols. Najaf: Matba'at al-Adab, 1955–8.

al-Majlisi II, Muhammad Baqir. *Bihar al-anwar.* Beirut: Mu'assasat al-A'lami li al-Matbu'at, 2009.

al-Majlisi I, Muhammad Taqi. *Lawami'-i sahibqarani.* Tehran: Bardaran-i 'ilmi, 1963.

——. *Rawdat al-muttaqin.* Qum: Bunyad-i Farhang-i Islam, 1973–99.

Makdisi, George. "Ibn Taymiyya: A Sufi of the Qadiriyya Order." *American Journal of Arabic Studies* I (1973).

Makki, Hasan. *al-Sayyid Ahmad ibn Idris al-Fasi.* Khartoum: al-Markaz al-Islami al-Ifriqi bi al-Khartoum, 1986.

Mallat, Chibli. *Renewal of Islamic Law, Muhammad Baqer as-Sadr, Najaf and the Shi'i International.* Cambridge: Cambridge University Press, 1993.

Mamaqani, 'Abdullah. *Nukhbat al-maqal*. Unpublished.

——. *Tanqih al-maqal fi ahwal al-rijal*. Qum: Mu'assasat Al al-Bayt li-Ihya al-Turath, 2002.

Mandaville, Peter. *Global Political Islam*. New York: Routledge, 2007.

Marjani, Haydar. *al-Najaf al-ashraf qadiman wa hadithan*. Baghdad, 1986.

Marsot, Afaf Lutfi al-Sayyid. *Women and Men in Late Eighteenth-Century Egypt*. Austin: University of Texas Press, 1995.

Martin, Vanessa. *Creating an Islamic State: Khomeini and the Making of a New Iran*. London: I.B.Tauris, 2000.

——. *Islam and Modernism: The Revolution of 1906*. London: I.B.Tauris, 1989.

Mashkur, Muhammad Javad. *Tarikh-i Shi'a va firqaha-yi Islam ta qarn-i chaharum*. Tehran: Intisharat-i Ishraqi, 1976.

Matthee, Rudi. "Between Arabs, Turks and Iranians: The Town of Basra, 1600–1700." *Bulletin of the School of Oriental and African Studies* Vol. 69, No. 1 (2006): 53–78.

——. *Persia in Crisis: Safavid Decline and the Fall of Isfahan*. London: I.B.Tauris, 2012.

——. *Politics of Trade in Safavid Iran: Silk for Silver 1600–1730*. Cambridge: Cambridge University Press, 1999.

——. "Unwalled Cities and Restless Nomads: Firearms and Artillery in Safavid Iran." In *Safavid Persia*, Charles Melville, ed. London: I.B.Tauris, 1996.

Matthee, Rudi, Willem Floor, Patrick Clawson. *The Monetary History of Iran: From the Safavids to the Qajars*. London: I.B.Tauris, 2013.

Matthiesen, Toby. *The Other Saudis: Shiism, Dissent and Sectarianism*. Cambridge: Cambridge University Press, 2015.

Mazzaoui, Michel M. *The Origins of the Safawids: Shi'ism, Sufism, and the Gulat*. Wiesbaden: F. Steiner, 1972.

McCaffrey, Michael J. "Battle of Chaldiran." *Encyclopaedia Iranica* Vol. IV: 656–8.

McDermott, Martin. *The Theology of Al-al-Shaikh al-Mufid*. Beirut: Dar el-Machreq, 1986.

McNeill, William H. "The Age of Gunpowder Empires, 1450–1800." In *Islamic & European Expansion: The Forging of a Global Order*, Michael Adas, ed. Philadelphia: Temple University Press, 1993.

Menashri, David. *Education and the Making of Modern Iran*. Ithaca: Cornell University Press, 1992.

Metcalf, Barbara D. and Thomas R. Metcalf. *A Concise History of India*. Cambridge: Cambridge University Press, 2002.

Millward, William G. "Aspects of Modernism in Shi'a Islam." *Studia Islamica* 37 (1973): 111–28.

Mitchell, Richard P. *The Society of the Muslim Brothers*. Oxford: Oxford University Press, 1993.

Mitchell, Timothy, ed. *Questions of Modernity*. Minneapolis: University of Minnesota Press, 2000.

———. "The Stage of Modernity." In *Questions of Modernity*. Timothy Mitchell, ed. Minneapolis: University of Minnesota, 2000.

Modarressi Tabatabai, Hossein. *An Introduction to Shi'i Islam: A Bibliographical Study*. London: Ithaca Press, 1984.

———. "Rationalism and Traditionalism in Shi'i Jurisprudence: A Preliminary Survey." *Studia Islamica* No. 59 (1984): 141–58.

———. *Tradition and Survival: A Bibliographical Survey of Early Shi'ite Literature*. Vol. 1. Oxford: Oneworld Publications, 2003.

Moin, Baqer. *Khomeini: Life of the Ayatollah*. New York: I.B.Tauris, 1999.

Momen, Moojan. *An Introduction to Shi'i Islam: The History and Doctrines of Twelver Shi'ism*. New Haven: Yale University Press, 1985.

———. "The Social Bases of the Babi Upheavals in Iran (1848–53): A Preliminary Analysis." *International Journal of Middle East Studies* Vol. 15, No. 2 (May 1983): 157–183.

Moreen, Vera B. "A Shi'i-Jewish 'Debate' (Munazara) in the Eighteenth Century." *Journal of the American Oriental Society* Vol. 119, No. 4 (October – December 1999): 570–89.

Morier, James. *A Journey through Persia, Armenia, and Asia Minor to Constantinople in 1808 and 1809*. London: Longman, Hurst et al., 1812.

Morris, James W. *The Wisdom of the Throne: An Introduction to the Philosophy of Mulla Sadr*. Princeton: Princeton University Press, 1981.

Mottahedeh, Roy. *Loyalty and Leadership in an Early Islamic Society*. Princeton: Princeton University Press, 1980.

———. *The Mantle of the Prophet: Religion and Politics in Iran*. Oxford: Oneworld Publications, 2002.

Moussavi, Ahmad Kazemi. "The Establishment of the Position of Marja'iyyat-i Taqlid in the Twelver-Shi'i Community." *Iranian Studies* 18:1 (Winter 1985): 35–51.

———. *Religious Authority in Shi'ite Islam: From the Office of Mufti to the Institution of Marja*. Kuala Lumpur: International Institute of Islamic Thought and Civilization (ISTAC), 1996.

Mudarrisi, Murtada. *Shaikhigiri va babigiri*. Tehran, 1972.

———. *Ta'rikh-i ravabit-i Iran va Iraq*. Tehran, 1972.

Mudarris, Muhammad 'Ali. *Rayhanat al-adab*. 8 vols. Tabriz, 1967.

al-Mufid, Shaykh. *Awa'il al-maqalat*. Unpublished.

———. *al-Ifsah*, Najaf, 1950.

——. *al-Masa'il al-sarawiyya*. Unpublished.

——. *Tashth al-i'tiqad*. Unpublished.

Mu'man, Qadi. *Ikhtilaf usul al-madhahib*. M. Ghalib, ed. Beirut, 1973.

Mutahhari, Murtaza. "Ilhami az Sahykh al-Ta'ifa." *Hizara-yi Shaykh-i Tusi*. Qum: Dar al-Tabligh, 1970.

Muzaffar, Muhammad Husayn. *Ta'rikh al-Shi'a*. Beirut, 1982.

al-Muzaffar, Muhammad Rida. *The Faith of Shi'a Islam*. Qum: Ansariyan Publications, 1982.

——. *Usul al-fiqh*. Najaf, 1967.

Naff, Thomas and Roger Owen, eds. *Studies in Eighteenth Century Islamic History*. Carbondale: Southern Illinois University Press, 1977.

Nahavardi, 'Ali Akbar. *Khazinat al-jawahir fi zinat al-manabir*. Tehran: Kitabfurushi-ye Islamiyeh, 1962–3.

al-Najafi, Shaykh Ja'far "Kashif al-Ghita'." *Haqq al-mubin*. n. p., 1901.

——. *Kashf al-ghita' 'an khafiyyat mubhamat al-shari'a al-gharra'*. Najaf, 1800.

——. *Khatimat al-qawa'id*. Iran: Lithograph, 1898.

——. *Manhaj al-rashad li-man arada al-sadad*. Najaf, 1925.

Najafi, Shaykh Muhammad Hasan. *Jawahir al-kalam fi Sharh Shara'i' al-Islam*. Abbas al-Quchani, ed. 23 vols. Tehran: Dar al-Kutub al-Islamiyya, 1972.

Nakash, Yitzhak. "The Conversion of Iraq's Tribes to Shi'ism." *International Journal of Middle East Studies* Vol. 26, No. 3 (August 1994): 443–63.

——. *Reaching for Power: The Shi'a in the Modern Arab World*. Princeton: Princeton University Press, 2006.

——. *The Shi'is of Iraq*. Princeton: Princeton University Press, 2003.

Naraqi, Muhammad Mahdi. *Jam' al-sa'adat*. Sayyed Mohammad Kalantar, ed. 3 vols. Beirut, 1985.

Naraqi, Mulla Ahmad. *'Awa'id al-ayyam*. Qum: Maktaba Basirati, 1903.

——. *Mathnavi-yi taqdis*. Tehran: Amir Kabir, 1983.

——. *Mi'raj al-sa'ada*. Tehran, 1864.

——. *Mustanad al-Shi'a*. Tehran, 1856.

Nasr, Seyyed Hossein, Hamid Dabashi, and Seyyed Vali Reza Nasr, eds. *Expectation of the Millennium: Shi'ism in History*. Albany: SUNY Press, 1989.

——. *Shi'ism: Doctrines, Thought, and Spirituality*. Albany: SUNY Press, 1988.

Nasr, Vali. *The Shia Revival: How Conflicts within Islam Will Shape the Future*. New York: W. W. Norton & Co., 2006.

Nawras, M. K. *Hukm al-mamalik fi al-'Iraq, 1750–1831*. Baghdad, 1975.

Nawwar, Abdul Aziz. *Da'ud Basha wali Baghdad*. Baghdad, 1967.

Newman, Andrew J. "The Development and Political Significance of the Rationalist (Usuli) and Traditionist (Akhbari) Schools in Imami Shi'i History from the Third/Ninth to the Tenth/Sixteenth Century." PhD Thesis, UCLA, 1986.

——. *The Formative Period of Twelver Shi'ism: Hadith as Discourse between Qumm and Baghdad*. Richmond: Curzon, 2000.

——. "The Myth of Clerical Migration to Safawid Iran: Shiite Opposition to 'Ali al-Karaki and Safawid Shiism." *Die Welt des Islams* 33 (1993): 66–112.

——. "The Nature of the Akhbari/Usuli Dispute in Late Safawid Iran. Part 1: 'Abdallah al-Samahiji's "*Munyat al-Mumarisin*." *Bulletin of the School of Oriental and African Studies* University of London, Vol. 55, No. 1 (1992): 22–51.

——. "The Nature of the Akhbari/Usuli Dispute in Late Safawid Iran, Part 2: The Conflict Reassessed." *Bulletin of the School of Oriental and African Studies* University of London, Vol. 55, No. 2 (1992): 250–61.

——. *Safavid Iran: Rebirth of a Persian Empire*. London: I.B.Tauris, 2009.

——. "Towards a Reconsideration of the Isfahani School of Philosophy: Shaykh Baha'i and the Role of the Safawid 'Ulama'." *Studia Iranica* 15 (1986): 165–99.

Niebuhr, Carsten. *Voyage en Arabie et en d'autres pays circonvoisins*. Amsterdam, 1780.

Nieuwenhuis, Tom. *Politics and Society in Early Modern Iraq: Mamluk Pashas, Tribal Shaykhs and Local Rule between 1802 and 1831*. The Hague: Martinus Nijhoff Pulblishers, 1982.

Norton, Augustus Richard. *Hezbollah: A Short History*. Princeton: Princeton University Press, 2007.

Nuri Tabarsi, Husayn. *Mustadrak wasa'il al-Shi'a*. Tehran, 1900–03.

O'Fahey, R. S. *Enigmatic Saint, Ahmad Ibn Idris and the Idrisi Tradition*. Evanston: Northwestern University Press, 1990.

O'Fahey, Rex S. and Ali Salih Karrar. "The Enigmatic Imam: The Influence of Ahmad Ibn Idris." *International Journal of Middle East Studies* Vol. 19, No. 2 (May 1987): 205–219.

O'Fahey, R. S. and Bernd Radtke. "Neo-Sufism Reconsidered." *Der Islam* 70 (1993): 52–87.

Perry, John R. "Aga Mohammad Khan Qajar." *Encyclopaedia Iranica* Vol. I: 602–5.

——. "Karim Khan Zand." *Encyclopaedia Iranica* Vol. XV: 561–4.

——. *Karim Khan Zand: A History of Iran, 1747–1779*. Chicago: University of Chicago Press, 1979.

Peskes, Esther. "The Wahabiyya and Sufism in the Eighteenth Century." In *Islamic Mysticism Contested: Thirteen Centuries of Controversies and Polemics*, Frederick De Jong and Bernd Radtke, eds. Leiden: Brill, 1999.

Peters, Rudolph. "Reinhard Schulze's Quest for an Islamic Enlightenment." *Die Welt des Islams* New Series, Bd. 30, Nr. ¼ (1990): 160–162.

Pourjavady, Nasrollah and Peter Lamborn Wilson. *Kings of Love: The Poetry and History of the Ni'matullahi Sufi Order*. Tehran: Imperial Iranian Academy of Philosophy, 1978.

Pourjavady, Reza and Sabine Schmidtke. "Muslim Polemics Against Judaism and Christianity in 18th Century Iran: The Literary Sources of Aqa Muhammad Ali Bihbihani's (1144/1732–1216/1801) *Radd-i Shubuhat al-Kuffar*." *Studia Iranica* 35 (2006): 893–924.

al-Qazwini, Hamdu'llah Mustafa. *Ta'rikh-i Guzida*. E. G. Brown, ed. and trans. Leiden: E. J. Brill, 1910–13.

Quinn, Sholeh A. *Historical Writing during the Reign of Shah 'Abbas: Ideology, Imitation, and Legitimacy in Safavid Chronicles*. Salt Lake City: The University of Utah Press, 2000.

Qummi, 'Abbas. *Fawa'id al-ridawiyya*. Najaf, 1956.

Qummi, Mirza Abu al-Qasim. *Jami' al-shatat*. Tehran: Intisharat-i Kayhan, 1992.

——. *Mafatih al-janan*. Tehran: Nashr Farhang Islam, 1985.

——. *Qawanin al-usul*. Tehran, 1958.

Radtke, Bernd. "Erleuchtung und Aufklarung: Islamische Mystik und europaischer Rationalismus." *Die Welt des Islams* New Series, Vol. 34, Issue 1 (April 1994).

——. "Sufism in the 18th Century: An Attempt at a Provisional Appraisal." *Die Welt des Islams* New Series, Vol. 36, Issue 3 (November 1996): 326–64.

Radtke, Bernd, et al. *The Exoteric Ahmad Ibn Idris: A Sufi's Critique of the Madhahib and the Wahhabis*. Leiden: Brill, 2000.

——. "Two Sufi Treatises of Ahmad Ibn Idris." *Oriens* Vol. 35 (1996): 143–78.

Rafati, Vahid. "The Development of Shaykhi Thought in Shi'i Islam." PhD Thesis, UCLA, 1979.

Rahimi, Babak. *Theater State and the Formation of Early Modern Public Sphere in Iran: Studies on Safavid Muharram Rituals, 1590–1641 CE*. Leiden: Brill, 2012.

Rahman, Fazlur. *Islam*. Chicago: University of Chicago Press, 1979.

——. *Islam and Modernity: Transformation of an Intellectual Tradition*. Chicago: University of Chicago Press, 1982.

——. *The Philosophy of Mulla Sadra*. Albany: SUNY Press, 1981.

——. "Some Key Ethical Concepts of the Qur'an." *The Journal of Religious Ethics* Vol. 11, No. 2 (Fall 1983): 170–185.

Razavi, Mehdi Amin. *Suhrawardi and the School of Illumination*. London: Curzon Press, 1997.

Reichmuth, Stefan. "Arabic Literature and Islamic Scholars in the 17th /18th Centuries: Topics and Biographies: Introduction." *Die Welt des Islams* New Series, Vol. 42, Issue 3 (2002): 281–288.

Rentz, George S. *The Birth of the Islamic Reform Movement in Saudi Arabia.* London: Arabian Publishing, 2004.

Rieck, Andreas. "The Nurbakhshis of Baltistan: Crisis and Revival of a Five Centuries Old Community." *Die Welt des Islams* New Series, Vol. 35, Issue 2 (Nov., 1995): 159–188.

Rizvi, Sajjad. *Mulla Sadra Shirazi: His Life and Works and the Sources of Safavid Philosophy.* Oxford: Oxford University Press, 2007.

Rizvi, Sayyid Muhammad. *Shi'ism: Imamate and Wilayat.* Richmond Hill: al-Ma'arif Books, 2000.

Sachedina, Abdulaziz. *Islamic Messianism: Idea of the Mahdi in Twelver Shi'ism.* Albany: SUNY Press, 1981.

——. *The Just Ruler in Shi'ite Islam: The Comprehensive Authority of the Jurist in Imamite Jurisprudence.* New York: Oxford University Press, 1988.

Sadra al-Din Shirazi, Muhammad ibn Ibrahim. *Sharh Usul al-Kafi.* Tehran: Mu'assasa Mutal'at wa Tahqiqat Farhangi, 1987.

al-Sadr, Muhammad Baqir. *Durus fi 'ilm al-usul.* Beirut, 1978.

——. *al-Fatawa al-wadiha.* Beirut, 1978.

——. *Lessons in Islamic Jurisprudence.* Trans. and Introduction by Roy Parviz Mottahedeh. Oxford: Oneworld Publications, 2003.

al-Saffar, Muhammad b. al-Hasan, *Basa'ir al-darajat fi fada'il al-Muhammad.* Qum: Maktaba Ayat Allah al-Mar'ashi, 1983.

Said, Edward, W. *Orientalism.* New York: Vintage Books, 1979.

Sajdi, Dana, ed. *Ottoman Tulips, Ottoman Coffee: Leisure and Lifestyle in the Eighteenth Century.* London: I.B.Tauris, 2007.

Salmasi, Zayn al-'Abidin. *Mustadrek.* Unpublished.

Savory, Roger M. *Iran under the Safavids.* Cambridge: Cambridge University Press, 1980.

Sayeed, S. M. A. *Iran, Before and After Khomeini: A Study in the Dialectics of Shi'ism and Modernity.* Karachi: Royal Book Co., 1999.

Schulze, Reinhard. "Das islamische achtzehntes Jahrhundert: Versuch einer historiographischen Kritik," *Die Welt des Islams* New Series, Bd. 30, Nr. ¼ (1990): 140–159.

——. "Was ist Die Islamische Aufklarung?" *Die Welt des Islams* New Series, Vol. 36, Issue 3 (November 1996): 276–325.

Sedgwick, Mark. *Saints and Sons: The Making of the Rashidi Ahmadi Sufi Order, 1799–2000.* Leiden: Brill, 2005.

Shafti, Muhammad Baqir "Hujjat al-Islam." *Iqamat al-hudud fi zaman al-ghayba*. Isfahan: Maktabat Masjid al-Sayyid, 2005.

———. *Matali' al-anwar fi sharh Shara'i' al-Islam*. Unpublished.

Shahrudi, Nur al-Din. *Ta'rikh al-haraka al-'ilmiyya fi Karbala'*. Beirut: Dar al-'Ulum, 1990.

Shanahan, Rodger. *The Shi'a of Lebanon: Clans, Parties and Clerics*. London: I.B.Tauris, 2005.

Shibabi, Mahmud. *Taqrirat-i usul*. Tehran: Farbud, 1965.

Sirvani, Zayn al-Abedin. *Riyaz al-siyaha*. A. H. Rabbani, ed. Tehran, 1960.

Smith, Peter. R. P. *The Babi and Baha'i Religions: From Messianic Shi'ism to a World Religion*. Cambridge: Cambridge University Press, 1987.

Spence, Jonathan D. *The Search for Modern China*. New York: Norton, 1990.

Stearns, Peter N. *The Industrial Revolution in World History*. Boulder: Westview Press, 1993.

Stewart, Devin J. "An Episode in the 'Amili Migration to Safavid Iran: Husayn b. 'Abd al-Samad al-'Amili's Travel Account." *Iranian Studies* Vol. 39, No. 4 (December 2006): 481–508.

———. "The Genesis of the Akhbari Revival." In *Safavid Iran and Her Neighbors*. Michel Mazzaoui, ed. Salt Lake City: The University of Utah Press, 2003.

———. *Islamic Legal Orthodoxy: Twelver Shiite Reponses to the Sunni Legal System*. Salt Lake City: University of Utah Press, 1998.

———. "The Portrayal of an Academic Rivalry: Najaf and Qum in the Writings and Speeches of Khomeini, 1964–78." In *The Most Learned of the Shi'i: The Institution of the Marja' Taqlid*, Linda S. Walbridge, ed. New York: Oxford University Press, 2001.

Streusand, Douglas E. *Islamic Gunpowder Empires: Ottomans, Safavids, and Mughals*. Boulder: Westview Press, 2011.

al-Suwaydi, Abd al-Rahman. *Ta'rikh hawadith Baghdad wa al-Basra 1186–1192/1772–1780*. 'Imad A. Ra'uf, ed. Baghdad, 1978.

al-Suwaydi, 'Abdullah b. Husayn. *al-Hujaj al-qat'iya li-ittifaq al-firaq al-Islamiyya*. Cairo: al-Matba'a al-Halabiya, 1905.

Tabataba'i, Muhammad Husayn. *A Shiite Anthology*. Trans. William C. Chittick. Albany: SUNY Press, 1981.

Tabataba'i, Sayyid 'Ali. *Riyad al-masa'il*. Qum: Mu'assasat al-Nashr al-Islami, 1996.

Tabataba'i, Sayyid Muhammad Mahdi "Bahr al-'Ulum." *Bulghat al-faqih*. 4 vols. Tehran: Maktabat al-Sadiq, 1984.

———. *Rijal al-Sayyid Bahr al-'Ulum al-ma'ruf bi al-Fawa'id al-Rijaliyya*. Najaf, 1967.

Takim, Liyakat N. *The Heirs of the Prophet: Charisma and Religious Authority in Shi'ite Islam*. Albany: SUNY Press, 2006.

Thomassen, Einar and Bernd Radtke, eds. *The Letters of Ahmad Ibn Idris*. Evanston: Northwestern University Press, 1993.

Tihrani, Aqa Buzurg. *al-Kiram al-barara fi al-qarn al-thalith ba'd al-'ashara*. Najaf, 1954–68.

——. *Nuqaba' al-bashar fi al-qarn al-rabi' 'ashar*. Najaf, 1954–68.

——. *Tabaqat a'lam al-Shi'a*. 2 vols. Najaf: Matba'a 'Ilmiyya, 1954.

Trimingham, J. Spencer. *The Sufi Orders in Islam*. Oxford: Oxford University Press, 1971.

Tripp, Charles. *A History of Iraq*. Cambridge: Cambridge University Press, 2007.

Tucker, Ernest S. "Nadir Shah and the Ja'fari Madhhab Reconsidered." *Iranian Studies* Vol. 27, No. 1/4 (1994): 163–79.

——. *Nadir Shah's Quest for Legitimacy in Post-Safavid Iran*. Gainesville: University Press of Florida, 2006.

Tu'ma, Salman Hadi. *'Asha'ir Karbala' wa usaruha*. 2 vols. Beirut: Dar al-Muhajja al-Bayda', 1998.

——. *Turath Karbala'*. Beirut: Mu'assasat al-A'lami, 1983.

Tunikabuni, Muhammad b. Sulayman. *Qisas al-'ulama'*. Shiraz, 1964.

al-Tusi, Shaykh al-Ta'ifa. *'Uddat al-usul*. Tehran, 1894.

Ustan, Ismail Safa. "The Ottoman Dilemma in Handling the Shi'i Challenge in Nineteenth Century Iraq." In *The Sunna and Shi'a in History: Division and Ecumenism in the Muslim Middle East*, Ofra Bengio and Meir Litvak, eds. New York: Palgrave Macmillan, 2011.

al-Uthaymin, Abd Allah Salih. *Muhammad Ibn 'Abd al-Wahhab: The Man and his Works*. London: I.B.Tauris, 2009.

Vikor, Knut S. *Sufi and Scholar on the Desert Edge: Muhammad b. 'Ali al-Sanusi and his Brotherhood*. Evanston: Northwestern University Press, 1995.

Visser, Reidar. *Basra, the Failed Gulf State: Separatism and Nationalism in Southern Iraq*. Munster: Lit Verlag, 2005.

Voll, John Obert. *Islam: Continuity and Change in the Modern World*. New York: Syracuse University Press, 1994.

——. "Linking Groups in the Networks of Eighteenth-Century Revivalist Scholars: The Mizjaji Family in Yemen." In *Eighteenth-Century Renewal and Reform in Islam*, Nehemia Levtzion and John Obert Voll, eds. New York: Syracuse University Press, 1987.

——. "Muhammad Hayya al-Sindi and Muhammad ibn 'Abd al-Wahhab: An Analysis of an Intellectual Group in Eighteenth Century Madina." *Bulletin of the School of Oriental and African Studies* University of London, Vol. 38, No. 1 (1975): 32–39.

——. "The Sudanese Mahdi: Frontier Fundamentalist." *International Journal of Middle East Studies* Vol. 10, No. 2 (May 1979): 146–66.

——. "Two biographies of Ahmad Ibn Idris Al-Fasi (1760–1837)." *International Journal of African Historical Studies* Boston University, Vol. 6, No. 4 (1973): 633–45.

Walbridge, Linda S. *The Most Learned of the Shi'a: The Institution of the Marja' Taqlid*. Oxford: Oxford University Press, 2001.

Wallerstein, Immanuel. *World-Systems Analysis: An Introduction*. Durham: Duke University Press, 2004.

Wardi, 'Ali. *Lamahat ijtima'iyya min ta'rikh al-Iraq al-hadith*. 6 vols. Baghdad: Matba'at al-Irshad, 1969–76.

Weiss, Bernard, G. *The Spirit of Islamic Law*. Athens: University of Georgia Press, 1998.

Weiss, Max. *In the Shadow of Sectarianism: Law, Shi'ism, and the Making of Modern Lebanon*. Cambridge: Harvard University Press, 2010.

Wickham, Carrie Rosefsky. *The Muslim Brotherhood: Evolution of an Islamist Movement*. Princeton: Princeton University Press, 2013.

Wilson, Arnold T. *The Persian Gulf: An Historical Sketch from the Earliest Times to the Beginning of the Twentieth Century*. Oxford: Oxford University Press, 1928.

Zunuzi, Sayyid Muhammad Hasan. *Riyad al-jinna*. Unpublished.

INDEX